Silke Bartsch/Patricia Lysaght (eds.)

Places of Food Production

Origin, Identity, Imagination

PL ACADEMIC RESEARCH

Bibliographic Information published by the Deutsche Nationalbibliothek
The Deutsche Nationalbibliothek lists this publication in the Deutsche Nationalbibliografie; detailed bibliographic data is available in the internet at http://dnb.d-nb.de.

Library of Congress Cataloging-in-Publication Data
A CIP catalog record for this book has been applied for at the Library of Congress

Cover photo: Rape cultivation, an extensive regional crop in Germany
(Photo: Armin Wolf 2016)

Printed by CPI books GmbH, Leck

ISBN 978-3-631-72782-9 (Print)
E-ISBN 978-3-631-73022-5 (E-PDF)
E-ISBN 978-3-631-73023-2 (EPUB)
E-ISBN 978-3-631-73024-9 (MOBI)
DOI 10.3726/b11707

PL Academic Research is an Imprint of Peter Lang GmbH.

Peter Lang – Frankfurt am Main · Bern · Bruxelles · New York · Oxford · Warszawa · Wien

This publication has been peer reviewed.

www.peterlang.com

Dedicated to
Professor Dr.
Johanna Maria van Winter

Contents

Part III: Alienation and the Handling of Food

Foreword

This book represents a peer-reviewed selection of the papers presented at the 21st International Ethnological Food Research Conference held in the old university city of Heidelberg, Germany, from the 31st of August to the 2nd of September 2016. The conference theme was "Places of Food Production: Origin, Identity, Imagination", and its aim was to analyse the interaction between food, self-conceptions and region. Organised by Prof. Dr. Silke Bartsch, University of Education Karlsruhe, the conference lectures were held at the Dr. Rainer Wild-Stiftung, about which its founder, Prof. Dr. Rainer Wild, spoke at the opening session of the conference.

Three keynote speakers addressed the conference: Emeritus Prof. Dr. Konrad Köstlin, Institut für Europäische Ethnologie, Universität Wien, Austria (Opening Lecture), Prof. Dr. Stefan Bongard, Professur für Betriebswirtschaftslehre und Logistik, Hochschule Ludwigshafen am Rhein, Germany, and Prof. Dr. Jana Rückert-John, Professur für Soziologie des Essens, Hochschule Fulda, Germany.

The volume is arranged in three parts representing the three thematic streams of the conference discussion: Food and Region, Food and the Imagination, and Alienation and the Handling of Food.

Since food production has traditionally shaped the character and self-conceptions of regions, it is inevitable in the age of globalisation that global food production will affect regional foods and eating habits. How will this affect the self-identity of regions? (Part 1.)

Furthermore, although industrially-produced food has been of major significance in terms of food accessibility and food safety, this kind of food is now increasingly regarded as being unhealthy in contrast to locally-produced food which is viewed as being "good for the body". Thus the question arises as to how consumers manage the perceived risks associated with industrial food production and the products available on the market as a result. Do they have a sense of alienation concerning the origin of the food they consume because of the increasing invisibility of food-production and food-management processes? Are they concerned about so-called "hidden ingredients" and does this influence their imagination about food and food production in general? (Parts 2 and 3.)

In addition to the formal lecture programme the conference visited the Institute for Ethnology, Ruprecht-Karls-Universität, Heidelberg, where Prof. Dr. Guido Sprenger and Ph.D. students gave presentations on current research projects. The conference participants were also introduced to the city of Heidelberg and took part in a range of interlinked visits and events connected with the conference theme.

The conference was indeed an international, interdisciplinary event with participants – ranging from seasoned professors to graduate students – from 16 countries and 4 continents attending. It provided a forum in which to discuss and reflect on important questions, issues and anxieties concerning the impact on our lives of places of food production in this increasingly industrialized and globalised world.

Karlsruhe and Dublin, August 2017

Silke Bartsch and Patricia Lysaght

Opening Lecture

Konrad Köstlin

Kitchen Stories

Abstract: *Kitchens are surrounded by new stories since gender roles have lost clear perspectives and so convert the location into a battleground. "Stories" reflect and explain the location in terms of a representation of the self. Food and its production are under discussion as a matter of confessions (and confessionalists). The stories include a debate on responsibility in a world-wide perspective that can reach up to fundamentalism. In terms of sustainability the horizon of a new regionalism is sketched. The selling of stories is camouflaged as an offer of life-styles.*

New Perceptions

Until basic parts of food production were outsourced to the food industry, the kitchen, for a long period of time, was a primary location for its production. But it is not the history of the kitchen that I wish to talk about here. I will accentuate some aspects of "kitchen stories" that underline how the kitchen portrays important changes in values and general attitudes in modern Western societies. I will also comment on some aspects subtitled in the conference theme: Origin, identity and imagination could be mixed into one argument localised here, because the kitchen and our preferences in regard to food have turned into a place for confessing our attitudes – up to rigid forms of fundamentalism – towards the world around us (Köstlin 2013, pp. 37–45). This seems to be so pivotal, that lonely heart columns today present challenges in terms of food preferences, just as they did long ago for non-smokers.

Since I'm dealing with kitchen stories, I will not complain about congested stables, shredded chickens, young pigs castrated without anaesthesia, or about all of the other types of cruelties of mass production, or about additives and genetically-modified products, all of which have resulted in consumers' distrust of all branches of that globalised food industry.

During the last century, the household kitchen was a relatively small room, separated from other rooms in the house and serving as a location for storing, cooking and preparing food. It was also a place where everyday meals were eaten. The main utensils for food preparation and consumption were also often stored in the kitchen. It was mostly seen as an intimate, non-public, and a strictly separated, room. The housewife changed her apron, when she left it. Today, it tends to be an undetached, representative location. In many fields, a quantum leap in lifting secrets has occurred. In 1908, Georg Simmel, a German philosopher and sociologist, was already warning about the danger of "Entsekretisierung", a loss of secrets. He understood the secret as being very closely connected with the highest human potential of civilisation, such as love, creativity and phantasy (Simmel 1908). Today, on the contrary, everything seems to be in the public domain, and transparency is not only not an option, but also a must that has not only to be practised, but also to be demonstrated. This is evident in the pronouncement of a person's allergy restrictions in regard to food, a confession that confers distinction on the announcer. Some of those allergies may well have existed in the world before we inhabited it, but may not have been previously publicly announced. We live in societies of confessors. In this society, the kitchen is not only the place where more and more designed and shiny artefacts are on display. The artefacts and the cooking competences involved, are seen as a new form of identity-production for the owner. The kitchen often works as a place of performance, and in private households, this seems to be – and this is new – also a male terrain. The word terrain with its military background is chosen here quite carefully: It has become a field of tacit competition.

Alongside this functional and practical description, the word kitchen has further widespread meanings. It can be nationalized as in French cuisine, localized as in the "Wiener Küche", or regionalized as in the Nordic or Mediterranean kitchens. Quotations like these are on the rise in Europe, not only among shelf-nationalists who demand to "buy British" or German, but also among those who stress the typical, the own, the regional nearby, for ethical reasons. Kitchen can also be understood as a type of diet – like the vegetarian, the paleo, the stone age, the flexitarian or the vegan. Kitchen is a place, as a location, and it is also a topos, an idea filled with many meanings and contents which are then materialized by "doing kitchen", however people treat the place and the idea.

Focus on Kitchen

The kitchen – and this is not only in terms of the local – is not anymore a marginal spot, a kind of a sideshow. This may have to do with the fact that more and more men are involved in this system, since it has been discovered to be the place of expressive presentation of the self, of what is mentioned as "identity". It is also supposed to be an important, if not "the" place for, and of, new forms of communication, which is connected with images and quotations of its historic forms. Lamenting about the loss of direct face-to-face-communication, and the lack of family-shared meals, belong together. The renewed appreciation of the shared meal as an icon of family communication has given rise to bunches of arguments. On the other hand, and as already stated, in these times of hyper-communication we are debating things, which once would have been a secret. A new ideology urges us to communicate, to talk about our confessions. So the kitchen and its new meaning can act as a place for communication, as a place for being together in terms of deceleration, and as a place in which "real cooking" can work as a demonstration of resistance, as an explicit alternative to the use of convenience food.

Almost every journal, magazine, newspaper, or TV-station today, has a cookery programme, a debate about food, and worldwide nutrition facts. Likewise, every newspaper has recipes from home and abroad, both of which are nowadays equally exotic. One food-hype seems to hunt the next. This is not such a new phenomenon. An early one has survived and may serve as an example. This is the brunch, that mixture between a late breakfast and an early lunch that has been successfully reformulated or revitalised in manifold variations. In 1895, the British author (and hunter) Guy Beringer, published the article entitled "Brunch: A Plea" in *Hunter's Weekly*, where he was pleading for an alternative to the English Sunday morning dinner, which he described as torture due to heavy meat and pastry dishes. The suggested alternative to the heavy, post-church Sunday meals, favouring lighter fare served late in the morning, was the playful blend "brunch". The brunch, Beringer wrote, stimulates conversation: "Brunch is cheerful, sociable and inciting.... It is talk-compelling. It puts you in a good temper, it makes you satisfied with yourself and your fellow beings, it sweeps away the worries and cobwebs of the week."[1] Thus a manual, as a form of direction for its use and its social interpretation, had already been included by Beringer in his definition of the brunch. So it indicated a new kind of information on the requirement of communication: A modern storm. A long-lasting effect like that provided by the brunch will not happen with new modes of presentation like the "spiralizing" of zucchini, or the forming of it into noodle-like stripes, and punning it into "zoodels", that are offered as a replacement for the high-carb pasta. Playing with words such as "Inspiralized", the name of the cookbook of the Italo-American author Ali Mafucci,[2] turns the kitchen into a location with more than verbal creativity.

I owe the title of my paper, "Kitchen Stories", to Bent Hamer. His film ("Salmer fra Kjökennet", 2003) focuses on the kitchen and its use by single male individuals. His story is based on the Swedish idea of clearness, efficiency and rationality: Around 1960, a group of interviewers (maybe ethnologists) enter Norway. They

---

1 "The Birth of Brunch: Where Did This Meal Come From Anyway?", retrieved 26.8.2016 from http://www.smithsonianmag.com/arts-culture/the-birth-of-brunch-where-did-this-meal-come-from-anyway-164187758/#WP7tx6t4QcHZgE2E.99.

2 "Inspiralized. A healthy food blog for spiralizer recipes." Malfucci 2015 is the definitive cookbook for using a spiralizer: the kitchen gadget that turns vegetables and fruits into imaginative, low-carb dishes (www.inpiralizing.com; retrieved 26.8.2016).

cross the border, change the side of the road on which they drive,[3] and enter the country in a long queue of PV444 Volvos with camping trailers attached. Their plan is to study the behaviour of Norwegian bachelors in their kitchens. These researchers do their fieldwork by sitting on an umpire's chair in the kitchen as participant, but silent, observers. As ethnologists we know that the observer's attendance has a strong impact on the field observed. The purpose of the research was to modernize home kitchens based on observing the behaviour of these bachelors in their own kitchens. Isak, a bachelor, deeply regrets ever having agreed to participate in the study. And so to counteract the research proposal he stops using the kitchen and instead observes the researcher, Folke, through a hole in the ceiling. The movie ends as a friendly Nordic story: The two men, both lonely, overcome their distrust and become friends.

Fig. 1: "Kitchen Stories" (https://www.google.at/imgres?imgurl, retrieved 28.6.2016).

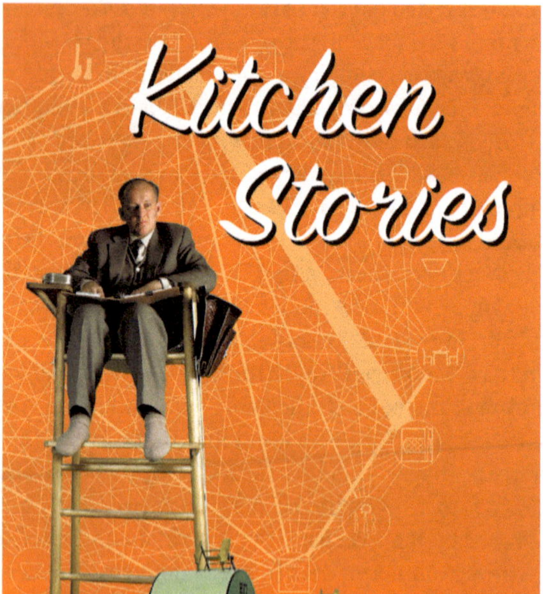

3 The change from the left to right side of the road occurred in September 1967 and it is called "H-day".

The Location and the Presentation of the Self

My emphasis is placed on the fact that kitchens are obviously seen as locations indicating the development of societies and includes the debate on gender relations. Once upon a time housewives used to say one sentence that expressed their martyrdom: "You have eaten within ten minutes what took me two hours to cook." This statement featured the accusation that the family had not found a successful way of appreciating the housewife's work. The point: It remained undiscussed that women were obliged to act in the kitchen.

We know that food has to be nicely done, has to please the eye, and so has to fulfil demands of creativity and communication. We have also learned that beauty is in the eye of the beholder – at least that is what we have thought. The eye is – as far as we know – connected to the brain. And this is connected to our Smartphones. People nowadays eat more often at a deli, in a burger-palace, or in a real restaurant; in general, they eat more food produced by professionals. And as such, it has to be photographed. According to current statistics, 61 % of Germans do this in restaurants. Food, prepared in a professional kitchen, seems to be of value in terms of being photographed. But – and this may be surprising only at first glance – 42 % of Germans also take pictures of food made by themselves (http://de.statista.com/statistik/daten/studie/577373/umfrage/umfrage-unter-deutschen-zum-fotografieren-ihres-essens/, retrieved 25.7.2016). Thus, the own creativity is also worthy of being documented and communicated. This is, without any irony – the marking out of a new perspective; it is a new insight into modern people's behaviour – without even taking into account the coincidence, that both the photos and the food increase in complexity, since both have to do with the phantasma called identity, serving as a confession: I let you know about what I eat; I want to let you to know all (?) about me.

Kitchen Stories, the presentation of food that has been eaten, is now in a new, and real, focus, since people take a photo of their food before they start eating. These are pictured kitchen stories. And they may well send this photo as a kind of testimonial to their followers. This is to inform family and friends about the quality of their lifestyle and also about their preferences in regard to food and circumstances. This indicates the importance of the eaten as a part of the presentation of the self, what people then declare as being "identity". Photos mark – as already stated – the extraordinary, and they let nice moments become even nicer. Almost nobody will watch them later on (evenings with slide-shows belong to history – thank God!). The new photos belong to the moment, and are made for the moment, not for eternity, but for a networking communication. Why do they and we do this? Maybe they believe they do so in order to communicate with all of their 94 followers, and to cater for them virtually. It seems – hopefully – that taking pictures of food encourages people to eat their food more carefully and with more fun, because they can communicate, and so share it, with others, and they let them know that everything is done nicely and decoratively. It produces good moods, self-control, and a good conscience as a fully accountable person: a confession.

Genderism and Changing Perspectives

Food was debated anew 50 years ago by French scholars, when Claude Levi-Strauss published "The Raw and the Cooked" in which he detected structures in cultural systems (Lévi-Strauss 1964). In "Mythology" Roland Barthes wrote essays such as "Ornamental Cookery", and formed structural oppositions, such as "Steak and Chips" or "Wine and Milk" (Barthes 1957; 1964; 1972). These scholars, interested in food and its structural oppositions, neglected the question of gender almost completely, as far as I can see. Questions of women's and gender history have expanded dramatically since the end of the twentieth century, showing great vigour and variety in the breadth of subjects tackled and the range of methodologies explored.[4] On exploring the evolution of historical writing about women and gender, we find a dominating female accent at the beginning of the twenty-first century, in terms of the application of theory in historical scholarship on gender.

It is necessary to remember that the kitchen, together with food, seen from a new angle, has turned out to be a major form of expression of self-conception within the last few decades, at least in Western societies. The kitchen has lost its strictness as a female place. Besides the production of meals, it can be characterized as a place in which feelings and representation, moods and attitudes, are produced. One of these is called "alienation", a word which was once brought into modern discourses by Karl Marx. The word now expresses the loss, and the lack, of direct contacts to foodstuffs. Seen as a critique, it can be understood as a process to regain this immediacy.

We live in times in which new perceptions of spaces are under discussion. In our world, the local (in all its forms) is being permanently framed anew. It is not only the ethnologists' league which is interested in regional or local food customs, anymore. Sciences witness this attitude by talking about the regional and the spatial turn (Bachmann-Medick 2014; 2016).[5] The local in general is being newly

---

4 Not so much in French or Polish Literature; see, for example, Bogucka 2004.

5 Beside the regional and the spatial turn, some other turns are discussed within cultural sciences, such as an interpretive turn, a performative turn, a reflexive turn, a literary turn, a postcolonial turn, an iconic turn, and a translational turn.

embedded in connection with the local in terms of sustainability, in categories like health and the body or the carbon footprint, among many others. And it is often that fundamentalistic compliance serves as a representation of the self in our contemporary identity-puzzle. Modern localism is the other side of the coin called globalism. It no longer consists only of the idea of the own because enhanced ethics or morality is now part of the representation of one's individuality.

Doing Kitchen

Doing kitchen can be materialized when strolling through cities. In German-speaking countries, one can observe that kitchen-shops of all kinds are developing and invading inner city locations, and that they are to be found next to the flagship stores of international clothing- and shoe-chains. These kitchen-shops offer a variety of specialized, and often shiny steel or copper equipment and machines. In contrast to the smallness of modern families, kitchen-utensils nowadays have reached huge dimensions. A kitchen, equipped like this, could easily feed a soccer team all at once.

But in these kitchens "real" cooking happens very seldom and only on special occasions. And instead of the self-evident sexual stereotyping of the past, modern role-divisions are not very clear anymore. It is a matter of arrangement as to who will be in charge of preparing food, for which kind of food, and for which occasion. The upgrading of the kitchen with manifold devices – often due to the invasion of that theatre by male actors – has developed as a new context in terms of gender.

Seen like this, my point of departure is the "crisis" of the old kitchen, and the ascension of a new perception of the place and image of the kitchen as an identity-producing locality and its ideology. Gender questions seem to be often converted, one to the other. Masculinity and feminism (and forms in between) have engulfed Western countries within recent decades, in Europe, at least. A new diversity has taken place and men and women re-conceptualize themselves and re-establish their place in permanently new emerging contexts. Constructs of gender seen in designed kitchens in this contemporary sphere enable an explorative analysis of the correlation between traditional attitudes as well as leftish-liberal constructs of gender and politics, to be made.

It is possible to bridge the many historical periods in relation to the kitchen by demonstrating the continued effects of different "identity" practices, since the times when the kitchen had to demonstrate status (when the word and the idea of "identity" were unknown) and fulfil basic needs, such as hunger – times that are long gone in Western societies. And this can demonstrate continuous effects on lifestyles and on societal conceptualizations of gender. By locating, analysing, and putting forward gender constructs that emerged in Western societies, one can put on offer multiple analyses and different perceptions of gender. My argument underlines the opinion that gender constructs are fluid and that they are responsive to many types of stimuli – social, political, economic, emotional – and that these realities remained true in changing contexts. My inquiry was seen through a lens of representations such as the location of kitchen-shops as a pictorial placement – and it was focused on material from journals, magazines, newspapers, and private, and not very systematic (but focused) observations to elucidate the variations on constructs of gender. We are always part of the fields we research – the privilege and the restriction of European Ethnologists.

Food and Its New Careers

Influenced by general opinion, constructs of gender seen in the kitchen and in society are brought into the contemporary sphere as a way of providing an explorative analysis of public picture-productions of activities in the kitchen. They show that conservative and liberal constructs of gender and kitchen politics are intertwined and a division between progressive and conservative has lost conciseness. It is not on an occasional basis that persons of public interest love to pose as defenders of family values and use the kitchen as a place of family representation. This pose, now more often done by men, can be one of remarkable hypocrisy. By locating, analysing, and putting forward concise models of gender constructs that emerged in the aftermath of the 1960s, we can see multiple perceptions of gender roles in regard to an increasing cross-gender use of the kitchen as an identity-producer. Here I underline my thesis again that gender constructs seem to be fluid and to represent contextual responses to many types of approaches – social, political, and economic on the one hand, and still historic ones on the other.

It is only human beings who need institutions that require aid and assistance from others, and also instruments when selecting, preparing and eating food. We fulfil our basic needs with methods learned and conveyed by others. This social coining of our habits we call culture. And, one of the important issues of this culture, we call kitchen, with its multiple meanings. It is not only the place where food is prepared. It is a system of materials, tastes and forms of food preparation, which seems to be a form of regional or national language, and also a form of description of attitudes. In other words, food and its context are about to make us readable. And we pretend that our (selected) food is "ours" in terms of being identifiable as "we". As a kind of an individual passport, food has made a new career. Its choice, understood as being individually shaped, serves more and more as a symbol of our shown or expressed identity. This is not really new, since food had always incorporated an often hidden language. But today it is staged in a new form, something to permanently talk about in order to display and to use it as individual potential, and as a medium to communicate with, and to communicate on.

Food is often promoted and perceived of as being local, and is often held out as being "Soul Food" – like the "Maultaschen". This noodle dough filled with meat or vegetables, and declared as being typical for the region Württemberg, has been turned into a unique selling proposal (USP) of, and for, the region: it serves now as a marker to make the region distinguishable from others.[6] UNESCO (which usually requires worldwide equality) supports, in cultural respects, this accent on differences, and has installed committees (to promote this crazy idea) which provide an imprimatur for these regional specialties. On a national level, Austria's government has recognized 113 such regions, so-called "Genussregionen", taste-regions (www.genuss-region.at/genussregionen/index.html, retrieved 21.9.2016). Focussed on tradition, the regulations are a kind of a demand, a sort of behaviour-setting requirement. Tradition in this case (and by law!) means three generations. This campaign (a military term, again) exists in order to support regional entrepreneurship with history as an argument. The new ascension of regional food is, in contemporary discourses, seemingly being contrasted with globalisation. The new implementation of the regions neglects the fact that both the new localism and the global are, as already stated, two sides of the same coin. Food has become the central argument in regard to the care of the own body. And the body is in focus, because of its new importance as an expression of responsibility, not only for the own body, but also as an expression testifying to the person's (= one's) own relation to the world, as an attitude towards nature, the world around us, and as a symbol of responsibility for future generations.

Today, doing kitchen is not limited anymore to a restricted room named kitchen. The kitchen story could be re-told under a title such as "the new living room", a room that combines functions of other rooms, including the former kitchen. But as a paradox, this living room has lost the somehow anarchic qualities of former times, having been upgraded in terms of functionality and efficiency. Since then, the kitchen, as a place of the highest symbolism has, in many respects, got a new and expensive reputation.

As a primary location of the "Production of Food", the kitchen itself, in the last century, was an indicator of basic change in societies that cannot be viewed as

6 They were indeed served as regional food during the conference!

being separate from broader reflections. The main change has been the outsourcing of household kitchen activities, and the new product-lines (oven-ready meals, food for children, women, elderly people etc., what is promoted as "individualisation") that have been developed as a result. All of these do their advertising with images of "real cooking". By pretending that this is the case, they evoke simultaneously the desire for this real cooking as a non-alienated form.

New Men in the New Kitchen?

The living-room-kitchen and the hearth are new places of celebration, places of representation, and the location where cooking competences within the living-room-area are to be displayed. This is a showroom for the new presenters of food and self-perception. The hearth-block, a quadrangle in the middle of a living-room, functions as an altar. Like a priest, the cook celebrates his High Mass, acting and talking with his face turned towards the parish. Similar to Catholic regulations, a male person is doing his *officium* like a priest, using the cookbook posed on a bookrack like the Holy Bible in church, and taking a sip from a wine-glass from time to time – wine indicates life-style. The living room has one of its shrines with the altar like an island positioned prominently as a centre, offering a platform for the creative cook as well for those bonded to the cookbook and its displayed contents.

But this festive position in the living room is restricted to special occasions only. Quite different to this exposure is the use of that kitchen on workdays, when women still have to prepare more or less processed food. It increases the gap between normal procedures and that "real" cooking dedicated to special events. This comes to be more and more the hour of the man of the house, if food is not prepared by professionals, hired caterers. New gender roles are not really under discussion here but induce genderized confessions. We can find prominent women who declare that they are proud of not cooking, especially not for a man. When women tend to give up the kitchen as their field, men tend to invade this field like a battleground, an area they occupy to display their quasi-professional competences.

In this perspective, "Slow Food" can be interpreted as an invention of, and for, the Italian man at weekends: Going to a market place with friends, judging meat, fish and vegetables; and at home celebrating food like a priest in male company. I want to be understood accurately here: The production of everyday food remains, in this context, the duty of the housewife, or the new soft houseman who replaces the housewife. This fits into the "do-it-yourself" category as a permanently re-done, often alternative movement that defines the kitchen as a place of production anew, as a place to bake bread, to dry apples and other fruits, and as a place where recipes, which include cucumbers and wild garlic, are communicated.

A survey I did some years ago about cooking classes in adult educational centres in Vienna showed that 80 % of those classes were booked by men – by educated men, not by lonesome bachelors. These clients represented the kind of "new" man who does the "real" cooking, a cooking procedure that takes time and care (Köstlin 2005, 101–117). This enabled him to present all the cooking skills designated as necessary by current discourses. But its clients felt in charge only for the extraordinary and expressive food performance that needs an audience, one that needs spectators. The new gender roles only seem to be new; the contrary is actually the situation, as the new man, in the new kitchen, is tightening old roles.

I have to admit that only a small sector of Western societies is affected by that new attitude. But discourses on the barbeque show how male practices seem to proceed in what is called the "sensual experience" when preparing food: Back to nature. In this very limited perspective, this identity-display very often turns out to be restricted to weekends, or events with friends, which portray mainly the cook. This identity has to be performed publicly because modern forms of identity-production remain senseless without an audience, without spectators. As a kind of performed identity, it has become popular, and is now to be displayed at times dedicated to leisure (as in the case of "Slow Food"). The importance of one's profession, though unspoken, tends to be secondary, but it is a non-debated precondition of that kind of leisure and its "real cooking" competences nearly approaching professionalism.

List of References

Printed

Bachmann-Medick, Doris: *Cultural Turns: New Orientations in the Study of Culture*. De Gruyter: Berlin/ Boston 2016.

Bachmann-Medick, Doris: *Cultural Turns: Neuorientierungen in den Kulturwissenschaften*. Rowohlt: Hamburg 2014.

Barthes, Roland: *Mythologies*. Paris: Éditions du Seuil, 1957.

Barthes, Roland: *Mythen des Alltags*. Frankfurt am Main: Suhrkamp, 1964.

Barthes, Roland: *Mythologies* (trans. Annette Lavers). London: Jonathan Cape, 1972.

Bogucka, Maria: *Women in Early Modern Polish Society, Against the European Background.* Aldershot: Ashgate 2004.

Köstlin, Konrad: "Essen als Lifestyle-Inventar und die Bekennergesellschaft: Fundamentalismus?" In Eberhart, Helmut / Berger, Karl / Wildling, Regina (Hg.): *Volkskunde aus der Mitte. Festschrift für Olaf Bockhorn zum siebzigsten Geburtstag*. Verein für Volkskunde: Wien 2013, pp. 37–45.

Köstlin, Konrad: "Neue Männer an neuen Herden : Zelebration am heiligen Ort". *Schweizerisches Archiv für Volkskunde* 101, 2005, pp. 101–117.

Lévi-Strauss Claude: *Le Cru et le Cuit*. Plon: Paris 1964 (= Mythologiques I).

Maffucci, Ali: *Inspiralized: Turn Vegetables into Healthy, Creative, Satisfying Meals*. Clarkson Potter: New York 2015.

Simmel, Georg: *Soziologie. Untersuchungen über die Formen der Vergesellschaftung*. Duncker & Humblot: Leipzig 1908.

Internet

"Kitchen Stories", retrieved 28.6.2016 from https://www.google.at/imgres?imgurl.

"The Birth of Brunch: Where Did This Meal Come From Anyway?", retrieved 26.8.2016 from http://www.smithsonianmag.com/arts-culture/the-birth-of-brunch-where-did-this-meal-come-from-anyway-164187758/#WP7tx6t4QcHZgE2E.99.

http://de.statista.com/statistik/daten/studie/577373/umfrage/umfrage-unter-deutschen-zum-fotografieren-ihres-essens/, retrieved 25.7.2016.

www.genuss-region.at/genussregionen/index.html, retrieved 21.9.2016.

www.inpiralizing.com; retrieved 26.8.2016.

Part I:
Food and Region

Déirdre D'Auria and Patricia Lysaght

"Town of Food": The Creation of a New Food Region in County Kilkenny in South-East Ireland.

Abstract: *This paper examines current efforts to create a "food region" in County Kilkenny in south-east Ireland, an area historically rich in natural resources and food production. It analyses the motivations behind this endeavour and asks whether these are concerned only with the improvement of economic and social conditions in the county or whether the creation of a sense of regional identity, based on food produce, is also implied.*

Introduction

Irish food has risen in reputation over the last decade, both nationally and internationally. A number of Irish foods have been awarded the PGI (Protected Geographical Indication) and PDO (Protected Designation of Origin) classifications (D'Auria / Lysaght 2015, pp. 78–80), by the European Union in recognition of their excellence and their importance for regional identity, and more applications for such designation are currently in process. Northern Ireland has declared 2016 a "Year of Food and Drink".[1] This Northern Ireland food-related campaign has included radio and television advertising concerning the food sector and a year-long programme of festivals and events to showcase local food-producers and restaurants. Last year saw the launch of the "Ireland's Ancient East" marketing campaign, a tourism project to attract visitors to the eastern counties of Ireland, as a follow-up to the highly successful "Wild Atlantic Way" promotion that has been responsible for a solid rise in tourism numbers in the West of Ireland in the last couple of years.[2] Food, drink, restaurants, pubs, cafés, food markets and festivals play a significant role in both of these campaigns, alongside historical sites, beautiful natural scenery, music, sport, and other cultural events, advertised in order to attract visitors to these areas. Although specific food items, or

---

1 For more information, see "Food NI – Our Food So Good!", retrieved 5.5.2016 from www.nigoodfood.com; and "Northern Ireland Year of Food and Drink 2016", retrieved 5.5.2016 from www.discovernorthernireland.com/yearoffoodanddrink2016.

2 See further "Ireland's Ancient East", retrieved 7.5.2016 from www.irelandsancienteast.com; and "Wild Atlantic Way", retrieved 7.5.2016 from www.wildatlanticway.com.

restaurants, are now beginning to draw tourists to an area in their own right, the idea of food "regions" is not as well developed in Ireland as it is in Italy or France (Hyman / Hyman 2003, pp. 31–49), for example, where the cuisines of Tuscany and Provence, respectively, are well-established and recognized internationally.

This paper will focus on recent initiatives to establish a "food region" of sorts in the south-east of Ireland, encompassing Kilkenny city, rural towns, and surrounding areas, the motivations behind such efforts, and their results.

Methodology

This essay will first of all examine the definition of "region" in the context of food, based on recent works dealing with this topic. It will then use online, tourism, and printed sources to investigate the historical background to food production and food culture in County Kilkenny, before looking at more recent initiatives to revive this particular sector, and to develop a cohesive strategy in order to create a "food region" in the area. Field work, involving recent input from local food producers in the county, provides a direct insight into the motivations behind this strategy.

"Food Region" and "Regional Food"

A "food region" is not easy to define as it is not necessarily just a geographic area, but can also be connected to many overlapping issues, such as matters of ethnicity, identity, culture, travel and tourism. In his 2008 article, Konrad Köstlin states that the idea of "region" has "gained a new reality in western countries" (Köstlin 2010, p. 37). He claims that "region" is now perceived as "providing a symbolic vision of possible regional autonomy" (ibid.), and that this perception can also be applied to a "food region".

Lucy M. Long has considered "region" in the context of the "Culinary Other", meaning something that is different from what is known and familiar to someone. She also asserts that it refers to "groupings within a culture, differentiated by geographic location and physical resources (Long 2003, p. 408), and that it has a clear role to play in the tourism industry (ibid.).

The idea of "region", and of "regional food" is also inextricably linked to that of identity. Food can be used as a powerful symbol, to unite people, both in their everyday lives, and on occasions of celebration. According to Lucy Long, it can also be used to indicate "national, ethnic, and regional identity and pride" (Long 2003, p. 376). She asserts that regional foods, because they stand in contrast to foods found in other regions, are essentially markers of differences rather than representing a culture (ibid.). They must accordingly serve to unite those living within that region and contribute to their sense of identity.

"Regional Food" is thus a complex concept, one which has "changed its character in recent decades" (Köstlin 2010, p. 11). According to Köstlin "regional food" has no longer simply to do with locally-sourced food, identity, and traditional values, but includes a broader philosophy, and an understanding of the ethical and responsible treatment of producers and the environment, and of the body itself (ibid., pp. 43–45).

This more developed understanding of "regional food" is reflected in several of the efforts being made to create a "food region" in County Kilkenny. The Slow Food Movement is active in this part of the country, and the "Four Rivers" chapter, which includes Kilkenny, often organizes events which bring those involved in the food sector together[3] in order to promote the concepts of "good", "clean" and "fair" in relation to food cultivation, production and consumption. Local food blogger Keith Bohanna, who is based in Kilkenny city, writes regularly about food-related businesses and events in the area. His blog, "Bia Beag" (meaning "small food" in the Irish language), focuses on small-scale, ethical and local food producers and he also organizes events bringing together small-scale food producers in order to give talks on various food-related themes, in which members of the public can participate.[4]

Local food producers, Helen Finnegan (a cheese-maker), and Mag Kirwan (a trout farmer) recognize that it is towards this broad understanding of "food region" discussed above, that County Kilkenny is moving, but both are also very much aware that much work still remains to be done in order to achieve this. The success of such a development would be impossible without the large-scale, dedicated support, coordination and investment currently being provided at local, regional and state levels.[5]

In recent times, efforts have been made to coordinate food businesses and related enterprises in County Kilkenny in order to make the food of this geographical area a focus for tourism, i.e. to construct a "food region" of sorts, similar

---

3 For more information on Slow Food in this area, see "Four Rivers. Slow Food Ireland", retrieved 20.5.2016 from www.slowfoodireland/four-rivers.

4 See also "Biabeag (Small Food): Exploring the world of small scale, ethical & local food producers", retrieved 20.5.2016 from biabeag.com.

5 In conversation with Helen Finnegan, founder of the Knockdrinna Cheese enterprise. See also www.knockdrinna.com, retrieved 20.5.2016. In conversation with Mag Kirwan, director of the Goatsbridge Trout business. See also in this connection www.goatsbridgetrout.ie, retrieved 7.7.2016.

to those in countries such as Italy and France that have occurred naturally over time. As will be evident from the next section, there are indications that the long history of successful food production in the County Kilkenny area has provided a natural basis for this development.

Kilkenny County – A Brief History of Food Production

Kilkenny is an inland county in the south-east of Ireland, with a current population of approximately ninety-five thousand people.[6] In recent times, the city of Kilkenny has become known for its nightlife, bars and festivals throughout the year, something which has led to significant growth in the hospitality sector in the city and surrounding areas. This has resulted in an increase in the number of restaurants, cafés, bars, artisan food producers, and most recently, cookery schools, in the city and county, respectively.

As well as being vibrant, busy, prosperous domestic and international holiday destinations, Kilkenny city and surrounding towns also have a rich and influential social, economic and political history. The town developed originally from an important sixth-century monastic settlement which was built around a church dedicated to St. Canice, who remains the patron saint of the city to this day. Kilkenny became a town of significance after the Anglo-Norman invasion of 1169, forming part of the Lordship of Leinster. Subsequently, a prosperous city developed which included a castle, a cathedral, city walls, and many other important historic buildings. It was even the seat of the Irish parliament in the fourteenth century.[7] It was given city status by Royal Charter in 1609. Local agriculture and food production were therefore apparently sufficient in order to enable a prosperous city to develop, to sustain a growing population over centuries, and to engage in trade in the food business.

Agriculture – Cattle and Crops

Environmental influences, over time, along with economic fluctuations, societal change and historical events, shaped the agricultural regions of Ireland. According to A. T. Lucas, the food system in Ireland was, from ancient times, based on cattle and corn, that is, on livestock (primarily cows) and grain products, thus

6 "Census. CSO. Central Statistics Office", www.census.cso.ie, retrieved 20.5.2016. Figure according to the 2011 Census.

7 For more information on the history of Kilkenny city, see "Kilkenny", retrieved 7.7.2016 from www.visitkilkenny.ie.

giving rise to the dairying, cattle-raising, and tillage areas still essentially discernible in Ireland today (Whelan 2011, p. 77). Thus milk, and milk products such as butter (Lucas 1960, p. 30) and cheese (the latter undergoing a revival since the second half of the twentieth century) (ibid., pp. 21–30), and corn products (derived mainly from oats, barley and wheat) such as bread and porridge, were the basis of the diet (ibid., p. 8). This was also the case for County Kilkenny, a largely fertile, inland area. While the county does not enjoy a coastline, the majestic river Nore runs through the county, which is also bordered by the river Barrow to the east and the River Suir to the south.[8] These rivers provided fish for food, and the fertile land of the alluvial river plains was suitable for growing crops, and raising livestock for meat. Thus, along with fish from the rivers, the land, with its livestock and grain-based agricultural economy, was, and is, the primary provider of food for Kilkenny city and surrounding areas. Kilkenny also lies in the commercial tillage area of the south-east of Ireland, and has benefited greatly over time from the demand for wheat for flour, and barley for the brewing industries.

Cider-making and Brewing

According to A. T. Lucas, the apple was one of the most important fruits in Ireland, both wild and cultivated, and apple orchards were frequently found around large houses and monastic settlements, where they were used for food and cider-making (Lucas 1960, p. 38). Lucas also states that on examining evidence from the sixteenth century, it appears every religious house mentioned had an orchard attached to it (ibid.). As County Kilkenny was home to many monasteries over the centuries – the early thirteenth-century Cistercian Duiske Abbey in Graiguenamanagh,[9] Inistioge Abbey, a settlement of the Augustinian order, possibly dating to the sixth century,[10] the twelfth-century Cistercian Jerpoint Abbey,[11] and the Dominican Black Abbey,[12] founded in the thirteenth century – it is likely that cider-making was well established in different parts of the county, a practice which is once again in evidence today.

8 "The Three Sisters". These three rivers (Barrow, Nore and Suir), are known as "The Three Sisters"; see for example: https://www.google.ie/search?q=Three+sisters+rivers&ie=utf-8&oe=utf-8&client=firefox-b&gws_rd=cr&ei=3bKXV4X8AeaNgAbLr4uABA, retrieved 23.7.2016.

9 "Duiske Abbey", at www.discoverireland.ie/duiske-abbey, retrieved 21.5.2016.

10 "Inistioge Abbey", at www.inistioge.ie/history_of_Inistioge, retrieved 21.5.2016.

11 For "Jerpoint Abbey", see www.heritageireland.ie/south-east/jerpointabbey, retrieved 23.5.2016.

12 For "The Black Abbey", see www.visitkilkenny.ie/black_abbey, retrieved 23.5 2016.

The brewing tradition is a long-established one in the south-east of Ireland, for example in Dungarvan, County Waterford,[13] Carlow town,[14] Enniscorthy, County Wexford,[15] and also in County Kilkenny where it was developed by the monks of St Francis Abbey in Kilkenny city in the thirteenth century.[16] The success of commercial tillage in the area also "generated heavy investment in processing facilities – mills, malt houses, breweries and distilleries, especially in towns commanding navigable waters and good hinterlands" (Whelan 2011, p. 80) of which Kilkenny was one. The most famous beer to originate in Kilkenny bears the family name of Smithwick's, a clear, red-coloured, ale-style beer.[17]

County Kilkenny was clearly a "region" where the raising of livestock, the cultivation of crops, the growing of certain fruits and vegetables, and brewing, had been successfully carried on for centuries, to the extent that not only were the surrounding natural resources sufficient to support a growing population, but some crops were also used for trade (Martin 1993, p. 151), and for export. Therefore, it is possible to suggest that there was an "idea" of a successful "food region", if predominantly in a geographical sense, and a tradition of food and drink production in this area over the centuries.

Kilkenny Today – The Kilkenny LEADER Partnership

The Kilkenny LEADER Partnership (KLP), currently in operation, is a community-led, independent, not-for-profit, local development organization, established approximately twenty-five years ago, with the intention of leading and facilitating "the creation of an integrated local development strategy to improve the economic, social and cultural quality of life of the people, communities and small enterprises of County Kilkenny".[18] This has included supporting many small food businesses and food- and drink-related projects, alongside other community-centred training courses and work-placements. LEADER supported the TRAIL

13 For brewing in Co. Waterford, see "Dungarvan Brewing Company", retrieved 22.7.2016 from www.goodfoodireland.com/place/dungarvan-brewing-company.

14 For more information on brewing in Carlow, see "O'Hara's. Carlow Brewing Company", retrieved 22.7.2016 from www.carlowbrewing.com.

15 For brewing in Wexford, see www.blackstairsbrewing.com, retrieved 22.7.2016.

16 See www.smithwicksexperience.com, retrieved 22.7.2016.

17 For more information on Smithwick's Brewery, Kilkenny, see "Smithwick's Experience Kilkenny", www.smithwicksexperience.com, retrieved 22.7.2016.

18 For the vision, aims, and programmes of the Kilkenny Leader Partnership see www.cklp.ie, retrieved 15.4.2016.

Kilkenny initiatives consisting of arrranged or self-guided tours with various themes, including one concentrating on "food and drink", around the county.[19]

In 2013, the Kilkenny LEADER Partnership also ran a competition for the title "Town of Food", for which several towns in the county entered, and Thomastown, a small rural town situated a few miles outside Kilkenny city, succeeded in winning the award. The town's application for the title, and the associated grant-aid available for the winners, included a plan to create a new school, the "Kilkenny School of Food," for training chefs and catering staff. As part of the prize, the organising committee secured significant funding to establish this school, which offers a wide range of accredited professional courses, as well as amateur cookery classes throughout the year.[20]

Food Initiatives in Kilkenny

Alongside the high-quality artisan food production and eating establishments now found in the city of Kilkenny and surrounding areas, there is a number of other food initiatives to draw the interested tourist to the area, and to help to promote the "town of food", and the "food region" ideas. There are several operational cookery schools, delivering many different training and educational courses,[21] a tourist-oriented food trail that takes the visitor around the county to various food-related destinations,[22] and there is also an annual food festival, which brings artisan producers together in one place to exhibit their produce.[23]

The "Taste Kilkenny" trail website provides a free, downloadable map, which pinpoints the location of several restaurants and cafés, delicatessens, food producers who are open to visitors, and other "food destinations and experiences".[24] The list of food producers ready to receive visitors includes those managing an orchard, a free-range poultry farm, a trout farm, and a cheese production enterprise.

---

19 For the "TRAIL Kilkenny" initiative, see www.trailkilkenny.ie, retrieved 24.5.2016.

20 See "Thomastown wins 'Town of Food' Title", retrieved 20.7.2016 from www.knockdrinna.com/thomastown-wins-town-of-food title; see also www.visitkilkenny.ie?School-Of-Food, rerieved 20.7.2016.

21 See "Cookery Schools in Kilkenny" at www.visitkilkenny.ie/cookery, retrieved 22.7.2016.

22 See "Trail Kilkenny. Taste of Kilkenny Food Trail / Themed Trails" at http://www.trailkilkenny.ie/themed-trails/taste-of-kilkenny-food-trail/, retrieved 22.7.2016.

23 For the "Savour Kilkenny, Festival of Food", see www.savourkilkenny.com, retrieved 22.7.2016.

24 See further, http://www.trailkilkenny.ie/themed-trails/taste-of-kilkenny-food-trail/, retrieved 22.7.2016.

The "Savour Kilkenny Food Festival"[25] is an annual weekend-long event, celebrating its tenth anniversary in 2016. The festival programme includes talks, lectures, demonstrations, workshops and dining events organized by local food-industry representatives, and nationally-known chefs and cooks. The events cover a wide variety of food-related themes, including sustainability, health and wellness, foraging, distilling and brewing, superfoods and their benefits, food photography, "forgotten" meat cuts, and international ethnic food. Part of the programme is dedicated to children, and includes baking competitions, educational talks and workshops to get the younger generation interested in food, cooking, and food provenance.

These opportunities, in particular the food trail and the food festival, with the financial support of the Kilkenny LEADER Partnership, make networking between small and new businesses easier, while providing them with a forum in which to showcase their produce to members of the public and to other business people.

Case Studies:

1. Goatsbridge Trout Farm

Mag Kirwan, a third generation farmer, runs Goatsbridge Trout Farm near Thomastown, Co. Kilkenny, and has been heavily involved in the LEADER-sponsored strategy to develop County Kilkenny as a destination for food-oriented visitors, for several years. The farm includes a visitors' centre, and a shop in which the trout products, including smoked, and barbecued trout, a trout pâté, and a trout caviar, can be sampled and bought. Her trout farm is listed on the "Taste Kilkenny Food Trail" and is open to visitors. Mag lives on the farm with her family, and they pride themselves in the maintenance of this farm and on upholding their traditions of "purity" and "sustainability" in food production.[26]

Kirwan explains that there was more to the coordination of efforts to promote the Kilkenny region as a food destination than a response to an economic need. Those who got involved early on in the process, including herself, had a vision for the area. They saw other parts of Ireland develop their local and artisan food industries, including West Cork, for example, and they agreed that Ireland, and in particular the south east, has undoubtedly some of the best natural food produce in the world. Their pride in that natural produce drove them to market it

25 For more information on the festival, see www.savourkilkenny.com, retrieved 20.5.2016.

26 www.goatsbridgetrout.ie/about, retrieved 23.5.2016.

alongside the arts, crafts and other elements of culture that had already made Kilkenny a popular tourist destination. Now the "Taste of Kilkenny" brand is often seen alongside the well-known, longer-established "Made in Kilkenny" brand.[27]

Having been involved in these food and tourism-oriented initiatives for several years, Mag Kirwan recognises that, although she has seen an expansion in tourism, this increase is not all food-related. "There is a cross-over", she explains, as people might take in "a bit of the food trail while on the cycling trail". She sees Kilkenny city as being most certainly a "foodie town", having been publicly acknowledged in this context by food writers, and by also having two Michelin-recognised restaurants among the many eateries to be found in the county; but she is also aware that much more work still remains to be done to enable the Kilkenny area to be recognized as a food region.

The "Savour Kilkenny" food festival is in its tenth year, and although new and innovative at the time of its inception, it now has to compete with many more similar food festivals in many other counties.[28] Kirwan asserts that the challenge lies in maintaining momentum in asserting the identity of Kilkenny as a "food region", and in staying ahead of food-related innovations in other parts of the country. This, she believes, is the best way to ensure that local food businesses remain viable. To that end, the network of food producers involved in the "Taste Kilkenny" group are pushing for a more coordinated approach, a county-wide strategy that will support them all in their continued efforts to keep the Kilkenny area on the food-tourist's map.[29]

2. *Knockdrinna Cheese*

The well-known television cook and blogger, Donal Skehan wrote on his blog as follows concerning Helen Finnegan's Knockdrinna Cheese:

> The world of good food production is as much a story of sharing as it is about business plans. Our ancient cheese-making history was all but lost until people like Veronica Steel of Milleens came along and from that grew our world-class cheese industry. Helen Finnegan is one of the inheritors of this new tradition as well as an inspiration to part-time artisans wondering if it's worth striking out into the foodie world full-time.[30]

---

27 For the "Made in Kilkenny" brand, see www.visitkilkenny.ie, retrieved 8.7.2016.

28 See, for example, the "West Waterford Festival of Food, Dungarvan", retrieved 22.7.2016 from www.westwaterfordfestivaloffood.com; and "Galway Food Festival", retrieved 22.7.2016 from www.galwayfoodfestival.com; also "Bite Food Festival [Dublin]" retrieved 22.7.2016 from bitefoodfestival.ie (Dublin).

29 In conversation with Mag Kirwan, director of Goatsabridge Trout Farm, 4.7.2016.

30 See further, www.donalskehan.com/blog, retrieved 22.5.2016.

A former civil servant, Helen Finnegan made her first batch of cheese in 2004, using a few simple utensils from her own kitchen, and a small amount of goat's milk sourced from local man, Hugh Daniel's small herd of six goats.[31] After some experimentation, she produced and marketed "Knockdrinna Snow", a goat's cheese camembert, and the business grew successfully from there.

The Knockdrinna cheese company benefited from the supports for such projects put in place by the Kilkenny Leader Partnership, and Helen believes that the KLP's success with food-producing businesses stemmed from the keen interest shown in the sector by a particular board member, and from the dynamic, almost-immediate success of the "Savour Kilkenny" food festival. Although she feels that as a small business owner, her own enterprise has to be her priority, she considers that being part of a network makes everyone stronger, and encourages the idea of an "identity" for the region.[32]

Conclusion

Kilkenny, due to its abundant natural resources, has always been an area of successful food production. Today, many of the small food businesses in the area – breweries, artisan cheese-makers, and a trout farm, for example – are reminiscent of food production strategies of an earlier time.

The resurgence of interest in food, and in particular in "regional food", has led to a large number of small food-related businesses being established in the Kilkenny area. Whereas this is a common development in many parts of Ireland, the Kilkenny food scene, in contrast, is emerging as a coordinated, organized development, one with the support of local government and enterprise boards.

The motivation behind this, from the KLP's point of view, has been to improve the economic, social and cultural quality of life in the county. However, local food businesses appear to have a broader "vision" than just the economic benefits for themselves arising from an increase in tourism in Kilkenny city and county. They speak of linking pride in their own food-related businesses to that of the "region", as a whole, thus implying a sense of "regional" identity based essentially on food produce.

Although not yet an acknowledged "food region" with the historical and cultural recognition that that entails, the efforts described above – seeking to assert county Kilkenny's identity through its food produce, thereby celebrating its

31 See "Discover Farmhouse Cheese – Versatile, Natural & Delicious", at www.discoverfarmhousecheese.ie, retrieved 22.5.2016.

32 In conversation with Helen Finnegan, founder of Knockdrinna Cheese, 21.5.2016.

long history of food production and natural resources – form a contemporary construct of the more traditional understanding of the term "food region", thus bringing Ireland slowly in a new direction, where outstanding natural resources and food produce draw visitors to the country, and maybe, in the first place, to Kilkenny and the south-east.

List of References

Printed

D'Auria, Déirdre / Lysaght, Patricia: "The Online Promotion of Irish Food as a Tourist Attraction". In Krawczyk-Wasilewska, Violetta / Lysaght, Patricia (eds.): *Food and the Internet*. Peter Lang: Frankfurt am Main 2015, pp. 77–91.

Hyman, Mary / Hyman, Philip: "Food and Cuisine in France". In Katz, Solomon H. / Weaver, William Woys (eds.): *Encyclopedia of Food and Culture*, vol. 2. Charles Scribner's Sons: New York 2003, pp. 31–49.

Köstlin, Konrad: "A New Ascension of Regional Food". In Lysaght, Patricia (ed.): *Food and Meals at Cultural Crossroads. Proceedings of the 17th Conference of the International Food Commission for Ethnological Food Research*, Oslo, Norway, September 15–19, 2008 (Oslo: Novus Press, 2010), pp. 36–45.

Long, Lucy M.: "Symbol, Food as". In Katz, Solomon H. / Weaver, William Woys (eds.): *Encyclopedia of Food and Culture*, vol. 3. Charles Scribner's Sons: New York 2003), pp. 376–378.

Long, Lucy M.: "Tourism". In Katz, Solomon H. / Weaver, William Woys (eds.): *Encyclopedia of Food and Culture*, vol. 3. Charles Scribner's Sons: New York 2003), pp. 407–409.

Lucas, A. T.: "Irish Food Before The Potato". *Gwerin* 3(2), 1960, pp. 8–43.

Martin, F. X.: "John, Lord of Ireland, 1185–1216". In Cosgrove, Art (ed.): *A New History of Ireland II, Medieval Ireland, 1169–1534* (Oxford: Clarendon Press, 1993), pp. 127–155.

Whelan, Kevin, "The Modern Landscape: From Plantation to the Present". In Aalen, F. H. A. / Whelan/ Kevin / Stout, Matthew (eds.), *Atlas of the Irish Rural Landscape*. Toronto University Press: Toronto. 2011, pp. 67–103.

Internet

"Biabeag (Small Food): Exploring the world of small scale, ethical & local food producers", retrieved 20.5.2016 from biabeag.com.

"Bite Food Festival [Dublin]", retrieved 22.7.2016 from bitefoodfestival.ie.

"Black Abbey", retrieved 23.5.2016 from www.visitkilkenny.ie/black_abbey.

Department of Agriculture, Food and the Marine, retrieved 24.5.2016 from www.agriculture.gov.ie.

"Census. CSO. Central Statistics Office", retrieved 20.5.2016 from www.census.cso.ie.

"Cookery Schools in Kilkenny", retrieved 22.7.2016 from www.visitkilkenny.ie/cookery.

"Discover Farmhouse Cheese – Versatile, Natural & Delicious", www.discoverfarmhousecheese.ie, retrieved 22.5.2016.

"Donal's Journal", retrieved 22.5.2016 from www.donalskehan.com/blog.

"Duiske Abbey", retrieved 21.5.2016 from www.discoverireland.ie/duiske-abbey.

"Dungarvan Brewing Company", retrieved 22.7.2016 from www.goodfoodireland.com/place/dungarvan-brewing-company.

"Food NI – Our Food So Good!", retrieved 5.5.2016 from www.nigoodfood.com.

"Four Rivers. Slow Food Ireland", retrieved 20.5.2016 from www.slowfoodireland/four-rivers.

"Galway Food Festival", retrieved 22.7.2016 from www.galwayfoodfestival.com.

"Goatsbridge Rainbow Trout Farm", retrieved 20.5.2016 from www.goatsbridgetrout.ie and www.goatsbridgetrout.ie/about.

"Inistioge [Abbey]", retrieved 21.5.2016 from www.inistioge.ie/history_of_Inistioge.

"Ireland's Ancient East", retrieved 7.5.2016 from www.irelandsancienteast.com.

"Jerpoint Abbey", retrieved 23.5.2016 from www.heritageireland.ie/south-east/jerpointabbey.

"Kilkenny", retrieved 7.7.2016 from www.visitkilkenny.ie.

"Kilkenny LEADER Partnership", retrieved 24.5.2016 from www.cklp.ie.

"Knockdrinna Farmhouse Cheese Co.", retrieved 20.5.2016 from www.knockdrinna.com.

"Made in Kilkenny", retrieved 8.7.2016 from www.visitkilkenny.ie.

"Northern Ireland Year of Food and Drink 2016", retrieved 5.5.2016 from www.nigoodfood.com, or www.discovernorthernireland.com/yearoffoodanddrink2016.

"O'Hara's. Carlow Brewing Company", retrieved 22.7.2016 from www.carlowbrewing.com.

"Savour Kilkenny, Festival of Food", retrieved 20.5.2016 from www.savourkilkenny.com.

"Smithwick's Experience Kilkenny", retrieved 22.7.2016 from www.smithwicksexperience.com.

"The Three Sisters" [Barrow, Nore and Suir Rivers], retrieved 23.7.2016 from https://www.google.ie/search?q=Three+sisters+rivers&ie=utf-8&oe=utf-8&client=firefox-b&gws_rd=cr&ei=3bKXV4X8AeaNgAbLr4uABA.

"The School of Food", Thomastown, Co. Kilkenny, retrieved 20.7.2016 from visitkilkenny.ie/School-Of-Food.

"Thomastown Wins 'Town of Food' Title", retrieved 20.7.20167 from www.knockdrinna.com/thomastown-wins-town-of-food title.

"Top Ten Breweries in Enniscorthy" retrieved 22.7.2016 from https://www.yelp.ie/search?cflt=breweries&find_loc=Enniscorthy%2C+Co.+Wexford.

"TRAIL Kilkenny", retrieved 24.5.2016 from www.trailkilkenny.ie.

"Trail Kilkenny. Taste of Kilkenny Food Trail / Themed Trails", retrieved 22.7.2016 from http://www.trailkilkenny.ie/themed-trails/taste-of-kilkenny-food-trail/.

"West Waterford Festival of Food, Dungarvan", retrieved 22.7.2016 from www.westwaterfordfestivaloffood.com.

"Wild Atlantic Way", retrieved 7.5.2016 from www.wildatlanticway.com.

Maja Godina Golija

Slovenian Cheeses Mohant, Tolminc and Nanos, and their Importance for Local Food Production and Regional Identity

Abstract: *Slovenia's considerable geographical diversity led to numerous differences in the food culture of its regions and produced four distinct food regions. An important part of the Alpine food region consists of different cheeses. The making of the Mohant, Tolminc and Nanos cheeses is important for the economy of local farms, for tourism, and for the culinary offer of the Slovenian Alpine region.*

Traditional food and festive dishes, their preparation, variety, and regional diversity are the themes most often dealt with in ethnological literature. Apart from spiritual culture, ethnographers were already interested in certain elements of material culture in the 19th century, and believed that foods expressed special characteristics and original features of a nation or an ethnic group. But food is not only a component of the material world; it also plays an important role in the culture and the social life of the community. Collective preparation and consumption of food connects people, creates new relations, and strengthens the position of an individual within the community. Günter Wiegelmann, a German ethnologist and one of the founders of modern research on food culture, once wrote that food, in addition to speech and clothing, is the only cultural element that is realized on a daily basis (Wiegelmann 2006, 13). His opinion is shared by a number of researchers who maintain that on all levels and in all periods of European civilisation, shared meals were one of the most significant forms of daily, as well as occasional, and particularly festive, communication among people. Eating is therefore not just a way of satisfying a basic biological need; it is also a social activity and an act of communication between the sharers of food, which is strongly linked to a host of cultural values (Godina Golija 1996, p. 11).

Food as a Segment of Slovenian Lifestyle and Culture

Food culture is also an important part of national and regional heritage, and thus has not just economic, but also political and social importance. As a segment of the lifestyle and culture of Slovenes, it has not been particularly closely studied by Slovenian ethnologists. Shorter texts on the food culture of the Slovenian rural population were published in comprehensive reviews of Slovenian popular culture in the 1960s and 1980s – for example, in *Slovenska ljudska kultura* ("Slovenian Folk Culture") in 1960 (Novak 1960, pp. 167–170) and *Slovensko ljudsko izročilo* ("Slovenian Folk Heritage") in 1980 (Angelos 1980, pp. 110–118). During the last two decades, Slovenian ethnologists have focused their research on typical local dishes and on regional food products.

Slovenia, as a part of Central Europe, is situated at the crossroads of important European cultures and diverse geographical areas. These heterogeneous geographical features and contacts with Slovenia's neighbouring, and predominantly larger European nations, have been determining factors regarding the lifestyle, economy, and certainly the regional food culture, of its inhabitants, for centuries. People inhabiting the Pannonian plain in the eastern part of the country, have typically used wheat flour, frequently preparing pasta, leavened pies, and breads not made anywhere else in Slovenia. Dishes were often flavoured with sour cream, milk, pumpkinseed oil, as well as, although to a lesser extent, cottage cheese, red pepper, and poppy seeds. Inhabitants of central Slovenia consumed a great variety of cereals and root crops (Godina Golija 2006, p. 51). Many dishes were made from millet and buckwheat gruel, dried fruit, sauerkraut, potato and sour turnip. In the Alpine north, an area studded with dairying mountains, the food consumed by the local population depended heavily on animal products, particularly on dairy foods such as milk, a variety of cheeses, and cream. Dishes were often flavoured with minced lard. The westernmost part of Slovenia is Mediterranean in character. Typical for this area was the use of olive oil, as well as a larger consumption of vegetables and fruit than in other parts of Slovenia, and also fish. Polenta replaced bread in every meal (ibid., p. 52).

Increasing industrialization, the introduction of railways and, as a consequence, greater mobility in the 19th century and at the beginning of the 20th century, gradually significantly diminished the regional diversity of Slovenia. The rural population started to purchase some of the staples used in their daily dishes in stores, something which considerably influenced the structure of their menus. These changes became much more pronounced at the end of the 1950s and in the 1960s, which was mainly due to the higher standard of living of the majority of the Slovenian population. No longer chiefly dependent on home-grown produce, the meals became more uniform in character and lost some of their regional characteristics.

Ethnological research on food culture gradually started to follow these changes. From the mid-1990s, scholarly interest in the subject increased once again, particularly among curators in regional museums (Mlakar Adamič 2004). The results of this interest are evident in studies that no longer concentrate solely on so-called popular food culture, but focus also on the food culture of townspeople and the working classes.

Designation and Promotion of Slovenian dishes

During the last two decades, Slovenian ethnologists have also focused their research on typical local dishes and rural food products, and on the protection of their geographical indications and designations of origin within the European Union. The search for, and the promotion of, typical Slovenian dishes is encouraged by the Slovenian Ministry of Agriculture, Forestry and Food of the Republic of Slovenia, whose primary aim is to promote Slovenian agricultural goods and certain food products. Several ethnologists have been participating in the preparation of documentation for the preservation of Slovenian food products within the European Union. The Ministry of Agriculture, Forestry and Food of the Republic of Slovenia adopted the Regulation on the Conditions for the Use of the Designation of Traditional Specialty Guaranteed (TSG) for various Slovenian foods, and awarded certain foodstuffs and dishes the designation of protected food product (Gašek / Kos-Skubic 2010, p. 25). In addition, foodstuffs may also have Protected Designation of Origin (PDO), as well as Protected Geographical Indication (PGI), status. Both emphasize the significance of the region in which a particular item of food has been produced and specify the kinds of ingredients used throughout its production process. The designation Traditional Specialty Guaranteed, however, focuses more on the original recipe for a dish, ensuring that it is prepared from traditional ingredients and in a traditional manner (ibid., p. 9).

During 2009, 2010 and 2014, the author of this study conducted fieldwork in the Slovenian Alpine region, collecting data, literature, and photographic material on the characteristic cheeses used in Alpine cuisine: Mohant cheese, Tolminc cheese and Nanos cheese. These cheeses represent an important element of what both agriculture and tourism have to offer in the Slovenian Alpine region, and serve to promote its local cuisine and heritage (Godina Golija 2010, pp. 56–59).

Slovenian Cheeses Protected in the European Union

Slovenia was able to protect three varieties of cheese in the European Union: Nanos, Tolminc, and Mohant cheese. All three kinds have Protected Designation of Origin status. They are protected, because they originate from a particular Slovenian place or region, which significantly affects the characteristics or quality of this agricultural product and distinguishes it from similar European products. Natural and human factors from the Alpine environment are important for the production of these cheeses, because they affect their colour, shape, texture and taste – thus all production processes must be performed in a particular geographic area.

Tolminc cheese has a round shape and has a smooth rind with a few holes about the size of lentils or peas. The first records of Tolminc cheese date back to the 13th

century. In these sources, the cheese was mentioned as a form of payment to landowners at that time. The cheese is only produced in the Upper Posočje area and has a very long and rich tradition. The beginnings of cheese production in that region are linked to the commencement of grassland farming on the high mountain pastures, because at that time the production of cheese was the only method of conserving milk. The unique taste of this cheese is the result of the climatic and geographic conditions of the mountainous regions, the cattle breed itself, as well as the method of cattle breeding. The taste of Tolminc cheese is at first sweet and milky and, as it matures, it becomes more intense, rich, aromatic, and sweetly spicy with the taste of walnuts. It has a smooth, light yellow natural rind, and, when cut, a few holes about the size of lentils or peas can be seen. It is matured on wooden shelves in a controlled environment. It has the shape of a wheel and weighs approximately 3kg.

Nanos cheese is produced on the outer edge of the Alpine region on the Nanos plateau, which borders on the Mediterranean world. In the vicinity of the plateau, there are the rich vineyards of the Vipava valley, as well as the Karst plateau, the Trnovo plateau, and the Idrija hills, from where the milk used for the production of the cheese comes. The milk is derived exclusively from brown cattle, which are bred in these geographical areas. Records show that the Nanos cheese was already being produced in the 16th century. It has an intense yellow colour, because the milk from which it is produced has a high beta-carotene content. Because of the special microflora of vineyard areas where the cheese maturing rooms are located, the Nanos cheese, after two months of maturing, gets its special spicy taste, which distinguishes it from other Slovenian and European cheeses.

Fig. 1: Mohant cheese as a part of an everyday meal (Photo: Maja Godina Golija, 2009).

Mohant cheese is a traditional dairy product, made in villages and on dairy mountains in Bohinj and its vicinity. Its distinctive, slightly tangy and bitter taste and strong smell, make it different from other kinds of cheese produced in Slovenia. Even before the First World War, the ethnologist Rajko Ložar wrote that it had a simple and very old production process, one which was practised even before the hard cheeses of Bohinj started to be produced in the mid-19th century (Ložar 1944, p. 202). Traditionally made in remote places far from main roads or milk-collecting locations, Mohant cheese was made from the surplus milk which the local farmers could not sell. The cheese is presently made on approximately fifteen farms situated in the municipality of Bohinj, either for the farmers' own consumption or as a registered supplementary economic activity. While in the first, and generally the more frequent, case, the cheese is made in people's homes, usually in kitchens, several farmers have also built small cheese dairies on their property.

The manufacturing process is as follows. When the milk is heated, the cheese-maker adds rennet. After twenty or forty minutes, the milk curdles. The curd is then roughly cut, stirred, and strained through a cloth or a sieve. After the whey has been drained, the curd is mixed with salt and placed in containers. Until the 1980s, the cheese was shaped into loaves, weighing two kg each, which were placed in wooden containers, and left to age. Thereafter, many farmers started to place layer upon layer of the cheese in plastic containers, as they still do today. The cheese was then pressed, covered with a linen cloth and a wooden lid, and, additionally, weighted. Then it was left to ripen at 20 °C for a period lasting from four to six weeks, with excessive whey being constantly drained away. During this period, the cheese acquired its typical sharp, pungent flavour, light-yellow colour, and plastic texture (Godina Golija 2010, p. 57).

Mohant cheese is generally consumed as a part of everyday dishes and meals. It is eaten with bread or with boiled sliced potatoes; it adds flavour to corn and buckwheat mush, roast potatoes, soups, and fried eggs. Home-makers have created and written down some modern recipes for its preparation – for pastries, cookies, omelettes, and main dishes, for example. These newly-created dishes with Mohant cheese serve to enrich the existing tourist offer and catering services, particularly on agritourist farms (ibid.).

The role of Mohant cheese in the life, and particularly in the economy, food culture, and folk medicine of the population of Bohinj and its vicinity, has not yet been researched in detail. The Cheese Making Society of Bohinj (*Sirarsko društvo Bohinj*), which had taken steps to gain the European Union Protected Designation of Origin for Mohant cheese, has been successful in the preservation of this heritage. Knowledge about the production of this cheese is generally transmitted within the family, from generation to generation; the recipes are disseminated in the same manner.

The making of Mohant cheese is important for the economy of local farms, for tourism, and for the culinary offer of Bohinj. Preservation of the knowledge of its production process, and its use in cooking, are of exceptional importance for the safeguarding, presentation, and improvement of ethnographic characteristics and cultural heritage in northwest Slovenia, particularly in Bohinj, and in the area of the Triglav National Park (Godina Golija 2012, pp. 91–104).

Fig. 2: Making Mohant cheese at home (Photo: Maja Godina Golija, 2009).

Despite the fact that the further financing of this research project – the Slovenian Register of Intangible Heritage – has been terminated, the work will nevertheless continue. It is in this manner that ethnologists try to draw attention to the significance of local products and dishes that are a part of the intangible heritage of a country. An important factor in the efforts made for the preservation of cultural diversity and a high quality of living, these elements represent a weighty counterpoint to globalisation and the unification of food culture.

Conclusion

Food culture as a segment of the lifestyle and culture of Slovenes had not been particularly closely studied by Slovenian ethnologists in the past. During recent decades, however, they have focused their research on several local products and on the protection of their geographical indications and designations of origin within the European Union. The important reason for this approach has been an increasing interest in regional food in connection with the tourist industry and economic development in certain regions.

When regional food becomes recognized as a local specialty and as a part of local heritage, a number of previously, seemingly unimportant, questions, come into focus. These relate primarily to the ownership of this heritage and to the dilemma concerning who has the right to use and exploit it, and also about who is the officially-recognized implementing agency for such culinary heritage. Another highly pertinent question concerns the geographical origin of food heritage, particularly in view of the ongoing process of heritage delocalization. It is therefore necessary to recognize as a matter of urgency that the act of determining what foods are regional food products, and how they should be commercialized, involves more than a simple, one-dimensional transfer from the local environment to the global market; new and intermediary factors also arise in the course of this process (Tschofen 2010, p. 119).

Similar processes were also evident during research on the production, safeguarding, and promotion of the Slovenian cheese, Mohant. Since some producers have also started to make Mohant cheese in other parts of Slovenia, thus attempting to delocalize a part of Slovenian cultural heritage, the Cheese-Making Society of Bohinj has taken steps to protect it within the territory of Slovenia itself, as well as in other parts of Europe. The cheese is now sold in its typical packaging furnished with the slogan proclaiming that "Mohant cheese is unique." The slogan emphasizes the territorial origin of the cheese, its exclusiveness, and its uniqueness.

The Mohant, Tolminc and Nanos cheeses, and their significance for the local population, are not purely economic; they are also symbolic. Proud of this part of their local identity, the people of the Alpine region present cheese to the public in various ways – on web pages describing the Triglav National Park and other local tourist attractions, for example. The manner in which local culinary knowledge is treated, popularized and advertised, is important; equally so is also the way in which it is disseminated. This is a multifaceted issue that involves new elements and experiences that have an impact on the construction of cultural complexes. According to Barbara Kirschenblatt Gimblett, all heritage interventions alter relations between people, their actions, and cultural elements: "They change how people understand their culture and themselves. They change the fundamental conditions for cultural production and reproduction" (Kirschenblatt-Gimblett 2004, p. 58).

Local, regional, and national food and meals have to be understood as arising from a combination of values, and in relation to the concept of how to use cultural heritage for economic and political purposes. It can be concluded that Slovenian cheeses have become an important element, not only regarding economic activity and tourism, but also in the creation of local identities and cultural heritage in the Alpine region of Slovenia.

List of References

Printed

Angelos, Baš (ed.): *Slovensko ljudsko izročilo* ("Slovenian Folk Heritage"). Cankarjeva založba: Ljubljana 1980.

Gašek, Vlasta / Kos-Skubic, Mira: *Slovenski zaščiteni kmetijski pridelki in živila* ("Slovenian Protected Agricultural Products and Foodtuffs"). Ministrstvo za kmetijstvo, gozdarstvo in prehrano: Ljubljana 2010.

Godina Golija, Maja: "Contemporary Appropriations of Culinary Tradition in Slovenia". *Traditiones* 41, 2012, pp. 91–104.

Godina Golija, Maja: "Mohant" ("Mohant Cheese"). In Križnar, N. (ed.) *Živa kulturna dediščina se predstavi*. Slovensko etnološko društvo: Ljubljana 2010, pp. 56–59.

Godina Golija, Maja: *Prehranski pojmovnik za mlade* ("Concepts of Food Culture for Young People"). Založba Obzorja: Maribor 2006.

Godina Golija, Maja: *Prehrana v Mariboru v dvajsetih in tridesetih letih 20. stoletja* ("Food Culture in Maribor in the 1920s and 1930s"). Obzorja: Maribor 1996.

Kirschenblatt-Gimblett, Barbara: "Intangible Heritage as Metacultural Production". *Museum International* 221 / 222, 56(1–2), 2004, pp. 52–65.

Ložar, Rajko: *Narodopisje Slovencev 1* ("Ethnography of Slovenes 1"). Ljubljana: Klas 1944.

Mlakar Adamič, Jana: *Teknilo nam je!* ("It Was to Our Taste!"). Zasavski muzej: Trbovlje 2004.

Novak, Vilko: *Slovenska ljudska kultura* ("Slovenian Folk Culture"). Državna založba Slovenije: Ljubljana 1960.

Tschofen, Bernhard: "Things, Senses, Practices: Experiencing Cultural Crossroads through Hospitality and the Culinary System". In Lysaght, Patricia (ed.): *Food and Meals at Cultural Crossroads*. Oslo: Novus Press, 2010, pp. 112–122.

Wiegelmann, Günter: *Alltags und Festspeisen in Mitteleuropa*. Waxmann: Münster 2006.

Daša Ličen

Culinary Experts' Horizon of Istrian Food

Abstract: *This article takes an ethnographic approach to the contemporary food movement on the Istrian Peninsula, which is, to a great extent, made coherent precisely by Istrian food. Regional gourmet heroes, who, through their discourses on the alternativeness of Istrian food, create and distribute ideas about what "authentic" Istrian cuisine is, are at the centre of this text.*

Introduction

> Fifteen years ago, I said mad cow disease had emerged because of [wicked] alimentary practices. I am now very worried that current trends might result in mad children, which is a big menace to a population that used to be healthy. The cherries are still there, the sun too, and sardines are in the sea.

The above quote from one of the culinary experts I interviewed as part of my research on Istrian-food experts, reveals her view of "long-established" Istrian cuisine as a means by which an individual, or an entire region, can break away from all overly modern, fake, artificial, unhealthy, and even dangerous practices typical of the modern world. This paper questions discourses such as this, which do not always distinguish between designations such as ecological, organic, healthy, good, traditional, or authentic, in food contexts, because, at least in the eyes of the culinary experts, that is, my interviewees, Istrian food combines all of these desirable traits. These local food experts produce gastronomic knowledge, which spreads among the inhabitants of the Istrian Peninsula, forming an intangible resource of Istrianess *par excellence*. Through their approach and food preparation, they establish themselves and regional cuisine in opposition to mainstream global food networks. Although *food in Istria* is clearly present in many forms and varieties, my interviewees talk of *Istrian food* as if it possessed a heaven-sent identity, and thus one with strong, long, and eternal roots. An ethnographic approach was used to examine this regional case, which partially follows global currents but also maintains its own particular features.

Debates on which foodstuffs are Istrian, how or when to prepare an "authentic" Istrian meal, and how to serve it, are dominated by a group of people whom I refer to as culinary experts. They are journalists, cooks, restaurant owners, and festival organizers, or all of these rolled into one, who are considered by themselves and by others to be knowledgeable when it comes to Istrian food. Although the experts often criticize each other and seek to stand alone at the apex of the Istrian food-expertise hierarchy, their views on Istrian cuisine and their activities are actually very similar to those of each other. They form a group of individuals who, in Bourdieu's terms, are considered to possess distinguished taste (Bourdieu 1984) and, for that reason are called on to judge what is, and what is not, Istrian, in a food context. In the remainder of this article, I will focus initially on the region itself, then deal with experts' discourses about, and their perception concerning how Istrian food integrates into an alternative market category.

The Istria Region

Istria lies at the intersection of Slavic, Romance, and Germanic settlement areas. The Istrian Peninsula, located in the very north of the Adriatic Sea, between the Gulf of Trieste and Kvarner Bay, is less than 90 kilometers wide and 100 kilometers long (north to south). It is currently divided among three countries, the largest share belonging to Croatia (89 %), then a Slovenian part consisting of three municipalities, and a rather small part belonging to Italy. It may come as a surprise to learn that, in the case of Istria, the hinterland coastline-division may be more meaningful in cultural and identity terms than the very recent international one (Rotar 1993, pp. 15–24); Darovec 1993, pp. 179–193).

Most studies of Istria depict situations with regard to national borders, or focus on either its Slovenian or Croatian part, but do not look at Istria as a region. Researchers tracing links between collective identities and food generally focus either on ethnic cuisines or national ones. Regional cuisines are often basically forgotten. My ethnographic study of Istrian food experts' discourses, argues for the significance of regions in food studies. I share the opinion that in most cases regions are cultural landscapes, the product of specific natural environments and history. This also holds true for Istria, which was split by international borders only after World War II. The purpose of the study is to show that regions (in this case, Istria) are largely homogeneous units, within which a specific natural, as well as a cultural, context can be discerned and followed.

Contemporary Changes

The birth of recent interest in cuisine and gastronomic festivals, and the discourses surrounding them, are often difficult to comprehend. Even Sidney Mintz whom some regard as the father of food anthropology, has seemed puzzled by the increasing popularity of food as an international phenomenon during the last three decades (Mintz 2011, p. 1, retrieved 30.6.2016 from http://openanthcoop.

net/press/http://openanthcoop.net/press/wp- content/uploads/2011/01/Mintz-Devouring-Objects-of-Study1.pdf). The market for Istrian cuisine has been emerging since the early 1990s, and the number of associated food experts, as well as gastronomic festivals, has been growing exponentially since then. Resulting foodways, emerging as authentic Istrian cuisine, offer the discipline of anthropology a means by which to measure cultural change. For example, I am trying to understand *why* one of the experts I spoke to said "my goal is to destroy muffins and to save *buhteljni* [local sweet rolls filled with jam]."

Consistency within so-called traditional Istrian cuisine is commonly recognized among researchers, whereas contemporary Istrian food homogeneity often remains ignored. Food changes not only with sites, but also through time; it is repeatedly born, each time a bit differently. Consequently, in the case of Istria, I aim, not simply to indicate that there is historical interweaving within food culture in the region, but also to provide an idea about current regional food discourses – which are indeed present in the entire region nowadays. It must be recognized that in the food experts' minds, authentic Istrian food is inextricably linked to notions of traditional, ecological, and alternative, markets. It is thus regarded as being in opposition to the mainstream agro-industrial market and hence considered as an alternative to it.

Istrian and other authenticity-seeking food movements arise out of an uneasiness with the food industry and its, to them, perturbing "universalism", or application to the masses. However, a complex geography of food survives in Europe and in other places as well. Quality is seen as being an inherent trait of local and natural foods. In Miele and Murdoch's terms (2003, pp. 25–41), culinary experts like those in Istria are against food as fuel and in favour of food as pleasure, linking cultural life to biodiverse production-spaces that aim to diffuse knowledge about typical products and local cuisines. In this context, and in France and Italy in particular, regional cooking has achieved iconic cultural status, something which Istria is striving for. Praise of such regional culinary diversity is not just a form of nostalgia for the past, but rather a way of looking at present culinary development in Istria and of assessing its possible future.

In a very broad way, this article is an anthropological study of "grassroots" responses to more global changes. Regional, authentic-food movements are, in fact, a reaction to accelerated dietary changes. This makes the culinary movement under investigation here, resist mass-market capitalism. In addition to being a response to the global, the Istrian culinary movement has its own unique characteristics, which have grown from a particular local context – Istria's established "in between" position, which Bojan Baskar (2002) calls "ambiguous".

Discourses

One of the most striking aspects that I noticed, when studying the culinary experts' discourses, was the arbitrary use of adjectives, such as *Istrian*, *authentic*, *traditional*, *natural*, *healthy*, and a number of others, associated with Istrian food. Such an oversimplified use of such terms creates obstacles for labelling the precise meaning of each. They all exist as interchangeable terms within the discourses on Istrian food, and are also used to characterize Istrian food itself. The point is, therefore, not to seek to understand each of them separately, because, even though all of the blended adjectives suggest something slightly different, nevertheless they are all merged or amalgamated under the "master-signifier" – "Istrian food". However, I believe that "authenticity" might be regarded as the most relevant term in this context as it seems to encompass the very kernel of culinary discourses in Istria. Ethnographic experiences have indeed proved that "authenticity" frequently serves as a code word for all of the other positive adjectives ascribed to Istrian food. Thus the keyword *authenticity* is a kind of Möbius strip on which all of the terms endlessly overlap but nevertheless have one broader meaning; namely, the "splendid" assortment of Istrian culinary characteristics.

I found the mixture of terms present in Istrian food discourses to describe the characteristics of Istrian food, to be reasonably coherent among all of the Istrian culinary experts, regardless of their citizenship. Certain differences do exist, but these are not based on national or ethnic divisions, but can be related rather to a person's essential "ruralness" or "urbanness" in outlook, something which I cannot go into further at this point. A consistent dietary pattern has existed within Istria for decades. However, a coherent and unified group of discourses on food also suggests the existence of a current unity in the Istrian dietary pattern. Istrian food is often described using concepts such as genuine, real, or true, thereby establishing itself in opposition to what is supposedly inauthentic and fake. Both extremes, the positive as well as the negative, are usually rejected altogether by the social sciences. Nevertheless, consideration of these positions can yield useful results if approached cautiously.

While the meaning ascribed to "authenticity" can shift from one context to the next, yet it tends to hint at something that is true, original, good, morally right, ecological, organic, part of a fair market, and so on. However, according to Jeffrey Pratt, "the totalizing character of this discourse hides the fact that the different qualities evoked for alternative foods do not in fact entail each other, and may pull in different directions" (Pratt 2007, p. 285). For example, in the minds of the culinary experts that I interviewed, dishes made from Istrian oxen (*boškarin*) turn out better than just "beef" dishes. These *boškarin* dishes are implicitly, but at times even explicitly, considered to be better, healthier, more environmentally friendly, and, of course, more traditional and authentic, than other "beef" dishes, which demands that they be accompanied by other "typical" products, and which allows the sellers to set their prices high – something which I will discuss below. This situation then of authentic/Istrian versus non-authentic/non-Istrian presents a challenge that can never be completely resolved. Nonetheless, commencing with a consideration of the dichotomy between "Istrian" versus "non-Istrian" as being more colourful than that between "bad" versus "good" is probably a helpful starting point.

The Alternative Market

The inner passion of culinary experts is not sufficient to provide them with economic stability; they need to make a profit in order to put bread on the table. However, it is the case that the majority of them are rather well off, precisely because of their culinary activities. They write books and articles, host TV shows, give lectures, attend food tastings, and lead workshops, and, of course, cook. Many of them are household names. Media recognition is of vital significance for them. Here I discuss how the experts tend to talk down the monetary factors connected with their activities, while in reality they are supporting precisely the mainstream economy they believe they are fighting against; they are in fact very much integrated into the mainstream global agro-industrial food system. According to the experts, the alternative food market contrasts with the mainstream one according to the manner in which it organizes production and distribution, and in terms of the cultural values integral to it (ibid.). The alternative food market is then characterized by the attention given to animal welfare, and to fair trade (Winter 2003, p. 24) – these are concerns which also hold true for the experts from the micro-region of Istria.

Some experts start out by saying that they are utterly against capitalism and its nuisances, but finish the interview with an invitation to look at the photos they took with Bernie Ecclestone on his yacht, or by saying that I should be thankful they are responding to my questions because other experts would demand money for such a conversation. Where I detect the greatest contrast, between their ideological pro-authenticity stance and their more concrete activities, lies, is when they talk about the future. On the one hand, they imply that what they do is for the future betterment of humanity, while, on the other, it would seem that their interest is directed mainly towards themselves and their families. They wish to return to the "genuine", to the era before the industrial revolution, but they simultaneously seek to earn enough money to enable them to purchase a BMW, or plan to build a hotel, expand a festival, enter foreign markets, or to be able to go abroad to participate in a large food fair.

The culinary experts commonly stated in the course of their interviews that their gastronomic endeavours have nothing to do with making money; on the contrary, they are really charitable activities on their part. The longstanding organizer of an Artichoke Festival stressed how much effort goes into coordinating such an event. At first glance, the organizer seems to be sacrificing himself for the community's wellbeing by doing unpaid work in his leisure time. However, this work brings him satisfaction because he believes he is doing a worthwhile job by promoting high-quality Istrian food. On the other hand, the organizer of the festival in question, is not only engaged in the role as a respectable well-intentioned villager; he is also in fact the largest local artichoke retailer and one of the initiators of the festival. This enables him to sell up to one-third of his yearly harvest at this merry event – not to mention, that the earnings thus arising are not at all bad, because the price of the home-grown artichokes, which, because they are organically produced, are presumed to be very healthy, is high. His retail activities thus make his assertions about the insignificance of the financial return arising from the festival somewhat debatable.

A few kilometers away, the Slovene "truffle king", as the media has labelled him and which he does not hesitate to use himself, operates in a similar fashion. The "poisonous" food that is transported from far away should, in the opinion of the owner of this truffle-serving restaurant, be replaced with local and seasonal products, which, in his view, would hinder the impact of the huge companies from abroad that interfere with traditional routines and exacerbate social inequality. The "truffle king" is in fact even a member of a rather radical local left-wing party that fights for the renaissance of the countryside, yet he simultaneously advertises his restaurant in shopping malls, where he sets up a stall, prepares truffle dishes, and sells the home-made pastes and jams that he and his family members make. The "truffle king" appears to strive to rule two kingdoms: the authentic, as well as the inauthentic one. And, it would appear there are plenty more such emperors among the Istrian culinary experts. In the eyes of my interviewees, Istrian food is part of the alternative food market that stands against the detested mainstream one. Jeffrey Pratt (2007, 285), however, denies the existence of such strong boundaries between the mainstream and the alternative market because, he asserts, the borders between the two are in fact quite porous.

Although I am certain that the culinary experts, to some extent, at least, do believe in the authenticity of Istrian food, they are, of course, also oriented towards increasing its consumption. Unpaid experts' activities are not necessarily of a purely benevolent nature, however, as they can also be regarded as an investment, granted, at times, a very long-term one, in their own future. Thus while experts' attempts in relation to Istrian food are promising efforts, they can hardly, in themselves, serve to reorient local marketing activities in this direction. In reality, it is probably the case, that however much alternative food movements – among them also Istrian ones – seek to distance themselves from the global market, they are almost inevitably a part of it. They believe in personal economic relations and discard the impersonal market, but the authentic knowledge they disseminate encourages exactly the market they ostensibly oppose. Even though I critically assess their quasi-charitable activities, I nonetheless respect them and their strong claims to have control over their market engagement. Even though they usually fail to provide a real alternative to the mainstream market, their attempts open up new spaces – in Harvey's terms, "spaces of hope" (Harvey 2000).

Conclusion

Istrian cuisine has recently been reborn as a symbol of a civilization threatened by globalisation – an icon of the past, but also of modernity. This brief article has examined the discursive *mélange* concerning Istrian food that gourmet experts proudly disseminate and that opposes the mainstream agro-industrial food market. However, at the end of the day, the mainstream agro-industrial food market is what actually triggered all of the alternative food movements, and the one to which they all return in the end. This is not only because the culinary experts do not, in fact, distance themselves from the neo-liberal market, but also because such strict division of the market into mainstream and alternative does not exist.

By and large, I have restricted my attention to the Istria region and aimed to rethink the world that the Istrian experts established, their alternativeness, their activities and approaches, and, most of all, their efforts to design an "authentic" food experience. Insisting on regional differences, and emphasizing a unique regional culinary identity, might seem backward in the modern world, yet the process of "contamination" or globalisation still affects every place differently and transforms it in its own unique way – as claimed by Jean-Luis Flandrin and Massimo Montanari (2013, pp. 548–554). Global experiences thus reshape, but also reconfirm, the "Istrianness" of Istrian regional cuisine.

List of References

Printed

Baskar, Bojan: *Dvoumni Mediteran* ("The Ambiguous Mediterranean"). Znanstveno-raziskovalno središče: Koper 2002.

Bourdieu, Pierre: *Distinction: A Social Critique of the Judgement of Taste*. Harvard University Press: Cambridge, MA, 1984 [1979].

Darovec, Darko: "Migracije in (etnična) dihotomija mesto-podeželje v Istri do konca 18. Stoletja" ("Migrations and [Ethnic] Dichotomy in Urban-Rural Istria until the End of the 18th Century"). *Časopis za kritiko znanosti* 158 / 159, 1993, pp. 179–193.

Flandrin, Jean-Luis / Montanari, Massimo: "Today and Tomorrow". In Flandrin, Jean-Louis / Montanari, Massimo (eds.): *Food: A Culinary History from Antiquity to the Present*. New York: Columbia University Press: New York 2013, pp. 548–554.

Harvey, George: *Spaces of Hope*. University Press: Edinburgh 2000.

Miele, Mara / Murdoch, Jonathan: "Fast Food / Slow Food: Standardizing and Differentiating Cultures of Food". In Almas, Reidar / Lawrence, Geoffrey (eds.): *Globalization, Localization and Sustainable Livelihoods* Ashgate: Basingstocke 2003), pp. 25–41.

Rotar, Drago Braco: "Kje je Mediteran?" ("Where is the Mediterranean?"). *Časopis za kritiko znanosti* 158 / 159, 1993, pp. 15–24.

Pratt, Jeffrey: "Food Values: The Local and the Authentic". *Critique of Anthropology* 27(3), 2007, pp. 285–300.

Winter, David: "Embeddedness, The New Food Economy and Defensive Localism". *Journal of Rural Studies* 19(1), 2003, pp. 23–32.

Internet

Mintz, Sidney: "Devouring Objects of Study: Food and Fieldwork". Open Anthropology Cooperative Press 2011, p. 2, retrieved 30.6.2016 from http://openanthcoop.net/press/http://openanthcoop.net/press/wp-content/uploads/2011/01/Mintz-Devouring-Objects-of-Study1.pdf.

Anikó Báti

Organic Farm: A Chance for Renewal
(An Example from North-Eastern Hungary)

Abstract: *The paper shows the present situation in an agricultural, multi-disadvantaged village in north-eastern Hungary, where external resources have had to become involved in order to teach people, once again, the very basics of agriculture. It focuses on how a social agricultural project, based on collective approaches to combat a lack of alternatives, has been used as an innovative way of finding an effective solution to the village's infrastructural and social problems, thereby ensuring its ongoing viability.*

Most of the territory of Hungary is well suited to cultivation.[1] For centuries, agriculture has been the basis of livelihood for broad strata of Hungarian society. However, political, economic and social transformations in the second half of the 20th century, utterly changed that situation. In this paper I would like to trace that process – drawing on the example of one village – to show how the present situation came about, that, in an agricultural region, external sources and specialists had to be employed in order to teach people, once again, the basics of agriculture. This paper focuses on a social and agricultural project used as an innovative way in which to find a solution in collective approaches, in order to combat a lack of economic alternatives in the village in question.

In the first part of my paper I shall briefly outline the economic and socio-historical background to the national processes which affected the whole of agriculture in Hungary during the twentieth century. In the second half I shall focus on the north-eastern part of the country, one of its multi-disadvantaged regions,[2] and in particular on a single settlement, Hernádszentandrás,[3] as an example of the processes of decline and revival of a village community in twentieth-century Hungary. On the basis of my recent short-term fieldwork, I would like to present this village as a case study of a settlement that succeeded in working out an exemplary solution to its economic and social problems, by placing the resources avail-

---

1 The author, Anikó Báti works for the Hungarian Academy of Sciences, Research Centre for Humanities, Institute of Ethnology, Budapest, Hungary.

2 For social agricultural projects and public work organized by municipalities and civil societies in the region see: Morell 2015, retrieved 1.8.2016 from www.socio.hu/uploads/files/2015en_food/asztalos_morell.pdf.

3 Hernádszentandrás; www.hernadszentandras.hu, retrieved 1.8.2016.

able to it (arable land and manpower) in the service of sustainable development. I conducted interviews with some participants in the programme concerning their work, and I was able to observe the daily operation of the organic farm. I also collected and used articles appearing in the media about the project. As I describe the operation of the organic farm, I shall also briefly indicate how all of this is related to traditional peasant knowledge and values, how far it builds on them, and in what ways it also differs from them.

Economic and Social Historical Background

The new boundaries drawn in the peace treaties after the First World War dealt a serious blow to the entire Hungarian economy.[4] The territory of the country was reduced to one-third of its previous size. The agricultural regions lost part of their markets, and the new borders cut across industrial, trade, and transport connections.

The uneven distribution of land ownership was a source of serious social tension in the inter-war years. Two-thirds of the population living in villages either owned no land or had only unviable micro-holdings. This large segment of the population was not in a position to carry out independent economic activity, and their main source of income arose from their work as hired agricultural labourers. For them, acquiring land was the key to social and material betterment.

Land reform was carried out after 1945 and many people became land owners. But from the end of the 1940s, after the communist takeover of power, the structure of agriculture in Hungary, like that in the other socialist countries of Central Europe, was gradually transformed in keeping with the communist political agenda. Individual land holdings were eliminated. By 1961, large-scale agricultural cooperatives had been organised throughout the country.[5] Only the small plots of land around the houses were left in private ownership. This was a huge social upheaval.

After 1948, the development of industry became the main direction of socialist economic policy and, to finance it, resources were withdrawn from agriculture. Many people subsequently left agriculture and took up another way of life, by moving to the towns, and by working in industry and in the service sector. The

4 For the history of Hungary see: Romsics 2016; Romsics 2009, pp. 250–272; Hoensch 1988.

5 For the changing rural society in Hungary, see: Sárkány 2005b, pp. 148–157; Valuch, 2005, pp. 135–159; Swain 1992. For information on one extraordinary village, see, for example: Hann, 1980; see further: Hann 1983, pp. 69–92.

number of active earners working in agriculture fell steadily. The self-esteem of the peasantry declined. Families that had previously lived from agriculture, now sent their children away to be educated, and these children did not return to the villages, even as adults. Many workers in industry commuted between their village homes and their urban workplaces. It also became the general practice for women to enter employment, thus fundamentally transforming the organisation of households. Traditional peasant society began to disintegrate: the knowledge, skills, behavioural forms and norms needed for independent farming activity, lost their importance, and were no longer passed down to the next generations. The villages were slowly depopulated and the age profile of the inhabitants gradually increased.

The large-scale agriculture structures that replaced family farming were based on mechanisation, modernisation, and the use of chemicals. The workers were employed as wage earners. Trained specialists with secondary and higher qualifications played an increasing role in directing the work. However, parallel with the large-scale agriculture structures, a system of strong, secondary, household-based production, based on household plots producing agricultural produce on a small scale, emerged. The land for this was made available by the cooperatives. Although the plots served primarily for the provision of food for the family, the goods produced became an important source of supplementary income throughout the 1970s and 1980s. The inhabitants of villages that were deliberately underfinanced by the state were able to use this income to buy prestige goods, not land as their forefathers had done, but rather new houses, electrical appliances, and cars.

After 1990, following change in the political system, a major new restructuring of ownership in agriculture, in line with the market economy framework, emerged.[6] Once again land passed back into actual private ownership. Previous owners received securities proportionate to the size of their original holdings, as compensation from the state, and those could be used to buy land. The agricultural cooperatives were dissolved, with the loss of many jobs. Together with this, the system of household plots also came to an end. Due to the restructuring of the agricultural system output fell by 50 % in the 1990s!

However, despite the political and agricultural-ownership changes, very few returned to the earlier form of agriculture as independent farmers; consequently, village society was essentially plunged into crisis. Many people were unable to

6 For more information on agricultural restructuring in Hungary post 1990, see: Sárkány / Hann 2003, pp. 117–141; Romsics 2012, pp. 37–52; Rainer 2009, pp. 9–17; Valuch 2014, pp. 2005–2014. In relation to one village, see, for example: Sárkány 2005a, pp. 143–151.

rebuild the household-based family farms because of the lack of sufficient capital to do so. In addition, the small plots that could be obtained as compensation could not be cultivated profitably, using modern methods. Furthermore, the knowledge needed for independent farming had been lost, or what still existed had become obsolete over the decades. Only those with sufficient expertise, and with the financial and relational capital necessary to buy cheap land and the machinery needed to cultivate it, were able to build up viable farms. For this reason, many people today do not cultivate their land but lease it to others. A narrow stratum of small-scale private producers have emerged, but their survival in this capacity remains very uncertain. Actually, their numbers have been falling in recent years.[7]

After 1990, industrial production also entered a crisis, with many factories closing down. Workers, who had earlier commuted to urban areas to work in industry, returned to the villages as they were unemployed. At the same time, the subsidiary industrial branches of agricultural cooperatives that had employed mainly women also disappeared, further adding to the number of villagers struggling with livelihood problems. Thus, by the early years of the 21st century, a substantial part of the population, mainly with a low level of education, who no longer wanted to live from agriculture but who could not find work elsewhere, gave rise to a permanent underclass – a marginalized population dependent on welfare subsidies. Municipalities, as redistributors of state resources, are responsible for providing welfare assistance for these people. Public works organized by the municipalities is a construct linked to state support for the long-term unemployed.[8]

The Example of Hernádszentandrás

Hernádszentandrás, the village with 445 inhabitants in north-eastern Hungary that is the focus of this paper, also followed the historical path outlined above. Today 70 %–80 % of working-age inhabitants are unemployed and live below the standard of living evident in other villages in the region. The village lies on the Hernád river, equidistant (35 km) from the two big cities in that part of the country, Miskolc in Hungary and Kassa / Košice in Slovakia. It has excellent

7 1.4 million households were engaged in agricultural production in 1991. This number had declined to 618,000 by 2007 and to 482,000 by 2013. Half of the farms produced products for self-consumption only, and an additional 32 % sold produce that was additional to their own consumption needs; see Morell 2015, retrieved 1.8.2016 from www.socio.hu/uploads/files/2015en_food/asztalos_morell.pdf.

8 On public works in Hungary, see further: Morell ibid.

quality soil. Historically, the source of livelihood here has been agricultural production and animal husbandry. The reorganisation of agriculture in the second half of the 20th century was followed by a considerable change in the population profile. Children, whose parents had been farmers, moved into the city, while the houses left vacant in the village were occupied by new, mainly Roma families, from neighbouring villages. Many of these engaged in a different life-strategy from the Roma who had previously lived there over a long period of time, in that they did not cultivate their gardens. Before 1990, Romas made up 5–10 % of the local population, a proportion that has now increased to 40 %. Families who have lived in the village for generations, and who could revive the values of traditional peasant farming, now constitute just a small minority of the inhabitants.

Life in the village was made difficult, not only by the sudden rise in unemployment from the 2000s and because of its ageing population, but also because of the unpredictable economic policy of the successive governments that had a negative effect on agricultural production. Small villages (with fewer than 500 inhabitants) were placed in an almost impossible position, and rural development policies still have not succeeded in solving the livelihood problems of the people. For example, primary schools have been closed down or merged. As a result, the possibility of gaining an education in Hernádszentandrás ceased in 1994, and children travel, by public transport, to school in a neighbouring village. The village has no kindergarten, medical care, pharmacy, post office, or library. It lacks civil organisations and an entrepreneurial stratum; actually, the only force holding the community together is the church.

By the 2000s, the village no longer had the material or intellectual potential that could have shifted it out of its rut, or which could have initiated, and helped, its integration into the market economy. This task was undertaken by the municipality, local government and its leader, the young mayor. (This very resourceful young man, in his thirties, had studied political science at university and saw it as a challenge to apply his knowledge to "revive" his native village.) He was elected mayor in 2006 and since then – together with his family – he has become the driving force behind and the key figure in, the village's development. In this context, he first had to shape the population into a community: for example, celebrations to revive their traditions, in which local dishes served to symbolize their sense of belonging together, were organised. To become the local leader accepted by the community, the young mayor demonstrated that, although he was a man, he could cook those dishes himself! Moreover, the municipality published a book summing up the past history of the village and its roots.

In 2010, when the programme for the organic farm was being developed, it was agreed that existing resources – good quality soil and existing manpower – needed to be utilized in order to set in motion the sustainable development of the village's economy. The people of Hernádszentandrás relearned the basics of agriculture, food production, self-sufficiency, and of how to achieve a sustainable economy. They set up an organic farm with the primary aim of providing the local population with affordable, good-quality food and, at the same time, of also providing work opportunities for the long-term unemployed. The municipality is aiming to combat welfare dependency resulting from marginalization, with a method-based social and agricultural project, to create new, market-based employment. It also aspires to combine the goals of ecological, social, and economic sustainability in a complex way in order to achieve a successful outcome for the people of the village. The municipality as entrepreneur – thus far exceeding its public administration tasks and responsibilities – strove to create jobs.[9] Most of the land that was used was owned by local government. The municipality created a farm that not only covers their own needs, but also produces food for the market, thus ensuring that those who work on the farm can also earn a living as a result.

Fig. 1: The organic farm in Hernád / Bioszentandrás: "Like a big family" (Photo: Anikó Báti, Hernádszentandrás, 2016).

9 On social farming see, see Morell 2015, retrieved 1.8.2016 from www.socio.hu/uploads/files/2015en_food/asztalos_morell.pdf.

To launch the project, the municipality applied for, and won, funding from the European Union. Further applications for funding enabled them to carry out developments and buy machines and equipment. They received professional advice on the setting up of the organic farm from a British agricultural engineer living in Hungary. And the daily work of the market garden is still directed by a retired agricultural engineer from the city of Miskolc. The participants in the programme learned the basics of chemical-free, ecological farming, from these experts in the course of several adult training courses.

When the organic garden was started, around 30 people from the village – independent of age group and ethnic identity – joined on a voluntary basis. At first they worked in the garden without payment and in their free time. In this way they became familiar with new plants and the basics of organic gardening. (They produce crops without using chemicals, only natural materials are applied to control pests, such as nettle, horsetail, comfrey, against which cow's milk is used as a spray; different plants are grown side by side in order to deter each other's pests.) Some of those working on the farm had already been cultivating the garden around their own homes, but it was only then that others among them began to do gardening at home and to keep small animals.

Today, a total of 20 people work in the various branches of the organic farm operation: production, processing and sales. The organic farm programme represents an opportunity for workers to earn additional income supplementary to the unemployment aid they receive from the state. In its initial years, participants received only a share of the produce of the farm for use in their own kitchens, but the revenues have now increased to a level where the organic farm operation is able to pay more and more workers an annual, regular wage. This trend will increase in the future, because, in addition to agricultural production, the produce is now processed in a small plant on the farm and it is then sold to produce extra revenue.

Vegetables, soft fruit, and 30 kinds of herbs, are grown on 2.5 hectares of the farm's land, and lavender on a further 2000 m^2 of ground. In 2015, the management planted fruit trees in a 1-hectare area. When selecting the varieties of fruit trees to be planted, it aimed to preserve the old gene stock typical of the region. In addition to outdoor cultivation, the farm workers are able to work throughout the year by using 9 polytunnels and a 150 m^2 glasshouse that can be heated. In summer, they are able to irrigate the ground with a drip system that waters the whole garden.

Those who did not join the organic farm initiative in its initial stages thought at the time that the whole venture was doomed to failure from the outset. Now, on seeing the current success of the farm, they envy the workers' permanent employment. "They envy the praise we get!"– said one of the workers proudly. Opinions in the village, regarding organic farming, are mixed. Some appreciate the fact that they have been able to combine their efforts in order to give new life to the village. But there are others who look down on them and fail to understand the whole purpose of the project: "My garden is organic too, I don't use sprays because they're expensive, but it doesn't have as many weeds as they do" – said a woman in the village who thinks that plants left between the cultivated rows are not there for the purposes of soil cover, but that they really are weeds that should be removed.

The mayor works as a manager (seeking funds, coordinating the work, and giving presentations on the results), and the other key person of the whole project is the commercial manager. Thanks to her training and experience in the area of product development and sales, she knows how to maintain relations with the customers and the workers. The secret of the farm's success is that the management very consciously built up its own brand. Its name was created from the name of the village, so that Hernádszentandrás became Bioszentandrás.[10] The management conducts continuous market research and maps buyers' demands, and it then adjusts the annual planting plan for the garden accordingly.

The range of products which the farm sells is expanding, and the workers' ideas and knowledge in terms of product development are incorporated into management planning, as well as the advice of experts. One of the Roma workers, for example, knows how to weave baskets from willow rods, an activity that is a family tradition. The idea of offering their produce at organic markets in these baskets was a big success and they now also sell the baskets themselves as handcraft products. Another idea came from a woman who had previously worked as a seamstress: they fill little sachets with lavender as gift objects that also popularize the Bioszentandrás brand.

Product sales are handled from the building known mysteriously as "Everything that", meaning everything related to sales. Vegetables ordered by customers are brought there from the garden, then they are carefully selected, weighed and packed, because only the best quality produce is sold. Since the summer of 2015, the organic farm has had a cool chamber for storage. (Any slightly faulty vegetables brought in from the garden now end up as rejects on the compost heap in quite large quantities. The management of the farm has not yet found

---

10 Bioszentandrás; retrieved 1.8.2016 from www.bioszentandras.hu.

a way to make use of less-then-perfect produce. Traditional peasant farming families had an entirely different attitude in this respect: nothing was allowed to go to waste.)

Fig. 2: Fresh, packed vegetables (Photo: Anikó Báti, Hernádszentandrás, 2016).

The annual order and structure of market gardening differs considerably from the earlier peasant farming traditions and are basically determined by constantly-changing market demands. The Bioszentandrás farm is a regular supplier to four restaurants, two of which belong in the fine dining category! The quality demands of these restaurants are the main yardstick for the farm's production standards and sales. The highest quality produce from organic farming is, at the same time, the farm's trademark; it needs such produce throughout the year and the demand thus overrides the cyclical nature of production. The schedule of work in the garden is largely regulated by these restaurants' requirements. For example, as soon as spring onions are harvested, the next crop is planted in their place to ensure a constant supply. The 30 kinds of herbs, and many different salad greens, also meet the restaurants' demands. Most of these herbs and greens were not known or used earlier by those working in the garden or by the villagers. Only a few of them have tried, and come to like, herbs with roast meats, for example. They had never tasted rucola or mizuma greens either. Even spinach was unknown to the villagers. They were surprised to learn that a plant they knew as a weed[11] was eaten by others as a salad. Salad as a dish is a novelty in Hungarian cuisine and it

11 For example, pigweed, *Amaranthus retroflexus*, retrieved 1.8.2016 from https://hu.wikipedia.org/wiki/Sz%C5%91r%C3%B6s_diszn%C3%B3par%C3%A9j.

does not yet have a permanent place in this context. In Hernádszentandrás, too, it appears only on the tables of the younger age group; older people, especially men, are not very fond of it.

Fig. 3: Products from the "House of Flavours" (Photo: Anikó Báti, Hernádszentandrás, 2016).

In September 2015, the municipality also built a processing plant and an organic kitchen that they call "House of Flavours". They modernized the interior of the 140-year-old former school building. Nowadays, modern machines are used to produce 10 to 12 products, such as jams, and they also have a 10-tray drying machine that operates on solar power. Some of the workers had earlier worked in the garden, but after attending further courses they undertook this work, as it is a big step forward and a source of great pride for them. Among other things they make ketchup, rose hip jam, aubergine and onion chutney, and pickles. The recipes were developed collectively, also incorporating the workers' ideas. (Several of the workers also made them at home for their families and the children liked them, but such relishes are not central elements of Hungarian cuisine. Among the workers' families, the men and older people are not so fond of them.) They are continually experimenting with flavours and products. For example, with diabetics in mind, they are trying to use the plant called stevia as a sweetener, instead of sugar, in their products. This plant is still a novelty in Hungary, but it is cultivated at the organic farm. Artificial preservatives are not used in the organic farm's products – in fact the cooking methods used resemble in many ways the cooking practices of old-fashioned peasant kitchens. But, at the same time, everything is measured very precisely and the most up-to-date kitchen technology is used in the processing plant. To ensure that it can operate throughout the year, the management of the farm has signed contracts with farmer suppliers in the region, and their produce is processed in this facility. The management has also built up a successful retail network because it sells not only fresh vegetables, herbs and products locally, but also does so in the bigger towns, even in Kassa / Košice in Slovakia. The success of the organic farm project has made the settlement attractive for business people. Recently, a private entrepreneur was just beginning to lay the foundations of a fruit and vegetable processing plant. When completed, this will also mean more jobs and sales opportunities for farmers in the region.

The gate of the organic farm is open to buyers and visitors. The management of the farm tries to inform as many people as possible about the approach they represent, that is, a health-conscious way of life. It organises "planting and gardening" days for families and schools, thus providing an introduction to the basics of chemical-free farming, new plants and flavours. A clear indication of the inclusive and open-spirited approach of the project and its community-creating role, is that on those "planting days" for example, healthy children and children with disabilities work together in the garden, helping each other. The garden also supplies a restaurant in Miskolc that is operated by persons living with disabilities.

The aim, which the management of the farm has for the future, is to expand the range of goods it produces as well as the circle of local farmers linked to it as suppliers, and also to increase the number of shops participating in sales of its products. The management would also like to expand the scope of services linked to the organic farm, by, for example, taking advantage of the possibilities offered by popular gastro-tourism. The system of production, processing and sales – based on the self-motivation and skills of participants – is now well established, and it is becoming independent of state subsidies. The municipality aims to gradually withdraw into the background from its coordinating role, once the venture is able to function wholly on a market basis.

The peasant knowledge, values, and norms needed for the cultivation of the land gradually lost their traditional worth and community validation in the course of the past 50–70 years. But now this knowledge has gained new life. It is capable, not only of renewing agriculture, but also of functioning as a community building force.

The Bioszentandrás project points far beyond chemical-free farming. The whole village has begun to develop and there have been major EU-sponsored improvements in infrastructure: mains water has been introduced, sewage drains and a telephone network have been built, and there are no longer any neglected, uncultivated household plots. The project is not only of outstanding importance for the development of the local market-based economy and for job creation, it can also be the key to community development, utilization of land, and to the very future of the village. It is an innovative way in which to become a self-help, collaborative community that can serve as an example for other villages in the region. It was the emphasis placed on community building and sustainable development that raised it above similar initiatives: it has also received recognition at European level – Bioszentandrás won a prize for social and welfare innovation in a competition announced by the European Investment Bank. The long-term impact of community building – including the integration of the Roma minority – requires further research.

The project is in line with new development directions in which sustainable agricultural development also serves to preserve and build the local community – represented, for example, by the collectively-cultivated gardens of housing estates in cities, or by the increasing number of eco-villages in the countryside.[12] Communities of producers and consumers are being built between cities and their agglomerations, based on personal connections between farmer and customer, on commitment to ecological sustainability, and on the turning away from, and the protesting against, the global product range of supermarkets.

List of References

Printed

Hann, Chris: *Tázlár, A Village in Hungary.* Cambridge University Press: Cambridge 1980.

Hann, Chris: "Progress Toward Collectivised Agriculture in Tázlár, 1948–1978". In Hollos, M. / Maday, B. (eds.): *New Hungarian Peasants. An East-Central European Experience with Collectivization.* East European Monographs 134. Brooklyn College Press: New York 1983, pp. 69–92.

Hoensch, Jörg K.: *A History of Modern Hungary 1867–1986.* Longman: London / New York 1988.

12 On eco-villages as a reaction to specific social problems, see Farkas, retrieved 1.8.2016 from http://tabula.neprajz.hu/neprajz.07.16a.php?bm=1&as=418&kr=A_10_%3D%222015%2016%281-2%29%22.

Rainer, M. János: "1989 in Hungary and in Central and Eastern Europe". In Rainer, M. János, (ed.): *1989: Year of Miracles in Hungary and Europe*. The Government of the Republic of Hungary: Budapest 2009, pp. 9–17.

Romsics, Ignác: *A Short History of Hungary*. Osiris Kiadó: Budapest 2016.

Romsics, Ignác: "Political and Economic Transformation in Hungary Since the Change of Regime". *Korea Journal of Central and East European Studies* September 2012, pp. 37–52.

Romsics, Ignác: "Interruption and Continuity in the Twentieth Century History of Hungary". In Marosi, Ernő (ed.): *On the Stage of Europe*. Balassi Kiadó: Budapest 2009, pp. 250–272.

Sárkány, Mihály: "Restudy of Varsány: Entrepreneurs and Property in Rural Hungary after 1989". In Skalnik, P., (ed.): *Anthropology of Europe. Teaching and Research*. Prague Studies in Sociocultural Anthropology 3. Set Out: Prague 2005a, pp. 143–151.

Sárkány, Mihály: "Studies on Changing Rural Social Structure in Hungary in the Second Half of the 20. Century". In Kilianova G. / Köstlin, K. / Nikitsch, H. (eds.): *Ethnology in Slovakia at the Beginning of the 21st Century. Reflections and Trends. Proceedings of the International Conference Dedicated to 55 Jubilee of Institute of Ethnology of Slovak Academy of Sciences*. Ustav etnologie SAV/UB: Bratislava-Wien 2005b, pp. 148–157.

Sárkány, Mihály / Hann, Chris: "The Great Transformation in Rural Hungary: Property, Life Strategies and Living Standards'. In Hann, Chris (ed.): *The Postsocialist Agrarian Question*. Halle Studies in the Anthropology of Eurasia 1. LIT Verlag: Münster 2003, pp. 117–141.

Swain, Nigel: *Hungary. The Rise and Fall of Feasible Socialism*. Verso: London / New York 1992.

Valuch, Tibor: "Social Transformation and Changes in Daily Life in Hungary, during the Period of the Change of System". *Metszetek. Társadalomtudományi Folyóirat* 3(1), 2014, pp. 2005–2014.

Valuch, Tibor: "From Long House to Squares. Changing Village Living Conditions in Sixties Hungary". In Rainer, M. János, Péteri, György (eds.): *Muddling Through in the Long 1960s: Ideas and Everyday Life in High Politics and the Lower Classes of Communist Hungary*. Studies on East European Cultures and Societies 16 (Trondheim Institute for the History of the 1956 Hungarian Revolution – Program on East European Cultures and Societies: Budapest 2005), pp. 135–159.

Internet

"Bioszentandrás", retrieved 1. 8. 2016 from www.bioszentandras.hu.

Farkas, Judit: "Nincsenek receptek". A magyar ökofalvak táplálkozásantropológiai vizsgálata ("'There are No Recipes.' Nutrition Anthropological Survey of Hungarian Eco-Villages"), retrieved 1.8.2016, from http://tabula.neprajz.hu/neprajz.07.16a.php?bm=1&as=418&kr=A_10_%3D%222015%2016%281-2%29%22.

Morell, Ildikó Asztalos: "Social Farming as a Means of Poverty Reduction in Rural Hungary", 2015, retrieved 1.8.2016, from www.socio.hu/uploads/files/2015en_food/asztalos_morell.pdf.

Pigweed (*Amaranthus retroflexus*), retrieved 1.8.2016 from https://hu.wikipedia.org/wiki/Sz%C5%91r%C3%B6s_diszn%C3%B3par%C3%A9j.

Astra Spalvēna

Gastronomical Exchange in Soviet Cuisine: On the Example of Latvia

Abstract: *One of the main features of Soviet cuisine was internationalization arising from the confluence or convergence of the different culinary traditions of the fifteen Soviet republics. Internationalization was facilitated by the Soviet state, and national dishes of the Soviet republics were gradually disseminated, through their provision in public catering services, into home cuisine in the different republics. In Latvia, however, significant modifications of these dishes arose due to the influence of locally-available ingredients, locally-practised cooking methods, and the customary taste-preferences of the region.*

My inspiration for engaging in research concerning culinary exchange processes in the territory of the USSR in Soviet times was the story of the Caucasian dish, *shashlik*, which, unexpectedly, became an integral part of the Latvian national celebration of the Midsummer Solstice, which is one of the most celebrated festivals in Latvia. The traditional celebration meal for this event includes simple, local, and long-standing traditional foods, such as bacon pasties, special cheese with caraway seeds called *Jāņu siers*, and beer. For a long time, and still even today, the Midsummer Solstice festival, with elements such as bonfires appearing in almost every yard as symbols of the sun, and the performance of magic rituals, ancient traditions, and folk songs, has traditionally been considered the most national of Latvian celebrations. At some period during Soviet times, the Latvian celebration of the Midsummer Solstice, because of its obviously nationalistic character, was suppressed. It is all the more peculiar, therefore, that around the 1970s a rather exotic dish from the Caucasian region, *shashlik*, a dish consisting of pieces of mutton roasted on a spit, was incorporated into this traditional feast. In Soviet times, however, the introduction of dishes from other socialist republics, into the national cuisine of the then USSR, was a common practice, often facilitated by the state. From their provision in restaurants and canteens, these dishes were gradually transferred to, or were adopted into, family meals and celebrations. In this way *shashlik* became the epitome of the de-sacralization and de-nationalization processes of Soviet get-togethers.

Introduction

Soviet cuisine was artificially synthesized from the cuisines of distinct regions of the USSR since a natural convergence or coming together of these cuisines was was a phenomenon unlikely to occur. The Russian food historian Vilam Pohlebkin (Вильям Похлебки) has used the term "Soviet Cuisine" in culture studies discourse, to refer to the characteristic features of the culinary scene in the Soviet Union. Pohlebkin has argued that basic features of the integrated Soviet cuisine were 1) the confluence of the dishes and cooking technologies of the different Soviet republics, and 2) the development of new cooking practices and gastronomic values influenced by new social conditions.[1] Gastronomic exchange was promoted among the fifteen Soviet republics with different culinary backgrounds and traditions, and with particularly diverse geographical and climatic conditions, in order to create a single unified Soviet cuisine for a single unified Soviet nation. The foundation of Soviet cuisine, therefore, was the outcome of the fusion of the cuisines of different gastronomic regions – such as the Russian and Ukrainian, Caucasian and Central Asian areas – with diverse culinary traditions. Gradually, the national dishes of these regions were further disseminated in the Soviet territory, often in the form of modified versions of those found in their home territories. The characteristics of the modifications, which occurred during transmission processes, will be discussed in detail later in this paper.

The Soviet Union, as a totalitarian state, set out to subjugate its citizens by having an effect on their private lives. Gastronomy, as one of the basic structures of everyday life, was considered a potent instrument of Soviet ideological influence and subjugation. The Russian historian, Irina Gluscenko (*Ирина Глущенко*), has carried out research on the development of the Public Food Service in the USSR, and has provided an account of the characteristics of Soviet gastronomic policy. The basic elements of this policy were: centralization (the imposition of state control from the centre, i.e. Moscow, over public catering enterprises in every republic), standardization (the provision of, and the obligatory adherence to, identical recipes and instructions in catering enterprises in the different republics in different situations), and democratization (the use of simplified recipes, easy cooking technologies, and inexpensive, widely-available ingredients, by the Public Food Service, in every republic) (Gluscenko 2014, p. 115).

As a state-sponsored mechanism, the Public Food Service (*Obshchepit / Общепит*) implemented the system of centralization. Already established in 1931, it took control of every enterprise in the food sphere, including trade and catering. To quote the historian Erik Scott: "It performed the dual function of responding to popular demand while cultivating public taste. Recipes and dishes adopted after careful deliberation by *Obshchepit* in Moscow later appeared in

---

1 See in this connection Pohlebkin, 2003, retrieved 12.05.2016 from http://www.e-reading.club/book.php?book=146524.

cafeterias and dining establishments everywhere from Tallin to Tashkent" (Scott 2012, p. 835). The food industry in the USSR did not exist as a network of different enterprises but more like a single hierarchically-structured establishment with regional branches.

The beginning of the 1950s saw the reorganization of the Public Food Service, which prescribed the standardization of public catering menus and the adaptation of dishes according to the availability of ingredients, already declared by governmental resolution (Pohlebkin 2000, p. 291). A unified collection of recipes, first published in 1955, the use of which was compulsory for every catering enterprise of the Public Food Service, was the obvious outcome of this governmental resolution.

"The Collection of Recipes" (*Сборник рецептур блюд и кулинарных изделий*) is a voluminous cookbook containing at least one and a half thousand recipes. What makes it remarkable and distinct from any other home cookbook, is not only its size, but also its form as a policy document. This form is noticeable in two aspects in particular. Firstly, its use was obligatory for Public Food enterprises and, secondly, its authors were not culinary practitioners. For example, in the 1968 edition, the "Introduction" to "The Collection of Recipes" was in the form of an order signed by the USSR Minister of Trade, Alexandr Strujev (*Александр Струев*), which decreed that the Trade Ministry of every Soviet republic was responsible for ensuring that the cookbook was used in every public catering enterprise, and that the recipes provided and, especially, the fixed quantities of ingredients mentioned for every dish, were adhered to. Furthermore, it was stated that recipes not included in the "Collection", could be used only with the permission of the Trade Ministry. The list of authors of the "Collection" included 36 representatives of the Research Institute of Trade and Public Catering and The Public Catering Department of USSR Trade Ministry. A few, unnamed, authors, described as "practitioners of public catering" were also included.[2]

From a contemporary free-market perspective, the notion of a menu, in every type of enterprise, in such a vast and diverse country, being constructed from one standardized collection of recipes, might sound improbable. However, such a centralized system was of great importance in creating a Soviet mythology – which did not correspond with historical reality – in which fifteen different republics had supposedly chosen, of their own free will, to consolidate their resources and values in order to create one egalitarian Soviet country. Representations of this myth included decorative elements such as national costumes or national cuisine

2 'Collection of Recipes of Dishes and Culinary Produce for Use in Public Catering', 1968.

to indicate that outwardly different peoples had been fused together in a united Soviet nation. In this scenario, therefore, internationalization became one of the main features of Soviet cuisine.

In creating a cuisine that would be "national in form" and "socialist in content", as Scott puts it, the Soviet state funded large-scale domestic production of national ingredients, and vigorously endorsed national recipes. "Ethnicity itself became edible and Sovietness – something one could consume around the table. The multi-ethnic nature of the Soviet Union was thus expressed deliberately but played out beyond the full control of the state" (Scott 2012, pp. 833–835).

The internationalization of Soviet cuisine was promoted through national restaurants. There were authentic menus, characteristic interiors, waiters in national costumes, and even cooks of genuine ethnic origin employed.[3] Furthermore, in order to broaden the scope of the process and to make it more democratic, international dishes were introduced in cafeterias and canteens, with the guidance of "The Collection of Recipes". Recipes of dishes of the different Soviet republics were included in the "Collection" in two different contexts. There were chapters on national cuisines, dealing with every Soviet republic apart from Russia, most likely because the latter was considered to be the central element of the Soviet Union, enriched by the diversity of Soviet "Others". National recipes were also included in the general section of the book, without any indication, even in the name of the dish, of their ethnic or geographical origin. This feature of Soviet cuisine, called *de-ethnicization* by Gluscenko, is exemplified by *shashlik* – the dish from the Caucasian region, which in Soviet tradition lost its origin as an Uzbek, Georgian or Azerbaijan national dish, and became just a general dish called *shashlik* (Gluscenko 2014, p. 127).

Methodology

In order to examine the process of gastronomic exchange in the territory of the USSR and how it impacted on Latvian cuisine, the main question to be asked is: which national dishes of other Soviet republics were cooked in public catering enterprises and promoted in cookbooks in Latvia; and were there local variations of these dishes created in the Latvian context?

To answer the question, 20 Latvian professionals who had worked in public catering enterprises during the Soviet period, were interviewed.[4] The material

3 For a description of Georgian restaurants in Moscow, see Scott 2012, pp. 840–846.

4 Interviews conducted between September 2015 and June 2016 (in the author's possession).

from these interviews was supplemented with data derived from an analysis of the content of five cookbooks of the period. In order to examine the process of the simplification of national recipes for use in public catering establishments during the Soviet era, recipes of particular dishes, ingredients and methods, in the chapters dealing with national cuisines in "The Collection of Recipes" (1968), were compared with the recipes for the same dishes in the general section of the book. Since the material arising from the interviews suggested that international dishes from public catering services were gradually adopted into home cuisine, recipes of the same dishes found in five cookbooks for domestic use, published from the 1960s to the 1980s, were also analysed.

International Dishes in an International Context

National dishes of the different Soviet republics entered Latvian cuisine in three different ways. Firstly, this arose from formal mechanisms used to encourage gastronomic exchange. Delegations of public catering professionals and administrative officials, mostly from the Public Food Service, went on gastronomic trips to far-away regions of the USSR; informants whom I interviewed frequently recalled going to the Caucasian republics. However, most of the informants were sceptical about the effectiveness of these trips in terms of gastronomic exchange:

> We went to Armenia in the 1970s. The food culture there was very different – they just cut the throat of a lamb right in the meadow and roasted it on the spot. This was not acceptable to us and of course it was impossible to repeat it in our restaurant. Therefore, yes, it was called an exchange of experience, but we did not bring home any recipes or we didn't learn anything. We have always made these international dishes according to local food habits.[5]

Secondly, informal exchange existed among cuisines as people migrated freely inside the Soviet Union and settled in different countries. They cooked their national food at home or at work in restaurants and cafés, thereby influencing the local cuisine to some extent, at least:

> There were immigrants everywhere – chefs in restaurants, cooks in canteens, women making their own national dishes at home. Neighbours visited each other, and guests surprised by unusual tastes, asked for recipes. I think that recipes are like folk songs – they are passed from mouth to mouth.[6]

5 Inara Klintsone, 76 years old, worked as a chef in a restaurant in Ogre.
6 Nina Masilune, 95 years old, cook, worked also as a culinary instructor in Rīga.

Thirdly, what I have termed a "semi-formal" mechanism of exchange was also involved. In this scenario, recipes of international dishes were included in "The Collection of Recipes", but cooks were not obliged to use them in their enterprises. Some informants explained that there were no demands to introduce these international dishes in the menu as they were considered trends, and that a particular repertoire of dishes was established during Soviet times which basically consisted of the recipes in the national chapters of "The Collection of Recipes".

Using the interview materials, I created a list of nine dishes from other Soviet republics, which were the ones most often mentioned and considered most popular in public catering enterprises. Most informants named at least three dishes from this list.

International dishes from Soviet republics popular in Latvia

Name of the dish	Region	Essential ingredients	Cooking method
Shashlik	Caucasian region	Mutton	Roasting on spit
Plov	Central Asia	Rice, mutton, fruits	Stewing
Soljanka	Russia	Different meats, salted cucumbers	Cooking (soup)
Borshch	Ukraine, Russia	Vegetables, esp. beetroot	Cooking (soup)
Rasolnik	Russia	Vegetables, esp. salted cucumbers, meat	Cooking (soup)
Ljulja-kebab	Central Asia	Ground mutton	Roasting on spit
Cepelini	Lithuania	Potatoes, meat	cooking
Azu	Central Asia	Meat, salted cucumbers	Stewing
Chicken tabaka	Georgia	Chicken	Roasting in a pan, with a heavy lid, on the stove-top

As the table suggests, the most popular dishes were those containing meat as they had a central role in Soviet cuisine in general. Likewise, cooked or stewed dishes were preferred since they were easy to make in large quantities for public catering.

Cooks who had worked in the Latvian public catering enterprises provided information about how these international dishes were cooked locally and whether they were made strictly in accordance with the recipes in the "The Collection of Recipes". They described several adaptations of these recipes. Firstly, the taste was customized, in that it was the milder forms of the usually hot and spicy dishes from the Caucasian region, that were made in Latvia, in consideration of the customary taste of local food. Secondly, local ingredients were used – for example, the more popular and better quality, pork or beef, were often used as a substitute for mutton. Thirdly, locally-available cooking techniques were used; thus instead of roasting on a spit, meat was roasted in the oven or in a roasting pan on the stove-top.

The practice of substituting unavailable ingredients with more easily-obtained ones, was rather common, because there were always shortages of various food items in the Soviet state. Thus, while "The Collections of Recipes" provided the frame for the recipes to be used, it still left some room for improvisation. As the informants explained, meat, for example, could not be substituted for fish, but pork could be used instead of mutton, and it was possible to reduce the amount and variety of spices mentioned in the "Collection" recipes.

Similar adaptations affected the recipes for the international dishes of the Soviet republics included in Latvian cookbooks. Dishes, which were made from mutton in their countries of origin, were made from beef, pork or even chicken in their Latvian manifestations. Similarly, naturally-fermented vegetables, especially cucumbers, were substituted for salt-preserved varieties. Roasting on a spit was rarely mentioned in the Latvian recipes, and almost every recipe included alternative cooking methods, such as roasting in the oven or in an electric appliance specially designed for roasting *shashlik*. These adaptations might have had an effect on the overall appearance and taste-structure of the dishes, giving them a sourer and less salty flavour, or a less spicy and savoury taste due to the lesser amount and variety of spices used. Salt and black pepper are often the only spices listed in the Latvian recipes.

While international dishes were accommodated to local tastes, they also brought new flavours to Latvian cuisine. For example, the use of tomato paste or purée combined with naturally-fermented cucumbers or other spicy-flavoured foods, enriched the former sour- and salty-taste register of Latvian cuisine. Starting from the 1980s, naturally-fermented vegetables were gradually replaced in cookbook recipes with marinated versions, as vinegar marinades had become more popular at that time.

To conclude, the strategy for the adaptation of international dishes in Latvian cuisine was rather simple – foreign dishes were made from available ingredients and tasted almost like everything else in this cuisine. Is it easy to recognize the national cuisine of the fifteen different Soviet republics in these Sovietized, standardized, and often bland, dishes? The answer is unfortunately "no" because when these dishes were made non-specific as to their origin, they also became *de-ethnicized*, which meant they were no longer connected with particular national traditions or cuisines, and remained exotic only by virtue of their names.

Conclusions

1. In the Soviet period an established repertoire of Soviet national dishes existed in Latvian cuisine. Today, some of these dishes, such as *shashlik*, have become surprisingly popular and have gained a place in local gastronomy, while some others, such as *azu*, which were not adopted into Latvian cuisine, remained a part of the repertoire of the Public Food canteen menus only.
2. These dishes were adapted to local resources – locally-available ingredients and locally-practised cooking techniques, something that made them more simplified, less authentic, and actually *de-ethnicized* in nature.
3. In Latvia, Soviet international dishes may have been different in taste and appearance to those same dishes in their countries of origin; this can be inferred from the descriptions of dishes in cookbooks. However, the national cuisines of other republics have also influenced Latvian cuisine.
4. The result of gastronomic exchange during the Soviet era was the provision of dishes simplifed in taste, easy to cook, and available to everybody. These dishes created the particular taste of Soviet cuisine.

List of References

Printed

Scott, Erik R.: "Edible Ethnicity: How Georgian Cuisine Conquered the Soviet Table". *Kritika: Explorations in Russian and Eurasian History* 13(4), 2012, pp. 831–858.

Gluscenko, Irina (Глущенко, Ирина): "The Ideal Shashlik" (Глущенко, Ирина, "Идеальный шашлык"). In Franz, Norbert / Frieß, Nina (eds.): *Küche und Kultur in der Slavia: eigenes und Fremdes im ausgehenden 20. Jahrhundert*. Potsdam: Universitätsverlag Potsdam, 2014, pp. 109–128.

"Collection of Recipes of Dishes and Culinary Produce for Use in Public Catering" (*Сборник рецептур блюд и кулинарных изделий для предприятий общественного питания*). Economica: Moscow 1968.

Pohlebkin, Vilam (Похлебкин, Вильям): "The Cuisine of the Century" (*Кухня века)*. Moscow: Polifakt, 2000.

Internet

Pohlebkin, Vilam (Похлебкин, Вильям): "The Great Encyclopedia of Culinary Art" (*Большая энциклопедия кулинарного искусства*). Centrpoligraf: Moscow 2003, retrieved 2.8.2016 from http://dic.academic.ru/dic.nsf/enc_pohlebkin/179.

Interviews

Interviews (20) conducted between September 2015 and June 2016 are in the possession of the author.

Interviewees mentioned in the text

Klintsone, Inara, 76 years old, worked as a chef in a restaurant in Ogre.

Masilune, Nina, 95 years old, cook, worked also as a culinary instructor in Rīga.

Zeynep Kılıç

Geography of Social Class on Istanbul's Dinner Tables

Abstract: *Interviews with discourse setters explore Istanbul's cuisine and how it interacts with ethnic identity, religious belonging and socioeconomic class. Findings show that the discourse setters see geography as crucial rather than national/ethnic identity. Issues of migration and social class appear as vague concepts where the informants avoid negative associations, while directing criticism at the larger global cultural trends. It seems inevitable however that the overall discontent with these cultural trends is connected intimately to social class and migration from Anatolia.*

Fig. 1: Fish sandwich stand at the Golden Horn, Istanbul (Photography by Zafer Sevener, ©Tables of Istanbul).

When I set out to make a documentary[1] about Istanbul's cuisine, I had many questions that related to my personal relationship with food as an immigrant in the United States. As I struggled to understand my own identity at my dinner table and in my kitchen, despite my academic persona, I ended up with migrant clichés. Gabeba Baderoon writes:

> In 1999 I left South Africa to take up a fellowship in the United States. The move left me disoriented and lonely. I turned to a familiar solution: cooking and sharing food. Making

1 "Tables of Istanbul", http://tablesofistanbul.com, retrieved 30.11.2016.

> what I knew as 'Muslim' food gave me a creative rather than a nostalgic relationship with South Africa; … Inviting others to share meals further lessened my sense of dislocation (Baderoon 2002, p. 4).

Additionally, as an immigrant, I was curious about the migrant city of Istanbul. After all, dislocation caused by the journey from a small city in Eastern Turkey to the megapolis of Istanbul may be even larger than the dislocation I felt moving from the capital city of Ankara to New York City. To answer these questions I pursued research that took me to Istanbul, Turkey, where I made a documentary about food, belonging and class.

I interviewed the most important characters of Istanbul's food scene to understand the cuisine from the point of view of the discourse setters. These interviews included people in four categories of food relationships: those who did *food as business* (chefs, restaurateurs), those who worked on *food as idea* (writers, bloggers, researchers, cookbook authors), and those who approached *food as cause* (activists, NGOs).[2] I completed twenty-five interviews.

In this paper I will first take up the question of "what makes a cuisine: ethnic or religious belonging?" And consider the possibility of social class as a determinant, and finally connect the two findings to pose a third question for future research.

Fig. 2: Spice Market, Istanbul (Photography by Zafer Sevener, ©Tables of Istanbul).

---

2 Additionally for an ethnographic peek, I interviewed those who experience *food as (daily) life* (families from various belongings in Istanbul), but in this analysis I focus on the discourse setters in the first three categories.

To understand Istanbul's cuisine, we have to understand its history and demographic composition. Istanbul has been an imperial city, and a capital to three empires. This meant that the best produce came to Istanbul, to the palace kitchens and pashas' mansions, which makes it a refined cuisine. Istanbul also has been the final stop on the "Spice Road" between Asia, Northeast Africa and Europe, which has allowed a large variety of spices to feature in its cuisine. Lastly it has always been a diverse city, where Greeks, Armenians, Sephardic Jews and Turks cooked, created dishes and ate together.

Even though Istanbul is no longer the capital of Turkey in the post-Ottoman Empire era, it remains the country's capital of food and diversity. Dwindling Armenian and Greek populations due to painful and dark political histories, coupled with the increasing rural to urban migration from Anatolia, created a different kind of ethnic diversity in today's Istanbul. Instead of taverns operated by Armenians and Greeks, a city that devoured seasonal fish and produce, the metropolis now houses every regional cuisine imaginable from the rest of Turkey, but particularly the many faces of *kebap* culture ubiquitously available at almost every street corner. Zafer Yenal discusses the discontent directed at the newcomers as a result of the tension between modernity and nostalgia (Yenal 2003, pp 98–101). Ünsal (2011) also mentions the dominance of *kebap* smells in the city, including the offending body odour that comes with the new migrants. So whose city is this Istanbul? What defines its cuisine today? The old nostalgic palace tables, or the *kebap*-eating migrants of a certain geographical background and social class?

As I pressed this point in my interviews with the discourse setters I got the same answer: that ethnic belonging or religious group membership is not the primary feature for understanding a cuisine. Everyone, except for one interviewee mildly disagreeing, pushed forward the idea of geography as the definitive and defining factors. In other words, they talked about how Istanbul, and its geography (and climate), was more important to understanding its dishes, rather than specific ethnic groups' influence.

> The effects of regional lifestyles run quite deep. Whatever difference exists between a Turk in Istanbul and a Turk in Malatya, also exists between Armenians and Greeks, and Kurds, Arabs, Abazas, Georgians. We need to recognize that geography can work quite differently even in cities in close proximity. Because it is the geography that gives you your soul, not the flag that flies over it (Başaran, Vedat. Chef / Ottoman Cuisine Researcher).

> Who makes stuffed mussels in Istanbul? Armenians do. Why? Think about it. When you look at history closely, geography is crucial. Armenians arrived in Istanbul in large numbers after the conquest. They settled, these people from Anatolia, in coastal areas of Istanbul. When they arrived, they already knew spices very well since they had been living on the Spice Road for thousands of years. And they already knew dolma (the stuffing technique). And they find a new ingredient – the mussel! So they utilized it by doing what they knew, which is the dolma by adding their ingredients like pine nuts, and spices, and created a new dish (Bağış, Levon. Wine expert, food writer).

At the same time, however, definitions of Istanbul cuisine inevitably rested on its historical ethnic composition: Greek, Armenian, Jewish and Turkish dishes of an imperial city that is situated by the Bosphorus Strait. In other words, the historical diversity was more defining to its cuisine than its ethnic composition today. The ethnic and religious diversity of yesteryear was seen as an important facet of Istanbul's cuisine.

> [Istanbul] housed the Greeks, the Armenians, and the Jews. Without these groups we cannot talk about Istanbul cuisine. But when I say Greek, Armenian, Jewish, I am talking about Istanbul Armenians, Istanbul Greeks and Istanbul Jews. Not talking about Jewish people from Israel (Denizsel, Şemsa. Chef).

> You have got to give credit to the people who do foster it, but not get too confused. It is not some sort of Armenian ingenuity that went into this dish or some Kurdish secret that made that cheese. … On the ethnic side of liver butchers, organ butchers, a lot of the old ones seem to be of Albanian origin. Wow, how did that work? And then you start finding out about … when they had the slaughterhouses down on the Golden Horn and the organ butchers would get the organs and they would wrap the kokoreç right there and that's why you have these sort of Albanian origin kokoreç vendors but it has nothing to do with Albania. I love it. It confuses me about what Istanbul's cuisine's roots are, but it is interesting (Mullins, Ansel. Food writer / Journalist, *Culinary Backstreets* founder).

Many of the dishes associated with Greek, Jewish or Armenian heritage as representative of Istanbul cuisine, for example, were created for specific religious dietary requirements. Yet the informants insisted that ethnic/religious membership is subsumed under what is essential to understanding Istanbul cuisine as part of the larger Turkish culinary landscape: its geography. The contextuality of geography over ethnicity is an interesting juxtaposition.

Fig. 3: Dinner in Istanbul with a migrant family from the Black Sea region (Photography by Zafer Sevener, ©Tables of Istanbul).

Fig. 4: Dinner in Istanbul with a Kurdish family from Adiyaman, southeastern Turkey (Photography by Zafer Sevener, ©Tables of Istanbul).

Today's Istanbul houses a different kind of diversity. This is a population that consists mostly of Anatolian migrants, from the Black Sea, from Central, Eastern and Southern Turkey; Laz, Arabs, Kurds, and also as of late, Syrian refugees. And they are mostly Muslims with few other ethnic / religious minorities mixed in. They are relatively new to Istanbul, but they may not know old Istanbul and what it stood for. For example, activist chef Defne Koryürek considers these residents to be only urban residents, not Istanbulites.

> Supposedly there are 2.2 million people registered as residents in Istanbul, among the 14–15 million population quoted in the city. If this is the number of real Istanbulites, I would say it is a huge lie. The real Istanbulite is aware of Istanbul's geography, can name its winds, knows which fish flows through the Bosphorus, when, and its order. The real Istanbulite walks in a certain place when the magnolias are blooming and takes time to smell the linden, goes down to the Bosphorus for Judas trees and laments over the disappearance of pines from the Bosphorus silhouette. Someone who doesn't know the geography, and has no relationship to it, is simply someone who lives in an urban setting, nothing more (Koryürek, Defne. Slow Food / Fikir Sahibi Damaklar, Leader).

When lamenting about old Istanbul, the disappearance of fish from the Bosphorus, orchards of lettuce, cucumber, citrus and dairy farms are mentioned, along with traditional Greek Orthodox and Armenian proprietors of charcuteries and taverns. The face of the city has changed drastically as the population exponentially grew. Combined with the mentions in the literature about tensions regarding newcomers, I was interested in understanding if social class was especially an issue: A rural, peasant, uneducated, Muslim takeover of an imperial, refined, educated, Levantine city? Many interviews touched upon newcomers retaining their old geographies and dishes, not adopting to Istanbul, but transforming Istanbul with their own culinary culture. On the one hand, this is seen as an enrichment of the city's culinary landscape, with the caveat that old Istanbul does not disappear. But who would do the safeguarding of this old Istanbul now?

Social class was a very amorphous concept in the interviews. How class mapped onto the city's food landscape varied a great deal across the interviews. There was, however, a clear avoidance of labelling the ongoing migration as a problem in general. In other words the discontentment and the tension mentioned in the literature did not appear in the interviews. There was widespread acceptance that things change all the time, especially in a metropolis like Istanbul, and that that is not something worth worrying over.

> This is an important place, with an important populace, and it is a melting pot. For example, there are people from Central Africa settling here and their children are going to grow up here. We are going to see very different kitchens in ten years, as their cuisines will affect ours (Bağış, Levon. Wine expert, food writer).

> The subject that I keep going back to is migration. I think that the food is a reflection of the people that live in the city, obviously, and Istanbul is the home of many millions of people who are fairly recent arrivals in the city. So the food cultures we are seeing are representative of all of the regions of Turkey, and more and more so these days, outside of Turkey. We are starting to see Syrian restaurants, it's a really interesting trend. Istanbul kitchen to me is that (Mullins, Ansel. Food writer / Journalist, *Culinary Backstreets* founder).

It was clear that the issue of how different social classes come to the table was not agreed upon. There were conflicting ways of understanding, how the poor, middle and upper classes ate and shopped for food in Istanbul, across the board. On the one hand there were the more romantic and pastoral notions of the lower socio-economic classes, where those who had migrated from Anatolia were seen as being closer to nature (or at least to their old rural geographies) compared to generations of urban elites.

> School lunches of the help's child and an upper middle class child are so different. That kid's mom (with the lower economic means) puts dried apricot, walnuts in the lunch box. Or she puts a wrap with flat bread she made, and cheese. But the wealthier kid brings packaged foods. Other one sends fruits and nuts for snacks.
> - So the wealthier kid's lunch is worse?
> - Yes of course, it is worse (Yavi, Ayfer. Slow Food / Yağmur Böreği, Co-president).

Alternatively there was criticism of the elites, for their affinity to Western cuisines at the expense of Turkish cuisine. However, the new trend in Istanbul points to a reversal of this, with increasing interest in regional foods being evident, which is a global trend in gastronomy.

> My people were detached from their own traditions. They didn't value them, turned their noses up at them. … So we had a Turkey where these were not acknowledged, weren't valued or seen as important. … In Istanbul, those class dimensions have been overcome. Those who identify as upper class now have a new interest. Peasant dishes from Anatolia now are on Istanbul elites' tables. Istanbul is no longer the same. Istanbul kitchen is moving towards a union with Anatolia. Istanbul is getting to know Anatolian cuisine (Başaran, Vedat. Chef/Ottoman Cuisine Researcher).

> You have a higher level of income. What do you demand? You demand Western cuisine. Well, the restaurant business is a business, not a public or cultural service. They approach it from a fiscal point of view and decide they should open up an Italian, Spanish or French restaurant so people would frequent it. Now, we've finally gotten over this (Kakınç, Zeynep, Turkish Friends of the Kitchen Association, President).

In many ways, Istanbul is depicted as being special because this is where the humble street-foods rub shoulders with the elevated cuisine. This is a place, like many other world cities, where every cuisine under the sun is available, and hence it is a vibrant food mecca. But I was curious about who actually consumed these foods in its ample variety: all social classes or just the upper classes? Again, the answers conflicted with each other. Half the interviewees talked about how people, especially those in the lower socio-economic classes, could not afford to eat out often enough to do this,[3] and hence stayed outside of these discourses. The other half disagreed, simply because of the size of the city making it impossible for workers not to eat, at least, lunch out. Some suggested that many in the lower socio-economic and middle classes ate bad food when out – either industrially-prepared, or cheap and fast food, such as *kebap* sandwiches made of suspicious meat or simple carbohydrates. Activists, on the other hand, argued that everyone eats terrible food these days, thanks to GMOs, dangerous environmental and industrial practices by the multinational food conglomerates, and the overall fast pace of modern, working, urban life stripping away seasonality and home cooking in favour of convenience. But in general, there was resistance against separation along class lines when it came to food.

> Return to rural, to natural products, to regional focus. This is present in all strata. I think everyone eats everything. Right now, we are having great coffee here, then I eat at Edirne liver place, then I get my beer from the corner, but sometimes it is Belgian beer. This is the way we live (Öney Tan, Aylin. Food columnist / Researcher).

> A wide range of people, regardless of their income level, eat at *kebap* places as well as at traditional Turkish cuisine or the fish restaurant. This is the average by and large. But some eat at places paying 90$ per person, others eat at more humble neighbourhood establishments, as they can afford it.
> – So we still have overlapping tastes?
> – Absolutely! Those women ordering 20$ salads for lunch in fancy neighbourhoods go home to order in "lahmacun" or "çiğ köfte" from the corner shop. We really shouldn't separate these (Durmay, Batur. Restaurateur [Âsitâne]).

Others also mentioned that it was not the money that mattered when it came to food, but rather priorities. The example of Turks in the lower classes preferring expensive technology purchases, instead of quality food, was identified as a problem of precedence, not economic power. Overall, when it came to *habitus* (Bourdieu 1984; 1990), it seemed that lower socio-economic classes had more problematic practices stemming either from a lack of education regarding food

3 Onurlubaş / Doğan / Gürler (2015, pp. 917–924) found that on average 11 % of total food spending was spent eating out, with cities like Istanbul approaching 22 %. Americans, on the other hand, spend half of their budget eating out (UPI. *Americans eat out about 5 times a week*. 2011, Sept. 19). http://www.upi.com/Health_News/2011/09/19/Americans-eat-out-about-5-times-aweek/54241316490172/, retrieved 1.12.2016).

issues, or economic inability to afford high quality food.[4] As Bourdieu (1984) suggested, class location does not solely imply class practices, but also the perceptions of and judgment on those practices.

Though there was very little blaming regarding food practices in the lower socio-economic classes, there were many issues identified as a major loss for Istanbul's food landscape. Issues most mentioned were loss of habitat, such as the environmental degradation in the Bosphorus, or loss of food production to real estate development. When we consider what happened to the old lettuce patch, we see that migration, and the expanding city footprint as a result of it, simply meant losing such green areas to housing development. There are of course two sources of culprits here: the outskirts of the city were mostly overtaken by the newcomers with limited means, and the gentrifying neighbourhoods that represented old Istanbul are renovated for the upwardly mobile middle classes. This is the city where residents spend their weekends at the fake grassy area in a shopping centre, which was built upon the actual green area that used to inhabit it. Hence it seems that the elephant in the city has some bearing on social class. Geography perhaps serves as a proxy to it. Though no one wants to directly implicate the poor/er residents, they are firmly planted on what used to be the orchard, living in a toxic environment, and choosing to spend their money on iPhones instead of free-range chicken. Do they care just as much about clean food or are they content with $1 fast food sandwiches? Are they concerned about the loss of fish in the Bosphorus, or is this too much of a luxury to consider in their daily struggle for survival? Are they truly rubbing shoulders with the elites, eating what they eat, or are they simply selling the humble foods to the elite?[5]

Lack of focus on social class is not entirely surprising. As Skeggs 2004 (p. 15) argues, "[p]lace-based identifications often emerge as a 'shorthand way of speaking class' that makes overt references to class unnecessary" (cited in Johnston / Rodney /Szabo 2012, p. 1093). Just so, social class on Istanbul's dinner tables emerged in this data as mostly vague and slightly confusing, but never as the

4 Johnston / Rodney / Szabo 2012, pp. 1091–1108) also showed that neighbourhood specific food cultures create and reproduce classed ways of eating where the lower socio-economic classes focus on cheap and fast food rather than healthy farmers' markets where the affluent shop, and to which they have easier access.

5 Social class can work in interesting ways when it comes to food. Goody showed for example that wealthy Ghanaians ate the same foods as poor ones, just more of it (Goody 1982). A sushi craze among Istanbul's upwardly mobile, young professionals, however, suggests that cultural capital can be at play by the distinction of what one eats (as in demonstrating knowledge); cf. Bourdieu, *Distinction*, 1984.

culprit. Overall, emphasis on environmental concerns trumped equal access to food and just food concerns. Blame was squarely placed on state policies or larger cultural trends, which shows an interest in macro issues, rather than groups of consumers.

My biggest take away from the interviews was a desire to frame food as a tool that brings people together rather than separate them. Hence some of my questions regarding ethnic, religious or social class diversity were initially downplayed. In its place they offered more celebration and less problematization, more coming together around the table across these differences as final sentiments, perhaps representing their hopes rather than the reality.

I am left with more questions regarding how social class reflects on dinner tables in Istanbul than when I started the research. Additional research on this is currently underway. In the absence of large-scale studies that identify and describe food behaviours in Istanbul across social classes, qualitative findings such as these are limited to perceptions. Though discourse setters have an excellent grasp of the large-scale issues, and they know Istanbul and food very well, it is safe to assume that they are not in close contact with the underclass or the working masses that commute to the city everyday from outerburbs (except for the food activists that may work with refugees, the poor etc.). However it is still important to understand their perceptions as they define and drive the food discourses, even national food policies. Food, beyond being a cultural connector, also functions as a marker of difference across various categories of belonging, including "regional, economic/class, religious, ethnic" (Cesaro 2000, p. 226). Hence this paper leaves us at the beginning of an important discussion: how may social class help define Istanbul's cuisine and perhaps override – or exacerbate – its historical identity imbued in ethnic and religious diversity?

List of References

Printed

Baderoon, Gabeba: "Everybody's Mother Was a Good Cook: Meanings of Food in Muslim Cooking". *Source: Agenda: Empowering Women for Gender Equity* 51, 2002, pp. 4–15. Special issue: "Food: Needs, Wants and Desires".

Bourdieu, Pierre: *Distinction. A Social Critique of the Judgment of Taste*. Harvard University Press: Cambridge, MA, 1984.

Bourdieu, Pierre: *The Logic of Distinction*. Polity Press: Cambridge, 1990.

Cesaro, M. Cristina: "Consuming Identities: Food and Resistance among the Uyghur in Contemporary Xinjiang". *Inner Asia* 2(2), 2000, pp. 225–238. Special Issue: "Xinjiang".

Goody, Jack: *Cooking, Cuisine, and Class: A Study in Comparative Sociology*. Cambridge: Cambridge University Press, 1982.

Johnston, Josée / Rodney, Alexandra / Szabo, Michelle: "Place, Ethics, and Everyday Eating: A Tale of Two Neighbourhoods". *Sociology* 46(6), December 2012, pp. 1091–1108.

Onurlubas, Ebru / Dogan, Hasan, G. / Gurler, Arslan Zafer: "Consumer Trends and Case of Food Consumption Away from Home in Turkey". *The Journal of International Social Research* 8(38), June 2015, pp. 917–924.

Yenal, Zafer: "Istanbul'da 'Yemek Kültürü' ve Gölgede Bıraktıkları ("Food Culture in Istanbul and what it Leaves in its Shadow"). *Istanbul Dergisi* 47, 2003, pp. 98–101.

Ünsal, Artun: *Istanbul'un Lezzet Tarihi* ("Istanbul's Taste History"). NTV Publications: Istanbul 2011.

Internet

UPI. *Americans eat out about 5 times a week*. 2011 (Sept. 19). http://www.upi.com/Health_News/2011/09/19/Americans-eat-out-about-5-times-aweek/54241316490172/, retrieved 1.12.2016.

Interviewees

Bağış, Levon: Wine expert, food writer.

Başaran, Vedat. Chef / Ottoman Cuisine Researcher.

Denizsel, Şemsa: Chef.

Koryürek, Defne: Slow Food / Fikir Sahibi Damaklar, Leader.

Mullins, Ansel: Food writer / Journalist, *Culinary Backstreets* founder.

Öney Tan, Aylin: Food columnist, researcher and historian.

Yavi, Ayfer: Slow Food / Yağmur Böreği, Co-president.

Naoto Minami

Promotion of Regional Food in Contemporary Japan: A Case Study of the "Shikoku" District

Abstract: *This study considers, first, the historical transition of the social evaluation of regional food, second, the geographical character of Shikoku Island and some examples of this district's regional dishes, and, third, attempts to promote local economies through regional food.*

Japan has been in a declining economic phase since the 1990s. In particular, local economies and societies have diminished strikingly compared to those of the capital city, Tokyo. To break this impasse, numerous local governments as well as central government have tried to present various measures and policies to energize the economies of their provinces. Among these "eating" plays an important role, because local food is not only a necessity of everyday life, but also a form of popular entertainment, and can therefore be an effective means by which to promote regional economies through tourism. Since "Washoku", as Japanese food and foodways are collectively known, was recognised by UNESCO as Intangible Cultural Heritage, in 2013, a variety of regional foods and foodstuffs have been introduced and advertised as a means by which to usher tourists from home and abroad into the Japanese countryside. To understand the multifarious nature of Japanese food culture, we have to explore the world of regional food in Japan. This study takes Shikoku, the smallest of the four main islands in the Japanese Archipelago, as an example of a declining region in Japan, introduces the variety evident in the traditional food products from this area, and examines endeavours to stimulate the local economy through food.

Regional Food: Its Evaluation and Social Position in Japan

Today, regional food is generally evaluated quite highly in Japan. For instance, it is regarded as a rich resource for tourism and as a symbol of regional identity. Seventy years ago, however, it was regarded in quite negative terms. In a guidebook published in 1944, regional food was described as "sounding rather unrefined" (*Kyoudo Shoku to Chouriho*), and a nationwide survey of contemporary regional food in 1940 stated that some food was questionable from the nutritional point of view (*Zen Nihon Kyoudo Ryouri*). This negative evaluation of regional food changed significantly from the 1960s and 1970s onwards, a period of rapid economic growth in Japan. As large numbers of people moved to urban areas, the countryside turned into an object of nostalgia, and regional food became a symbol of this positive image. During this period, several books were published that introduced various local dishes, mainly to readers living in cities.[1]

In the 1980s, a new favourable approach by the government helped regional food to survive in a highly urbanized society. The Japanese government, especially the Ministry of Agriculture, Forestry and Fisheries, and some nutritional scientists, as well as scientists in other academic fields, began to emphasise the nutritional, economic and cultural values of the so-called Nihon Gata Shokuseikatsu ("Japanese Style Dietary Habit") which is characterized by the use of fish and vegetables and the avoidance of animal fat. Against this background, some major publication projects, which tried to exhaustively investigate and introduce regional food in every prefecture of the Japanese Islands, materialized. The most important outcome of these projects was the "Complete Works of Japanese Food" (*Nihon no Shokuseikatu Zenshu* 1984–1993), consisting of fifty volumes, which reconstructed everyday meals, from approximately the previous fifty years, in the countryside of each prefecture, based on the oral history method.[2]

After the 1990s, several difficulties confronted the economy and society of Japan. This period is called "the lost twenties", during which some curious phenomena related to Japanese food culture occurred, such as the abrupt evolution of "Ramen", a noodle that originated in China but was popularized in post-war Japan. Among these phenomena, one of the most remarkable was the way in which regional food led the way in several attempts to promote and stimulate the economy and society. The concept of regional food gained a more positive social meaning and it got extensive recognition in the mass media. For example, as Table 1 shows, the number of articles in the *Asahi Shinbun*, a typical quality newspaper in Japan, dealing with regional food or dishes, has increased over the last twenty years.[3]

---

1 Because of limited space, only two examples are mentioned here: Terao, 1976, the author of which was a reporter for the Asahi Shinbun; and *Nihon no Aji: Atarashii Katei Ryouri to Kyoudo Shoku* 1973.

2 In addition to this, two major projects are to be mentioned: Ishige / Tsuji / Nakao: *Shuukan Asahi Hyakka Sekai no Tabemono* ("Weekly Asahi's Encyclopedia of World Food") 1982, of which vols. 81–97 treat of the regional food of Japan; also Isige et al.: *Nihon no Kyoudo Ryouri* ("The Regional Dishes in Japan"), 12 vols. 1986.

3 The author calculated these numbers himself based on data from "Kikuzo", the digital version of the *Asahi Shinbun* newspaper.

Table 1: Number of articles dealing with regional food or dishes in the Asahi Shinbun.

year	number of articles	year	number of articles	year	number of articles
1984	4	1995	70	2006	419
1985	6	1996	87	2007	325
1986	6	1997	251	2008	412
1987	9	1998	257	2009	381
1988	29	1999	318	2010	461
1989	43	2000	332	2011	409
1990	45	2001	301	2012	435
1991	69	2002	322	2013	388
1992	52	2003	310	2014	379
1993	43	2004	327	2015	390
1994	80	2005	365		

The boom in regional food was accelerated by several well-organised campaigns, such as the publication of "One Hundred Best Regional Dishes", which were chosen by the Minister of Agriculture, Forestry and Fisheries, in 2007. This list was partly artificially composed, with the specific purpose of energizing declining local economies through regional food, and also partly democratically selected by means of Internet voting. Containing very popular, but quite untraditional up-to-date, dishes, such as "Okonomiyaki", a sort of pancake from the Osaka district, or "Takoyaki", a round variation of pancake with octopus, this publication attracted wide attention, and soon regional food became one of the most popular themes in the mass media. Moreover, many public and private events for promoting regional food nationwide or locally were planned and executed, such as the "B-1 Grand Prix", a contest for local dishes mainly made with local foodstuffs, which has been held every year since 2006, and has received much media attention.

Last but not least, the registration of "Washoku" ("Japanese cuisine") on the UNESCO list of Intangible Cultural Heritage in 2013, might well expand the potential of regional food to be utilized for the benefit of tourism and the economy in the future.

The Shikoku District: Its Geography and Status Quo

Shikoku Island is located in the western part of Japan and has a generally warm climate. The Shikoku Mountains divide the island into two parts: the Inland Sea side and the Pacific Ocean side, and the island consists of four prefectures: Kagawa, Tokushima, Ehime and Kochi. Each has its own geographical character, and even within one prefecture, various environments can be found, such as seas, rivers, mountains and plains. Consequently, the Shikoku district has a great variety of distinctive regional food products that utilize materials produced in each region under different circumstances. In this sense, Shikoku Island is typical of the Japanese Archipelago, which has very diverse environmental factors, and the regional food and dishes of Shikoku Island typify those of Japan, at least as regards its western part.

However, the economic climate of the Shikoku district has gradually deteriorated since the 1960s, because it has neither large industrial areas nor big cities. Young people have moved from the island to Osaka or Tokyo, and, as a result, most rural areas have suffered from a continual decline in population.[4]

In order to confront such unfavourable conditions, the four prefectures of Shikoku Island try to promote tourism by means of the area's regional food. The next section focuses on this topic.

Regional Food in the Shikoku District

Based on the explanations in the four volumes of the "Complete Works of Japanese Food" that deal with the four prefectures of the Shikoku district (*Kikigaki Kagawa no Shokuji* 1990; *Kikigaki Tokushima no* 1990; *Kikigaki Ehime no Shokuji* 1990; *Kikigaki Kouchi no Shokuji* 1986), we can point to the geographical and environmental conditions, and the historical background, that have generated the district's typical regional food:

1) Fairly narrow plains, giving rise to a relatively high proportion of small farmers and a relatively low level of rice production.
2) Rivers, such as the Yoshino River, and many reservoirs, in the Sanuki plain, etc., providing people with various kinds of coarse fish.
3) Two contrasting seas, the Setonaikai ("Inland Sea") and the Pacific Ocean, providing a great variety of seafood, such as sea bream in the case of the former, and bonito in the case of the latter.
4) The relatively steep Shikoku Mountains located near the two seas, with the result that the inhabitants in this mountain area eat mainly millet and edible wild plants.

---

4 According to the 2015 census, the rate of decrease in the population was strikingly high in the Shikoku district, as well as in the Tohoku district; retrieved 1.3.2016 from http://www.stat.go.jp/data/kokusei/2015/kekka/pdf/youyaku.pdf.

Based on these accounts of the Shikoku district's regional food, this section introduces several examples of regional dishes from Shikoku. In the above-mentioned "One Hundred Best Regional Dishes", two dishes are selected per Shikoku prefecture, but the present author considers it necessary to make a few modifications. Consequently, eight typical dishes are selected, as shown in Table 2.

Table 2: Typical regional dishes per Shikoku prefecture.

Kagawa Pref.	**"Sanuki Udon"**	**"Shoyu Mame"**
Tokushima Pref.	"Naruto Wakame"	"Sobagome Zousui"
Ehime Pref.	"Uwajima Tai Mesi"	"Jako Ten"
Kochi Pref.	"Katuo no Tataki"	"Sawachi Ryouri"

Kagawa Prefecture produces one of the most famous regional dishes in Japan, i.e., "Sanuki Udon", a simple noodle dish. Sanuki is the old name of Kagawa Prefecture, and Udon is a thick type of noodle that is made from wheat. Because of the small number of rice fields in this prefecture, people survived on wheat and barley. The other typical food is "Shoyu Mame", broad beans marinated in soy sauce. People also ate beans as a valuable source of protein.

Two regional dishes are selected from Tokushima Prefecture: "Naruto Wakeme" and "Sobagome Zousui". Wakeme is a kind of soft seaweed growing in many parts of the Japanese Islands and is an ordinary ingredient of Miso soup, a very important dish for the Japanese. The Naruto area, which is located in the north-eastern corner of Tokushima Prefecture, is well known for its seafood, such as Wakame or sea bream. The other dish, "Sobagome Zousui" ("porridge"), can be said to symbolise this prefecture's environment of remote mountain areas. Sobagome is buckwheat wholegrain, which is eaten as a substitute cereal in the sterile lands of Japan. People living in the Shikoku Mountains were usually unable to eat either rice or wheat, and so their only food was buckwheat or barnyard grass. This dish, therefore, reflects the life of the poor in times past.

Ehime Prefecture has an extended coastline along the Inland Sea and is blessed with a variety of seafood. Two dishes made from fish are selected from this area. "Uwajima Tai Meshi" is a typical fish dish of Uwajima city, located on the west of this prefecture. Tai ("sea bream") is a typical highly-favoured foodstuff in traditional Japanese cooking, and there are many kinds of Tai dishes in the coastal areas along the Inland Sea. "Uwajima Tai Mesi" is a bowl of *meshi* ("rice") topped with slices of raw sea bream and spices, such as Welsh onion and sesame, and seasoned with soy sauce. The other dish, "Jako Ten", is an everyday food made from minced and deep-fried fish meat.

Kochi Prefecture, on the opposite side of Shikoku Island, also has a lengthy coastline along the Pacific Ocean. This rich ocean provides people with various marine products, such as bonito, called "Katsuo" in Japanese, a migratory fish that appears near the Kochi offing on the Black Current. "Katsuo no Tataki" is a typical traditional bonito dish, which is prepared by broiling a thick fillet of raw bonito for a few seconds, cutting it, and then seasoning it with soy sauce and ground garlic or ginger. This cooking method is called "Tataki" in Japanese. The other dish, "Sawachi Ryouri", is a superb festive meal, consisting of many kinds of food, such as sushi, a variety of raw fish, including "Katsuo no Tataki", some vegetables, and even some kinds of sweets. The most conspicuous characteristics of this meal are that it is put together using several kinds of food and that it is served in a large pottery dish.

To summarise, the Shikoku district has a wide range of regional dishes made from various local ingredients. These have the strong potential to stimulate tourism and local economies. The next section examines how these dishes are promoted and utilized.

Promotion of Regional Food in the Shikoku District: Prospects for the Future

An example of the tourism and economic potential of regional food in the Shikoku district is the success story of Sanuki Udon. After examining several guidebooks on regional food in order to find some explanations for the Sanuki Udon success story, the present author found that it was only infrequently referred to until the 1980s, but that it had been attracting much more attention generally since the 1990s, and that the "Sanuki Udon boom" broke out after 2000. The publication of a series of five-volume guidebooks (Mentsudan 1993–2002), with the apparently paradoxical title of *Osorubeki Sanuki Udon* ("Terrible Sanuki Udon"), seems to have played an important role in this phenomenon. The series introduces various types of Udon restaurants, buffets, cafeterias and small stands from all over the prefecture, in an informal and witty style, and in great detail, written as if the authors had explored many good but relatively unknown locations. After a local TV programme presented some of them, publicity for these guidebooks and Sanuki Udon increased gradually beyond the prefecture. At the same time, the reputation of Sanuki Udon was used by local government officials to promote the economy and tourism, and to try to commercialize its good name by every possible means. As a result of these successful campaigns, the name "Sanuki Udon" has become so well known nationwide, that today, even in Tokyo or Osaka, far from Kagawa Prefecture, a Sanuki Udon chain can easily be found, and many tourists visit Kagawa Prefecture in search of its genuine taste.

Except for Sanuki Udon, unfortunately, only a few dishes from the Shikoku district have gained nationwide publicity. "Sawachi Ryori" from Koch Prefecture is one of these, but it does not seem to have as strong an attraction as Sanuki Udon. On the Internet, however, many sites refer to regional food of the Shikoku district.[5] In the future, such sites could be an effective tool for making Shikoku's local food popular among the young generation.

List of References

Printed

Ishige, Naomichi / Tsuji, Shizuo / Nakao, Sasuke [editorial supervisors], *Shuukan Asahi Hyakka Sekai no Tabemono* ("Weekly Asahi's Encyclopedia of World Food"). Asahi Shinbun Sha: Tokyo 1982.

Isige, Naomichi / Okumura, Ayao / Kanzaki, Noritake / Yamashita, Yuichi (eds.):

Nihon no Kyoudo Ryouri ("The Regional Dishes in Japan"), 12 vols. Gyousei: Yamashita 1986.

Kikigaki Kouchi no Shokuji ("Record of Hearing about the Food in Kouchi Prefecture"). Noubunkyo: Tokyo 1986.

Kikigaki Kagawa no Shokuji ("Record of Hearing about the Food in Kagawa Prefecture"). Noubunkyo: Tokyo 1990.

Kikigaki Tokushima no Shokuji ("Record of Hearing about the Food in Tokushima Prefecture"). Noubunkyo: Tokyo 1990.

Kikigaki Ehime no Shokuji ("Record of Hearing about the Food in Ehime Prefecture"). Noubunkyo: Tokyo 1990.

Kyoudo Shoku to Chouriho ("Regional Food and Ways of Its Preparation"). Gakushusha: Tokyo 1944).

Mentsudan (ed.): *Osorubeki Sanuki Udon* ("Terrible Sanuki Udon"), 5 vols. Hot Capsule Publ.: Takamatsu 1993–2002.

---

5 See for example: "Welcome Shikoku" by the Shikoku Shinbun Sha ("Shikoku Newspaper Company"), retrieved 1.3.2016 from http://www.wel-shikoku.gr.jp; also the site introducing regional food in the sphere of "food" on the homepage of the Ehime Prefectural Offices, retrieved 1.3.2016 from http://www.pref.ehime.jp/kurashi/shoku/ryori/index.html); and "Shikoku no Migiagari", the information site managed by the branch office of the southern part of Tokushima Prefecture, retrieved 1.3.2016 from http://shikokunomigishita.jp.

Nihon no Aji: *Atarashii Katei Ryouri to Kyoudo Shoku* ("Tastes of Japan: New Home Cooking and Regional Food"). 6 vols. Yomiuri Shinbun Sha: Tokyo 1973.

Nihon no Shokuseikatu Zenshu ("Complete Works of the Japanese Food"). 50 vols. Noubunkyo: Tokyo 1984–1993.

Terao, Munehuyu: *Mikokuki*. "Topography from the Viewpoint of Taste". Tokyo: Shikishokan, 1976.

Zen Nihon Kyoudo Ryouri ("The Regional Food in Japan"). National Association of Headmasters of Girls' High School: Tokyo 1940.

Internet

[Census 2015], retrieved 1.3.2016 from http://www.stat.go.jp/data/kokusei/2015/kekka/pdf/youyaku.pdf.

Ehime Prefectural Offices ["Food" / "Regional Food"], retrieved 1.3.2016 from http://www.pref.ehime.jp/kurashi/shoku/ryori/index.html.

"Shikoku no Migiagari", Tokushima Prefecture, retrieved 1.3.2016 from http://shikokunomigishita.jp.

"Welcome Shikoku" by the Shikoku Shinbun Sha ("Shikoku Newspaper Company"), retrieved 1.3.2016 from http://www.wel-shikoku.gr.jp.

Hiroko Nakazawa

Production of Traditional Pickled Foods in Nagano Prefecture, Japan: *Nozawana-zuke* and *Sunki-zuke*

Abstract: *Two traditional pickles –* nozawana-zuke and sunki-zuke *– have been passed down through the generations in Nagano Prefecture, a mountainous area of Japan that suffers from very cold winters, in different ways. Interviews clarified that* nozawana-zuke *has been industrialized as a brand and is distributed throughout Japan, while* sunki-zuke *has been preserved as a local, unique, handmade product.*

Introduction

In traditional Japanese food culture, "pickles" are alternatively known as *koh-no-mono*, which means "aromatic side dishes". In traditional Japanese meals, pickles were not merely salted vegetables but an indispensable food item that provided "sour deliciousness", a pleasant savory taste (*umami*), and aroma. In fact, pickled food is an essential component of traditional Japanese food culture. Pickles are an ancient invention and the process of pickling enables the long-term preservation of vegetables by using salt, as well as by means of fermentation and drying, to be achieved. The ancient Japanese did not have the technology to prepare salt, and they therefore repeatedly dipped vegetables into seawater, and dried them several times, in order to make salted pickles that could be preserved for a relatively long time (Miyao 2013, pp. 30–35). Centuries later, in the Edo era (1603–1868), people prepared various kinds of pickles adapted to the climates and regional conditions of different areas of Japan; each household prepared and consumed these pickles which were regarded as important preserved food items.

After World War II, however, changes in Japanese dietary habits reduced the popularity of the making of traditional pickles in individual households, while simultaneously increasing the demand for commercial pickles.[1] On the other hand, the Ministry of Health, Labour and Welfare introduced strategies to reduce salt consumption, which were spurred on by the need to prevent hypertension among

1 See in this connection: "2015 Family Income and Expenditure Survey Results", *Statistics Bureau, Ministry of Internal Affairs and Communications*, retrieved 29.7.2016 from http://www.e-stat.go.jp/SG1/estat/List.do?lid=000001153656.

the Japanese population, thus resulting in a decrease in the salt concentration of pickles from about 13 % to 7 % (currently, it is less than 4 %).[2] Salt concentration in pickles was first reduced in 1979 when the recommended dietary allowance of sodium was set at less than 10g per day per person. In recent years, both pickle-production costs, as well as pickle consumption, have continued to decline.[3]

The present study focuses on two of the many Japanese pickles in existence, *nozawana-zuke* and *sunki-zuke*, both originating in Nagano Prefecture. *Nozawana-zuke* is a famous traditional local food and is renowned as constituting one of the three major Japanese vegetable pickles (*nozawana-zuke*, *hiroshimana-zuke* and *takana-zuke*). In contrast to this, *sunki-zuke* is known as a specialized local pickle prepared without salt. As mentioned above, both pickle production and pickle consumption are decreasing in Japan as a whole: however, in 2014, the base price of pickle production in Nagano Prefecture was still ranked fourth highest in Japan.[4] Therefore, the way in which knowledge of these two contrasting vegetable pickles has been handed down through the generations, from ancient ancestors to current residents in Nagano Prefecture, highlights the two typical, traditional methods of Japanese food-preservation culture, especially because of their contrasting production and industrialization processes.

Thus, the present study clarifies the effects of industrialization on traditional local food by comparing the roles of these two pickles in maintaining Japanese food culture. The study focuses on changes in production output, technology and quality, locations, uniqueness, local communities' recognition of their heritage in such food culture, and the power of invention, all of which are based on a literature review and on interviews conducted with production farmers.

Materials and Method

Nagano Prefecture, situated at the centre of Japan, is the fourth largest prefecture in width (having an area of 13,562 km^2). It has steep mountains higher than 2,000 m and thus has a very limited inhabitable area; its population is only

2 "Takuan-zuke no Rekishi" ("History of '*Takuan-zuke*', Pickled Radishes"), *Nozaki Tsukemo*, http://www.nozaki-p.com/blog/?p=167, retrieved 29. 7. 2016.

3 "2015 Shokuhin Sangyo Dotai Cyosa" ("2015 Statistics of Production by Food Industry"), *Food Marketing Research and Information Center*, retrieved 29.7.2016 from http://www.fmric.or.jp/stat/index.html.

4 "2014 Kogyo Tokei" ("2014 Industrial Statistics"), *Ministry of Economy, Trade and Industry*, retrieved 29.7.2016 from http://www.meti.go.jp/statistics/tyo/kougyo/result-2/h26/kakuho/saibunrui/index.html.

about 2.1 millions. Its geographic features vary and the area accommodates deep valleys, lakes, alluvial fans, river terraces, basins and volcanic highlands. As its length from north to south is approximately 215 km, it has a climatic range of heavy snows in the north and warm temperatures suitable for citrus farming in the south. In the northern snowy, mountainous area, people faced a high risk of food shortages during winter; therefore, long-term food preservation was essential for survival during the cold season. The development of various traditional local pickles throughout the prefecture indicates this necessity. Two representative examples of such local pickles are *nozawana-zuke* (or *oha-zuke*) developed in the northern area, and *sunki-zuke* developed in the Kiso area of the Ontake mountains.

More than four districts were selected for research (Table 1) from each of the four geographically distinct regions (*hokushin* in the north, *tohshin* in the east, *chushin* in the centre, and *nanshin* in the south). Farming women over 60 years of age, who have devoted themselves to maintaining the traditional food culture of the region, were recruited for interviews (N = 60+). Furthermore, participants of a seminar on making *sunki-zuke*, held on 24 November 2015, at the Kiso town community centre, in order to facilitate communication between urban and rural residents, were also interviewed about *sunki-zuke*.

Interviews were conducted from December 2014 to July 2016. Among the questions asked about *nozawana-zuke* and *sunki-zuke*, were the following: Do you currently make them? Why do you or don't you make them? How do you make them? Has the way you make them changed? How do you eat them? Do you know any activities that will help keep the tradition alive in the community?

Table 1. Districts considered for research for nozawana-zuke *and* sunki-zuke *(pickles) in Nagano Prefecture, Japan.*

Region	Names of districts (city, town or village)
North	Iiyama City, Iizuna Town, Nagano City, Chikuma City, Nozawa Onsen Village
East	Ueda City, Saku City, Toumi City, Aoki Village
Central	Ikeda Town, Azumino City, Hakuba Village, Otaki Village, Kiso Town (including Kaida, Mitake and Kiso-Fukushima districts)
South	Okaya City, Shimosuwa Town, Ina City, Yasuoka Village, Takagi Village, Iida City

Results and Discussion

Traditional Japanese dietary traditions were at risk of disappearing after World War II. Therefore, in 1983, Nagano Prefectural Education Committee selected and authenticated five typical cases of traditional food culture as intangible cultural folk properties or *aji-no-bunkazai*. The five *aji-no-bunkazai*s were *teuchi-soba* (hand-made soba noodles), *yakimochi* (baked rice cakes), *goheimochi* (skewed sweet rice cake with soy sauce and *miso* [fermented soy paste]), *nozawana-zuke* and *sunki-zuke*. Among these five, the present study focuses on *nozawana-zuke* and *sunki-zuke* ("Naganoken Sentakumukei Minzoku Bunkazai Cyosa Houkoku" 1984, pp. 41–54).

Nozawana-zuke

Owing to publication limitations, this report describes only the current situation of *nozawana-zuke*, one of the most famous commercial pickles in Japan, and its related culture in Nozawa-onsen village, rather than its general situation in Japan as a whole.

In 1918, a ski course opened at Nozawa-onzen, and skiers began to use *nozawana* as a nickname for pickles that were originally called *kabuna* (edible leaves of turnips). Nowadays, residents of Nozawa-onsen village usually call the pickles *nappa* (vegetable leaves). Sometimes, they also refer to these pickles as *ohazuke* (pickled leaves). In Nagano Prefecture, the pickles are commonly referred to as *ohazuke*, as many kinds of leaves are pickled in various regions. Among the most famous is *nozawana-zuke*, that is, *nozawana* leaves pickled with salt.

Fig. 1: Nozawana, *leaves of turnips for pickling (Brassica rapa var. hakabura) (Photo: Nagano Prefecture Agricultural Marketing Office, 撮影年を確認中).*

According to the oral history of the Kenmeiji temple, where the original variety of *nozawana* is now cultivated, the temple's eighth resident pastor brought *Tennouji* turnip seeds from Kyoto where he had gone to study Buddhism in 1756. These turnips were then cultivated (Miyao 2013, pp. 30–35). However, genetic studies have clearly shown that the *nozawana* variety of turnips is more closely related to the European variety of this vegetable, called *hakabura*, than to Asian turnips such as *Tennouji* (Takashi 1964, pp. 65–72). Indeed, European turnips, *var. hakabura*, have more cold-tolerant characteristics than Asian turnips.

After harvesting, residents of the Nozawa-onsen village commonly wash *nozawana*, or *ona-arai* ("washing nozawana leaves") in the water of a hot spring as it helps the leaves to avoid the cold, and to remove the insects from the leaves, as is traditionally required. Today, however, people use a blue vinyl sheet to form a warm-water pool on a light truck and then stand and wash *nozawana* in this pool.

In each household, methods of pickling have been orally transferred from mothers to daughters or from mothers-in-law to housewives, although traditionally, only methods for the preparation of salted *nozawana* have been thus transferred. A common proverb, *sanzoku-isshou*, which means strewing 1.89 kg (*isshou*) of salt on 45 kg (*sanzoku*) of washed *nozawana*, supports this. After spreading the salt, picklers add sufficient water to the leaves and place a stone weight on top in order to dehydrate the leaves overnight. The traditional pickling method used is *honzuke* (true pickling), which includes the process of fermentation which requires sophisticated skills for judging accurately the amounts of salt and water to be used.

Current *honzuke* methods vary greatly from household to household: different amounts of salt and water along with various additives are used in the various households, thus bestowing importance on "mom's cooking" in every household. Today, *hayazuke* (pickles made quickly and easily), or *shoyuzuke* (pickles made with soy sauce, that is, pickled in one night using sufficient amounts of soy sauce, sugar and vinegar), or *asazuke* (quickly-made pickles, using sufficient amounts of salt and other seasonings), are popularly eaten together with or instead of *honzuke*. The salt concentrations of *hayazuke* and *asazuke* are as low as approximately 3 %. Some commercial factory-produced *nozawana-zuke*, improved to retain the fresh green colour of the leaves, and thus differing from the homemade ones that eventually change colour, have now become available.

If stored in a refrigerator after March, *honzuke* can be eaten until early May. However, in most households, the eating of *honzuke* ceases much earlier because it becomes too sour in taste in the spring, due to fermentation. Another reason for a shortened period during which *honzuke* is eaten – which also means that less is consumed – is the increased availability of other foods.

While it was almost exclusively made for home use in the past, large amounts of *honzuke* are currently being factory-produced as souvenirs of Nozawa-onsen. In Nozawa-onsen village households, more than 100 bundles of *nozawana* (1 bundle = 8 kg) were pickled in the past. The current number of bundles of locally produced *honzuke* is approximately half of that amount; however, almost all village households still make *nozawana-zuke*. In fact, throughout Nagano Prefecture, the number of households making *honzuke*, and the amount made, have declined. Furthermore, some households have stopped making *honzuke* altogether, and have started making *hayazuke* instead. Commercial production of *hayazuke* and *asazuke* in Nagano Prefecture uses *nozawana* which has been transported from other prefectures. However, the taste of *nozawana* is not favoured by younger people and many other foods have now become available, even in winter. These two factors have contributed to reducing total *nozawana* consumption.

Nonetheless, ways of eating *nozawana-zuke* have remained unchanged: Most residents in Nozawa-onsen village eat *honzuke* with steamed rice or tea. In season, *honzuke* is an indispensable side dish for tea and meals. *Honzuke*'s flavour changes rapidly, within 30 minutes, and therefore people take it from the container just before a meal begins. If the taste becomes too sour in the spring, *honzuke* can be stir-fried with seasoning spices. It can also be cut and used as an ingredient in baked flour-balls or croquettes and eaten with steamed rice or tea. *Asazuke* is eaten as a salad with or without steamed rice or tea.

During the Meiji era (1868–1912), cultivation of *nozawana* spread to all districts in Nagano Prefecture and to many other prefectures also, including Hokkaido to the north and Kumamoto to the south. This was due to its advantages which included good taste, high yield, and ease of production.

The original *nozawana* seed species from Kenmeiji temple is continuously conserved as a temple seed. Improved cultivars, with smaller rhizomes and more stems than leaves, have become less expensive and have thus gained the favour of current consumers.

Farmers in Nozawa-onsen cultivate *nozawana* on their farms so that their families can use the *honzuke* method of pickling. But commercial *nozawana-zuke* products, all of which are *hayazuke*, are produced in factories in all other Japanese areas. Although *nozawana-zuke* is commonly recognized as a pickle originating in Nagano Prefecture, the pickle is now very popular throughout Japan. However, residents in Nozawa-onsen village still recognize its name as *nappa* or *ohazuke*. Commercialized *nozawana-zuke* products, available elsewhere in Japan, are mostly *hayazuke* or *asazuke* (shallow pickling) and not traditional *honzuke*. Although the amount of *honzuke* and the number of households making it are decreasing, it is still an important traditional fermented pickle, and it is considered to represent the flavour of "mom's cooking". The spread of *nozawana-zuke* was actually triggered by the invention of *asazuke*, whose increase largely contributed to the recent upsurge in *nozawana-zuke* consumption in Japan. *Nozawana*'s high yield and the softness of its leaves makes it suitable for *asazuke* preparation. Most urban consumers eat *hayazuke* or *asazuke* as *nozawana-zuke*, unaware that the best season for *nozawana-zuke* is winter.

In conclusion, it can be asserted that although *nozawana-zuke* has become one of the most famous pickles in Japan, the essence of traditional pickles prepared using fermentation, such as *honzuke*, has not spread. Thus, *honzuke* consumption and production have decreased, suggesting that people's traditional taste for the fermented smell and/or sourness of this pickle has not been passed down to younger generations. If another leafy vegetable suitable for *asazuke* becomes available, *nozawana* will very likely be replaced in this context. Thus, conserving *nozawana-zuke* may be necessary to popularise *honzuke*.

Sunki-zuke

In this study, the definition of *sunki-zuke* has been taken from a previous report on Nagano Prefecture dating to 1983 ("Naganoken Sentakumukei Minzoku Bunkazai Cyosa Houkoku" 1984, pp. 41–54): pickled red turnip leaves without salt but fermented using a specific lactobacillus species in the cool climate of the Kiso mountain region. The origin of the pickle, in this study, has also been taken from the same previous report: due to a scarcity of salt, the local people of the region developed a method for making pickles without salt. These pickles differed qualitatively from Kyoto Prefecture's *suguki-zuke*, from where *sunki-zuke* is rumoured to have originated. However, this is unlikely because the *suguki-zuke* made in Kyoto Prefecture used large amounts of salt (Miyao 2013, pp. 30–35). Another study reported that *sunki-zuke* existed in the Kiso region more than 300 years ago and, therefore, *sunki-zuke* seems to have been originally developed in the Kiso region only.[5]

The procedure for making *sunki-zuke* was reported to involve the preparation of alternate layers of the Lactobacillus source and boiled red turnip leaves, without salt; the Lactobacillus source was some *sunki-zuke* made the previous year and dried during the cold winter. These turnip leaves and Lactobacillus source mixture shortened the fermentation process and prevented the increase of putrefying bacteria, which were also suppressed by the cold winters in the Kiso region. According to the participants who gave the interviews, methods of obtaining the

5 See: "Nyusankin to Hakko Kin's 11" ("Lactic acid bacteria and Fermentation Kin's, vol.11"), *Calpis Ltd.*, retrieved 29.7.2016 from http://www.asahigroup-holdings.com/research/report/kins/digitalbook/vol_11.html.

Lactobacillus source have changed significantly. Today, many people use frozen *sunki-zuke* or its dipping sauce after it has been thawed. Furthermore, since 2009, four Lactobacillus species have become commercially available in the form of powders for the making of *sunki-zuke*.

In the past, *sunki-zuke* was made from October to November, especially in the high mountain villages, such as those in the Kaida district, for instance. According to interviewees, however, global warming has affected the temperatures of the Kiso region and the making of *sunki-zuke* has been forcefully delayed to avoid the activity of putrefying bacteria. Now, *sunki-zuke* is made from November to mid-December, before the first snow of winter comes.

The residents reported that the containers they used for fermentation were specifically-prepared wooden barrels called *sunki-oke*, which helped to maintain a similar taste in the *sunki-zuke* prepared each year. According to the interviewees, although some farmers still use these special wooden containers, many others now use smaller plastic containers. It was noted, through direct observation, that small-scale factories and the training facility for the making of *sunki-zuke* used polystyrene containers for making *sunki-zuke*, as they have the advantages of maintaining a stable temperature and being lightweight.

As to the source of leaves for *sunki-zuke*, the same five varieties of red turnips have always been used: Otaki, Kaida, Hosojima, Mitakekurose and Yoshino turnips from the Kiso region. In May 2007, Nagano Prefecture certified all these turnip varieties as "traditional food of Shinshu". The fermentation method has also remained unchanged, except for the slight difference in the method used for maintaining temperature; previously, containers were covered with blankets, but due to the change of the type of container used, that is no longer necessary.

Fig. 2: Kiso red turnips: Otaki, Mitakekurose and Hosojima in order from the top (Photo: Nagano Prefecture Agricultural Marketing Office, 撮影年を確認中).

Another change is in the preferred taste from "amber-coloured *sunki-zuke* [that] is more delicious as it is sourer", to a crispy texture with *umami*. For the latter taste, the *sunki-zuke* process used focuses on maintaining environmental conditions that will favour the Lactobacillus: avoiding having temperatures too high for the boiling of the raw leaves; using a good Lactobacillus source; and preventing oxidation by covering *sunki-zuke* using a container containing boiling water, after the leaves have cooled. In addition, the repetitive use of *sunki-zuke* sauce as the Lactobacillus source is believed to be the key to making *sunki-zuke* more delicious.

People in the Kiso region believe that making good quality *sunki-zuke* is difficult: according to an interview with a *sunki-zuke*-making instructor, everyone in the Kiso region enthusiastically attempts to make *sunki-zuke* every year; however, only a third succeed. Even today, a precise method of making good *sunki-zuke* has not been authoritatively established, and therefore each individual household tries to make good *sunki-zuke*, and hopes that it will have a very sour flavour.

The tradition of eating *sunki-zuke* has changed slightly from the previous report: usually, the period in which *sunki-zuke* is consumed is until March, but according to the interviewees in this study, the period has now been extended until April. Even so, *sunki-zuke* is still basically considered to be preserved vegetables that help people to survive the cold winters in the Kiso region. *Sunki-zuke* was historically stored outside in the cold, according to a previous report, but is now refrigerated indoors because of the effect of global warming and because changes in home-building that have resulted in higher room temperatures. The amount of *sunki-zuke* made on the same occasion has also changed, declining from one to three large wooden barrels (about 18–54 litres) to much smaller plastic or styrene containers, although several batches of *sunki-zuke* tend to be made at different times during the season.

Owing to its no-salt feature, *sunki-zuke* is still used in various ways in cooking: shaved dried bonito with soy sauce is sprinkled with *sunki-zuke*; *sunki-zuke* is added to miso soup (*sunki-jiru*) and to *soba* noodles in soup (*sunki-soba*). Some interviewees reported that they ate *sunki-jiru* every day during the winter while others reported new uses for *sunki-zuke* in cooking, for instance, in pizzas or traditional baked wheat-flour cakes (*oyaki*).

Sunki-zuke's distribution is basically limited to the Kiso region, particularly the Mt. Ontake area, owing to the availability of the red turnip leaves necessary for its production in this region. For the handing down of the traditional technology and taste of *sunki-zuke* to future generations, "*Kiso sunki kenkyu-kai*", a *sunki-zuke* study group in the Kiso region, was founded in December 1997. This is a citizenship activity-group working in cooperation with the Nagano Prefecture

Kiso Agricultural Extension Centre and researchers at the Tokyo Agricultural University and Shinshu University. These bodies have managed the "*Kiso sunki* contests" occurring annually since 2005. As a result of their activities, red turnips and *sunki-zuke* in the Kiso region were registered with the Ark of Taste by the Slow Food Association for Biodiversity in April 2007.

Fig. 3: Sunki-soba, *traditional Japanese soup with soba noodles and sunki-zuke (sour pickles) (Photo: Hiroko Nakazawa, 2015).*

Furthermore, as a transmission activity for *sunki-zuke*, local elementary schools and high schools provide students with opportunities for making *sunki-zuke*, from seeding onwards. In addition, specific facilities in the Kiso region offer seminars to the general public during which participants learn how to make *sunki-zuke*; these seminars begin in mid-November when many tourists visit the Kiso region and they often participate in these seminars. The number of participants usually exceeds 300 and many of them are repeat attendees.

The recent "healthy food" boom in Japan has accelerated the commercialisation of *sunki-zuke*: production by the eight major manufacturers, which rose from 13.5 t in 2013, to 25 t in 2014, and then to 35 t in 2015. However, some uncertified providers outside the Kiso region have begun to sell these pickles by flavouring them with seasonings rather than through *sunki-zuke* fermentation, which can potentially cause problems linked to inferior quality. To prevent such "piracy", manufacturers in the Kiso region, in cooperation with local village governments and *Kiso sunki kenkyu-kai*, plan to register *sunki-zuke* in the governmental "Geographical Indication" system in the near future.

In conclusion, due to the limited supply of red turnip leaves and resources, and problems related to production procedures and distribution, *sunki-zuke* is still strongly preserved in the Kiso region, especially around Mt. Ontake; furthermore, this preservation activity is supported by extensive cooperation among local citizens, government officers and university researchers. Thus, *sunki-zuke* is still considered to be a fascinating local product because of its no-salt characteristic, usability in many kinds of cooking, and its potential health-promotion properties.[6]

Conclusion

Knowledge about the traditional pickles, *nozawana-zuke* and *sunki-zuke*, both of which have been registered as intangible folk cultural properties by Nagano Prefecture, that is, as *aji-no-bunkazai*, in 1983, is still handed down to the younger generations in their locations of origin. However, the traditions associated with these pickles differ. *Nozawana-zuke* has become very famous in Japan and is made in many prefectures; however, popular methods of making *nozawana-zuke* (*haya-zuke* or *asauzuke*) differ greatly from the original method (*honzuke*). Original *honzuke*, which uses fermentation, is still made in Nozawa-onsen village, although both its production and consumption have largely declined. In contrast, *sunki-zuke* is not very well known in other prefectures, its production area is restricted to the Kiso region, and its production methods are highly conservative.

Differences between the two pickles can be attributed to several factors. Large amounts of salt are required in the making of *nozawana-zuke*, and salt was readily available in Nozawa-onsen as it is relatively close to the sea. However, in the Kiso region, salt was not so easily acquired. Therefore, people in the Kiso region needed other kinds of preserved foods for survival during the cold winters. They developed *sunki-zuke*, utilizing Lactobacillus for fermentation. In addition, *sunki-zuke* can be prepared from five limited varieties of red turnips, which can be cultivated only in Kiso and its surrounding regions. In contrast, the source plant for *nozawana-zuke*, *nozawana*, can grow in many prefectures.

According to interviewees, the transfer of the traditional pickle culture to the young generation appears to be difficult to achieve. Therefore, research on recognition and awareness of traditional pickles targeted at the younger generation is required. Such research can clarify why the transfer is difficult and can thus contribute to the conservation of local, traditional pickled-food culture.

6 Ibid.

List of References

Printed

Miyao, Shigeo: "Nihon zenkoku tsukemono tutu uraura" ("Pickles All Over the Country in Japan"). *Shokuseikatu: Magazine of Food* 107, 2013, pp. 30–35.

"Naganoken Sentakumukei Minzoku Bunkazai Cyosa Houkoku" ("An Investigation and Report on the Nagano Prefecture Selected Intangible Folk Cultural Properties"), *Nagano Prefectural Education Committee* (1984), pp. 41–54.

Takashi, Aoba, "Honpo Sosai Zairaihinsyu no Chiritekibunpu to Bunrui ni Kansuru Kenkyu, 4" ("Studies on the Classification and the Geographical Distribution of Local Varieties of Vegetables in Japan, 4"). *Journal of the Japanese Society for Horticultural Science* 32, 1964, pp. 65–72.

Internet

"2014 Kogyo Tokei" ("2014 Industrial Statistics"), *Ministry of Economy, Trade and Industry*, retrieved 29.7.2016 from http://www.meti.go.jp/statistics/tyo/kougyo/result-2/h26/kakuho/saibunrui/index.html.

"2015 Family Income and Expenditure Survey Results", *Statistics Bureau, Ministry of Internal Affairs and Communications*, retrieved 29.7.2016 from http://www.e-stat.go.jp/SG1/estat/List.do?lid=000001153656.

"2015 Shokuhin Sangyo Dotai Cyosa" ("2015 Statistics of Production by Food Industry"). *Food Marketing Research and Information Center*, retrieved 29.7.2016 from http://www.fmric.or.jp/stat/index.html.

"Nyusankin to Hakko Kin's 11" ("Lactic acid bacteria and Fermentation Kin's, vol.11"), *Calpis Ltd.*, retrieved 29.7.2016 from http://www.asahigroup-holdings.com/research/report/kins/digitalbook/vol_11.html.

"Takuan-zuke no Rekishi" ("History of '*Takuan-zuke*', Pickled Radishes"), retrieved 29.7.2016 from *Nozaki Tsukemo*, http://www.nozaki-p.com/blog/?p=167.

Ken Albala

The Artisanal Food Movement and How the Values of Fresh, Local and Sustainable are Co-opted by the Food Industry

Abstract: *This paper examines the use of buzzwords such as craft, artisanal and handmade in the advertisement of modern food products such as cured meats, cheese, beer and spirits. It argues that these terms are largely meaningless when used by large industrial corporations, though they may still work in attracting consumers who purchase these products as a mark of distinction. The paper calls for closer legal definition as a way to protect truly small-scale craft producers.*

Since the global economic downturn of 2008, the cultural landscape of the food scene has gradually shifted away from technologically driven avant-garde high-end restaurants like elBulli towards a decidedly artisanal small-scale craft aesthetic. This was not merely a matter of needing to downscale restaurants to serve an increasingly strapped clientele, find markets for exotic consumer goods lower on the price scale, and appear less elitist at a time when bankers and large corporations were perceived as being the root of the crisis. It was also an ideological shift toward populist values gastronomically, toward locally made, artisanal, small batch consumables, that even though they may have fetched prices exceeding those of previous decades, they at least gave the impression of being righteously craft-ish. Combined with newly heightened awareness of environmental issues, animal rights, justice for workers in the wake of the publication of books like the *Omnivore's Dilemma* (Pollan 2006), this food movement, much like earlier iterations in the late 1960s counter culture hippie aesthetic, was informed vaguely by concerns over health, but even more powerfully by the spirit of the creative individual operating beyond the constraints of corporate greed, crafting unique products that spoke of local communities, even local bacteria when it came to fermented products.

Part and parcel of this shift was the craft beer movement rising from 5 % in 2000 to over 12 % of the US market today. Artisanal cheeses gained an increasing presence, craft manufacturers of charcuterie La Quercia, Fra Mani, Olympia Provisions, Boccalone, and much the same happened with chocolate, vermouth and bitters used in cocktails and spirits in general. The quite sudden appreciation for small batch and local products was flavoured without explicit recognition or even realization, by an ideology that is fundamentally Marxist. It begins with the assumption that in a capitalist workplace the worker, although not perhaps still the appendage of flesh on a machine of iron, is nonetheless beholden to corporate values, shareholder profits, and a marketplace that is necessarily driven by growth rather than creative expression or personal connection to consumers. The social element and possibility of direct feedback to the producer is key: knowing your farmer, baker, cheesemaker, beer master is an indispensible facet of the artisanal culture.

Whereas Budweiser and Kraft (the company) American cheese stood for the aesthetic debasement of the American palate, the small craft brewery and local artisanal cheese represented the reawakening of the collective taste buds, a sometimes nostalgic return to products in which human hands and quirky values could find expression in foods that would appeal to those whose taste went beyond the complacent masses. That is, this was a new kind of elitism based not on cost rarity or the intellectual frisson that comes from deconstructed high-end restaurant dishes, but from discovering the odd, unknown craftsperson perfecting the trade with timeworn traditions connected to the soil, the community, and the circle of consumers who can discern righteous food.

I say this only half tongue in cheek, to point out that a populist aesthetic is often anything but democratizing. The cost of artisanal products is often much more expensive and justified by the need to source local ingredients and pay workers well and operate outside of the gas guzzling distribution networks that make much of the US food supply so cheap. Moreover the cultural capital that is gained by the patronage of these craft foods is far more prestigious than goods that mere money can buy, because it demands knowledge and discernment. For example an artisanal loaf of bread usually costs at least 3 times a much as what is made in a factory. (I compared the $6 Bay Area Acme 1 lb. loaf with the Safeway $1.99 rustic ciabatta.) At my local Bevmo a 6 pack of Bud in 12 ounce glass bottles is $6.99, while a single bottle and the Allagash Curieux 25 oz is $20.99. That is 10 times the price. The 10th Anniversary 1.5 litre bottle of beer sells for $69.99 which ranks with some of the most expensive wines the store sells.

The inherent irony in this situation is that both the Acme bread and the Allagash beer are distributed fairly widely, Acme through much of California and Allagash nationally. Whether the company loses its artisanal spirit when it becomes a huge industrial company with many employers serving a mass market is a philosophical question. It is one that concerns companies like La Brea Bakery, a small L.A. operation that hit the big time and is now in every supermarket. It is the same question posed to William Morris over a century ago, does it matter if your artists design beautiful wallpaper if its made in a factory and anyone can buy it? Of course for the consumer the product loses its power to confer status if it is mass marketed, but does the craftsperson cease to exist once there are no longer human hands involved in the process? On the other hand, can you blame a manufacturer for success and expansion? It is reminiscent of the intrepid restaurant hunter who wants to tell everyone about his latest discovery, knowing full well success would make it popular and ruin it. Or the Slow Food advocate who rescues a threatened traditional product only to find it later expands and is sold to a large manufacturer.

An equally fascinating phenomenon, beyond selling out, getting too big, or going corporate, is that the food industry itself capitalizes on the shift in consumer values. They create knock-offs, fakes that imitate the artisanal, often calling them just that. Rather than compete with these little upstart start ups, they often buy them out, and continue to sell them under the original label even though the directive comes now from corporate headquarters. The Safeway supermarket bread, although basically just a misshapen white Wonderbread, was labeled "Artisan" and wrapped in a paper sack and stacked in a rustic bin rather than on the shelf.

Co-opting the craft aesthetic is nothing new though. Today we find faux hipster pickles, pasteurized though probiotic kefir and kombucha, and even distilled grain spirits simply bought in bulk from Archer Daniels Midland (the same ethanol that goes into gas tanks) and then by adding a few flavourings it is marketed as artisanal gin, vodka, etc. Roughly 40 years ago the same thing happened as mass produced yoghurt, tofu and hummus muscled in on the hippie-driven health food market and went mainstream. This process was recorded in Warren J. Belasco's classic *Appetite for Change* (1996), but it is not generally recognized how effective corporations have since become in selling this aesthetic today by employing the language of the craft food movement, but none of its actual philosophy or techniques.

That is, because of a largely unregulated sphere of advertising, words which convey the craft aesthetic are slapped all over advertisements in an attempt to draw consumers in. This phenomenon has been recorded with the word "fresh" by Suzanne Freidberg in her book of the same name (Freidberg 2009). Studies have also been conducted on how corporate advertising uses certain buzzwords such as "healthy" "lite" and whatever it may be "free" from – growth hormone, GMOs, nitrates, gluten – simply to sell products, even though most products labelled gluten free would never have had any in the first place. Uncured bacon on a label is an outright lie, a legal loophole allows manufacturers to use nitrates from celery.

In this study I will examine the ways that industrial scale food advertisements have co-opted the craft aesthetic with certain key buzzwords such as craft, artisan, small batch, local, and related words such as traditional, or increasingly in the past few years "farm to fork". I have examined the print advertisements in several popular mainstream food magazines of the last 5 years including *Bon Appétit*, *Food and Wine* and *Saveur* and have focused on products which lend themselves to consumer confusion – specifically cured meats, cheese, bread, alcohol, and chocolate. I saw no point in tracking how products that have never been artisanal use this language. It is precisely the line of confusion that interests me most. To this end I have used the methodology of discourse analysis, and close textual reading or decoding of the buzzwords for select products. Although I will mention the images in passing it is primarily a linguistic analysis I am conducting, even though there are some very powerful visual cues that conjure up the craft aesthetic more effectively than words. At least in the US, a hipster with a beard and flannel shirt, in a makeshift wooden bar or workspace is an immediate marker. A friendly farmer is beginning to displace him now.

The first impression of the advertisements in these magazines is that they are aspirational, usually for travel or luxury goods that are slightly above the economic status of the magazine's content. In other words, whereas the recipes and stories generally do not include rare exotic ingredients or great expense – in fact they are generally fairly thrifty – the advertisements urge purchases that appeal to the socially rising aspirant and often have very little to do with food, but are more about insurance, travel (especially food related), luxury housewares (especially oven and kitchenware). The logic is that the advertisement should not simply confirm a purchase the reader would likely have made anyway, but goad them into a more expensive purchase, indulgence, or adventure that they would not have known in the first place. The food advertisements are completely different because they have to appeal directly to foodie sensibilities.

Let me start with an advertisement that appears in the current September 2016 issue of *Food and Wine* (p. 27). A new product, so self-proclaimed on the package, comes from Lorissa's Kitchen. It is "Ginger Teriyaki Premium Chicken Cuts" though the product description is in tiny letters in the advertisement.

The name of the company itself implies that there is a woman named Lorissa if not making the product in her own kitchen, then at least directing the company that began there. The squares of dried chicken product are pictured on a worn wooden cutting board further emphasizing that it is home made. Mismatched pottery bowls reiterate craftsmanship. The package shouts "chicken raised without antibiotics" since most educated foodies would know that this is the latest health concern – growing antibiotic resistance of pathogens. The projected consumer thus cares where her food comes from, is concerned about the ingredients, and the advertisement assures that it contains no MSG (but if you have a microscope it reads "except for that naturally occurring in soy sauce and yeast extract"). No added Nitrates (likewise "except for that naturally occurring in sea salt"), and no growth hormones (which Federal law prohibits anyway), and the package says gluten free (although chickens normally do not contain gluten).

It is indeed a new product since chicken jerky is unknown to most consumers. (Though the word jerky is not used because it implies low socio-economic status and junk food.) The lead copy is most interesting and reads "From Farm to Table to Carry On to Wherever". "From Farm to Table" implies that the product is somehow fresh or has moved directly to a meal with minimal intervention or processing, though clearly a shelf stable preserved product would not match that description. The "Carry On" explicitly implies that this is a consumer on the move, hurrying to catch a flight without time for a proper meal and just in case, the "to wherever" phrase suggests that even if there is no flight to catch, busy important people need to have snacks, but not just any snacks. Only those that are free from everything bad and contain everything good – a craftswoman behind the scenes who gets healthy chickens right from the farm and makes up batches of this truly unique product.

There is also an unstated context which is not necessarily paleo-dieting, but definitely the new dietary emphasis on protein for people who exercise. On the website the farm connection is far more explicit as it shows bucolic pastures and the outlines of animals labelled 100 % grass fed beef, chicken raised without antibiotics, and a pig raised responsibly (http://lorissaskitchen.com/?gclid=CMCmsYra1c4CFcdgfgodX2YMyQ&gclsrc=aw.ds, retrieved 25.8.2016).

A small amount of digging revealed that Lorissa's Kitchen is not a little craft farm raised start up, but a new brand spun by the largest manufacturer of jerky in the US – Jack Link's which can be bought in any convenience store; they hold a 50 % share of the 3 billion dollar US meat snack market (http://www.bakeryandsnacks.com/Manufacturers/Jack-Link-s-on-grass-fed-beef-Lorissa-s-Kitchen-and-retail-outlets, retrieved 25.8.2016). The new product line was rebranded and launched in February, and the company did in fact buy a grass fed beef supplier. Their logic was to expand their market to young women and appeal to a demographic of consumers that long ago stopped eating jerky out of concern for health and animal welfare. That is, the artisanal spin was created out of fear of losing profit margins, and is related to marketing makeovers happening now everywhere from fast food outlets to junk food. The most interesting part of the story is not that a large company is offering a healthy option, which makes perfect sense, but that they are spinning it as an artisanal product.

Admittedly, no one but a large corporation would be able to afford advertisements in these magazines. The smallest advertisement space available, and I know because I inquired, is $116,000 which is enough to start a small business. Advertisers are caught between wanting to appear to give time and care to products but also risk not attracting customers with an unknown brand. Sometimes their strategy to have it both ways falls completely flat, as it does in a bacon ad in the same magazine issue that claims "bacon takes time. It's always cured for 12 hours and smoke-housed for 12 hours, because bacon this good can't be rushed". The advertisement is for Oscar Meyer, the quintessential mass-produced brand, so it is difficult to imagine an actual smokehouse. In another advertisement they claim "some things are artificial, we're not" beneath a street sign for Hollywood. This is an advertisement for natural slow-roasted turkey breast (*Bon Appétit*, June 2016, p. 86). On some level many companies are redesigning their products for people who want a healthier alternative, but it is fascinating nonetheless that this is inextricably tied up with the image of slowness and being real food.

The word craft is also bandied about in ways that I cannot imagine anyone takes seriously. In the April issue of *Bon Appétit* there is an advertisement for Starbucks which claims that "our place or yours" – meaning in a store where an actual person makes the coffee, or at home "the same craft and care go into every cup" next to which is a box of Pike's Place Roast Keurig cups (*Bon Appétit*, April 2016, pp. 8, 31). Just a few pages later there is a Peet's Coffee advertisement which shows the brew pouring slowly from the machine and the copy reads "the original craft coffee" – though of course you can also buy it pre-ground and in Keurig cups. What makes either of these the product of craftsmanship is unclear – certainly not human hands, scale and locale is irrelevant, even the care and time spent on each cup. You could argue that in an actual coffee shop there is the social connection that is implied by the word, but not when it is made at home in a virtually instant machine.

The appeal of tradition is also tied into the craft aesthetic, especially as concerns cheese. Most supermarkets carry cheeses that at least began as truly artisanal like Laura Chenel and Coach farms goat cheeses, and nowadays, at least on the west coast, Point Reyes Blue, Humboldt Fog, and Cow Girl Creamery varieties. But other huge conglomerates are not beyond tapping into this source of implied artisanship. A long battle between California and Wisconsin went far in blurring the lines between artisanal, real, local cheese, and that made in a factory, and the confusion is being capitalized by other manufacturers. A few years ago the Italian cheeses like mozzarella and ricotta sold under the brand name Precious on the West coast and Sorrento on the East suddenly changed to Galbani. Otherwise they are the exact same products. A Galbani advertisement (*Food and Wine*, September 2016, p. 71) emphasizes that "over 130 years of Italian craftsmanship is part of every product we make". The logo reassures us that it is Italy's favourite cheese brand since 1882. The implication is that these are Italian cheeses, though they are clearly the same American cheeses. The Galbani company, moreover is owned by the huge conglomerate Groupe Lactalis, which is French and the largest dairy and cheese group in the world with 17 billion dollar turnover in 2015 (http://www.lactalis-international.com/en/the-lactalis-group.html, retrieved 25.8.2016). This is as large scale and industrial as cheese can possibly get. And yet the package shows rolling Italian hills, poplars, a farmhouse and a very clear message that this is somehow a traditional artisan product. (Incidentally, Egidio Galbani the actual company founder, invented Bel Paese which is the quintessential industrial cheese.)

The market for spirits also taps into this desire for artisanal products. This happened largely because of the loosening of very strict laws on distillation. The so-called microshiners have increased from about 600 to 1000 this past year, about 1 % of spirits sold in the US, or as much as 3 % if you include those that call themselves craft but produce a million cases a year – like Tito's out of Texas. It's very difficult to tell who might be an actual microdistiller since different criteria are applied. Sometimes independent ownership is important, sometimes actual distilling is from grain, which most gin manufacturers do not do.

So let us examine Prairie Vodka, which was launched in 2008 by Phillips Distilling in Minneapolis. An advertisement in the same *Food and Wine* issue (September 2016, p. 85) boldly pronounces "Farm Crafted Certified Organic" and with an image of a farmer's hands planting corn seedlings right next to the words, the connection is made explicit that this is a product of the soil, of direct human intervention that bespeaks the unique gastronomic properties of heartland prairie *terroir*. Every bottle exclaims not only certified organic but the words "handcrafted" vodka, gin, etc. Now the organic part is USDA certified, but the craftsmanship involved? Hand crafted implies that someone's hands were involved in the product, perhaps the owner or distiller operating a copper alembic still in a small batch. The Distilled Spirits Council and the American Distilling Institute define craft production as under 40,000 cases for the former and the latter 100,000 gallons, which is about the same (http://punchdrink.com/articles/what-exactly-defines-a-craft-spirit/, retrieved 25.8.2016). Beyond that there is little consensus about what the term means and no legal definition, which is why Prairie can use it. Some manufacturers purchase bulk ethanol, flavour and rebottle it (http://www.thedailybeast.com/articles/2014/07/28/your-craft-whiskey-is-probably-from-a-factory-distillery-in-indiana.html, retrieved 25.8.2016). Prairie on the other hand is actually distilled by a cooperative owned by 900 farmers, so there is a direct connection to the farms. The company's website features 3 organic farmers in detail. The vodka wins numerous awards such as the 2016 World Spirits Competition Gold Medal in San Francisco, so clearly this brand is not a hoax or corporate makeover. The size of the company might disqualify it from anything approaching the crafts-like manufacture of spirits, but otherwise everything the company claims appears to be true. But how many consumers are going to spend the time to research this?

There are many other spirits manufacturers that appropriate the language of craftsmanship but little more than that. Patron Tequila for example boasts "Unlike other tequilas, Patron is handcrafted in small batches under the watchful eye of our respected master distiller" (*Bon Appétit*, December 2012, p. 1). It also reads "Harken back to the days when all gifts were handmade in small quantities". There are traditional small-batch methods of growing blue agave, roasting the piñons and distilling in copper stills, and Patron was one of the oldest distilleries, but the name was bought out by a much larger US company and moved into a modern facility. The marketing team also began promoting it as a luxury drink, to change the reputation of tequila as a cheap mixer, and part of that was conveying the message that it is a small-scale artisanal product. If you go to the website you see the hacienda, the agave being cut by hand, roasted, crushed, etc. But if you simply do some math, you will realize the majority of the tequila (2.2 million cases in 2015–9 litres per case = 19.8 million litres or 445 million shots – more than a shot for every person in the US), has to be made exactly like any other tequila (http://www.statista.com/statistics/311758/patron-tequila-global-sales-volume/, retrieved 25.8.2016). Does this mean it is bad? Not in the least, it is very good, but the pretence of small quantities and craftsmanship is hard to swallow.

The most notorious story on this subject in the past few years was the scandal when it was discovered that the bearded Brooklyn hipster Mast Brothers selling ten dollar bars of artisanal chocolate which they advertised as being hand made, carefully sourced, bean to bar and so on, were actually buying mass produced chocolate from another company and repackaging it (http://www.eater.com/2015/12/23/10657022/what-the-mast-brothers-scandal-tells-us-about-ourselves, retrieved 25.8.2016). The worst sin an artisan can commit is to violate the rule of authenticity. The company survived the scandal, but the greater irony is that they did thereafter exclusively make their own chocolate, which according to most reviews is pretty bad. This story points to a larger theme, not that the words craft and artisan can be used by anyone or even faked outright, but that people buy food not necessarily for the taste and quality of the product but because of the story it tells about the manufacturer, and the message it communicates to the consumer and those who witness it being consumed. When it is said that food must be first good to think (to paraphrase Claude Levi-Strauss) it is not merely that we imagine it being palatable, healthy, just or whatever, it is that the food itself tells a story which confirms our values, which elevates our cultural capital, which make us seem better in the eyes of others. In the end it does not matter whether artisanal foods are well defined and legally protected, if that were even possible. All that matters is that people believe the stories and buy into the lifestyle, and apparently many people still do.

I would predict that as with all food trends, even those explicitly connected to larger ideologies, the craft aesthetic will become worn and will eventually be replaced by another movement whose faith in science and progress will embrace the technological again. If past patterns are any indication we have another 5–10 years (http://www.history.ac.uk/podcasts/anglo-american-conference-2013-food-history/toward-historical-dialectic-culinary-styles, retrieved 25.8.2016; Albala 2014, pp. 581–590).

List of References

Printed

Albala, Ken: "Toward a Historical Dialectic of Culinary Styles" *Historical Research* 87, November 2014, pp. 581–590.

Belasco, Warren J.: *Appetite for Change: How the Counterculture Took on the Food Industry*. Cornell University Press: Ithaca, NY 1996.

Bon Appétit, December 2012, p. 1.

Bon Appétit, April 2016, pp. 8, 31.

Bon Appétit, June 2016, p. 86.

Food and Wine, September 2016, p. 27; full page advertisement.

Food And Wine, September 2016, p. 27.

Food And Wine, September 2016, p. 71.

Food and Wine, September 2016, p. 85.

Freidberg, Susanna: *Fresh: A Perishable History*. Harvard University Press: Boston 2009).

Pollan, Michael: *The Omnivore's Dilemma: A Natural History of Four Meals*. Penguin: New York 2006.

Internet

http://lorissaskitchen.com/?gclid=CMCmsYra1c4CFcdgfgodX2YMyQ&gclsrc=aw.ds, retrieved 10.8.2016.

http://www.bakeryandsnacks.com/Manufacturers/Jack-Link-s-on-grass-fed-beef-Lorissa-s-Kitchen-and-retail-outlets, retrieved 10.8.2016.

http://www.lactalis-international.com/en/the-lactalis-group.html, retrieved 20.8. 2016.

http://punchdrink.com/articles/what-exactly-defines-a-craft-spirit/, retrieved 20.8.2016.

http://www.thedailybeast.com/articles/2014/07/28/your-craft-whiskey-is-probably-from-a-factory-distillery-in-indiana.html, retrieved 20.8. 2016.

http://www.statista.com/statistics/311758/patron-tequila-global-sales-volume/, retrieved 10.8.2016.

http://www.eater.com/2015/12/23/10657022/what-the-mast-brothers-scandal-tells-us-about-ourselves, retrieved 25.8. 2016.

http://www.history.ac.uk/podcasts/anglo-american-conference-2013-food-history/toward-historical-dialectic-culinary-styles (published as Albala 2014, retrieved 25.8.2016.

Shirley Cherkasky

Wild Rice and Maple Syrup: Native American Foods from the Western Great Lakes Region

Abstract: *Wild rice and maple syrup, both indigenous and traditional products of the Western Great Lakes Region of the United States, so far have survived the economic challenges of cheap imitation, mechanization, and genetic engineering. Will ecological challenges such as pollution and global warming overcome their ability to survive in the future?*

Wild rice and maple syrup are iconic foods of the Upper Midwest and Western Great Lakes region of the United States. Both were being harvested and consumed by humans in North America for generations before the first European explorers began sending back reports from the New World in the 17th century.

Fig. 1: Map of Great Lakes region (Courtesy of University of Wisconsin Cartography Laboratory).

This paper will focus on two U.S. states: Minnesota, where wild rice has been designated the "state grain", and Wisconsin, where the sugar maple is the "state tree". At the outset I want to recognize the definitive work of Thomas Vennum, Jr., *Wild Rice and the Ojibway People*, which provided much of my information on wild rice and, I suspect, that of many of the subsequent sources that have been cited in footnotes (Vennum 1998).

At the time of European arrival, wild rice, *Zizania aquatica*, an aquatic cereal grain as its name indicates, grew all over the eastern part of the United States, extending into areas around Lake Superior, the westernmost of the Great Lakes. After the end of the Ice Age, the retreat of the glaciers in this part of North America left the earth's surface pockmarked with indentations that filled with water to become thousands of small, usually shallow, lakes connected by winding, slow-moving rivers that provided the lakes with a supply of pure, fresh water. Today Minnesota and Wisconsin each claim to have more than 10,000 lakes within their borders. These lakes' alluvial mud-coated bottoms differ from European lakes which generally have lime- or sand-coated bottoms. The alluvium provides a rich base for the wild rice, which is not related to *Oryza sativa*, the common Asian rice.

The sugar maple tree, *Acer saccharum,* which produces a clear, just faintly sweet sap, is plentiful in the Upper Midwest's woodlands but mostly unknown in Europe. The trees are still found all over the Northeastern part of the U.S. and as far west as the Mississippi River area, beyond which the Great Plains begin. The maple sap was collected and evaporated by the Indians to become a sweet syrup or sugar. Maple sugar was almost the only seasoning the Indians used, with venison and other meats, with wild rice, with fish, and with their garden vegetables such as corn, squash, and potatoes, until they were introduced to salt by the Europeans.

Maple syrup and wild rice both played cultural and ceremonial roles in the diet of Upper Midwest Native Americans, among them the Ojibway Indians. The Ojibway language name for wild rice is *manoomin*, meaning (approximately) "good seed" (ibid., pp. 6–7). Other Indian tribes had their own names for it. Early French explorers and fur traders called it *folle avoine* (fool/crazy oats). After the English began to dominate the area, they called it wild rice because of its aquatic origin. As the European explorers, fur traders, and settlers traded with the Indians for maple sugar and wild rice to supplement the meat they hunted and the foods they brought with them or had to import from Europe, they found both the sugar and rice tasty and nutritious, and readily adopted them into their own diets.

The Ojibways, while still living east of Lake Superior, had begun trading with the European newcomers for furs, eventually becoming interpreters and middlemen. They began to move westward into the lands occupied by several other tribes, among them the Sauk, the Fox, the Menominee, and the Dakota

Sioux who were reliant on wild rice as a year-round diet staple. The resultant bitterly fought battles over the ricing areas caused much turmoil and, by 1827, the new American government began to forcibly remove the Dakotas to areas further west of the Mississippi River, leaving much of the ricing areas to the Ojibways who also had come to value and rely on wild rice as a staple. As the Indians were moved to government-designated reservations, the land they had formerly freely roamed, and used as a source for all their food and other daily needs, was offered for sale to the new European settlers who were eager to acquire good land for farming.

As part of their new farmlands, many of the settlers also acquired a grove of sugar maples, still commonly referred to in the Midwest as a sugar bush. Having acquired a taste for maple sugar, then a relatively cheap sweetener compared with cane sugar imported from the Caribbean or refined in Europe, the settlers began to process maple sap into syrup, as they had learned to do from the Native Americans. At first, it was only for their own use or to trade with their neighbors and others who wanted it.

Originally, the Indians collected the sap by simply gashing the tree bark with an axe and attaching a birch bark receptacle to catch the flow, and boiling that down over a slow steady fire until it was dehydrated sufficiently to be used as a sweetener. This required a plentiful supply of wood but, if wood was not easily available, the sap also could be dehydrated by setting it out in large shallow containers on freezing nights and then breaking and removing the ice that formed. After repeating this procedure several times, the remaining, very sweet, brown syrup was ready for use. To produce maple sugar, the syrup was boiled again until it crystallized into hard lumps that had to be pounded, very like cane sugar in early times, into granules.

Today's maple trees will produce, over a season, an average of twenty to sixty litres of sap per tree. It requires forty litres of sap to produce one litre of syrup with the desired sugar concentration of about two parts sucrose to one part water. In earlier times during the harvest, carrying the many sap-filled pails to a central collection point in the sugar bush was a tedious process and required many hands. At sugaring time family members and friends were enlisted to help. Over the years, new equipment and more efficient methods have been devised, and today each tree, once it reaches ten inches or more in diameter, is tapped with one or two metal spiles drilled into the trunk at least a few feet off the ground.

Fig. 2: Collecting maple sap in plastic bag (Courtesy of Carter Family).

The sap flows into a blue plastic bag attached to the spile or is carried by lengths of plastic tubing from the tree to a storage tank. After filtering, the boiling begins, either over a steady wood fire in the sugar shack out in the sugar bush or, in a commercial venture, the boiling may be done in an evaporator at the processing plant. When the measuring gauges indicate that the sucrose concentration is approximately 65 per cent, the hot syrup is ready to be bottled.

Ordinarily the amount of maple syrup produced does not vary much from year to year except in case of a severe drought, or if unusually frigid or warm temperatures occur during the harvest season from late February through April. But in 2013, the best year on record in Wisconsin since 1992 when such record-keeping began, the yield was five times that of the poor levels of 2012 (Lewis 2014, p. 9E).

To ensure a good harvest the conditions needed are a cold winter that freezes the tree roots and leaves snow on the ground to keep the roots cold, and varying daily temperatures, from freezing nights to a succession of days consistently warmed by the sun of early spring that causes the sap to rise in the trees.

At the end of the 19th century when cane and beet sugar became very cheap, maple sugar cost much more because harvesting it was so labour intensive. By that time it had become an alternative for honey, and was such a favourite, especially for topping American standbys such as pancakes, or as a flavouring for desserts, that commercial interests began, as usual, to seek cheaper substitutes. In the early years of the 20th century, one of these cheap imitations, called Mapleine, was marketed in small bottles like vanilla extract and could be used to flavour a specified quantity of a homemade simple sugar syrup to produce the consistency and appearance of maple syrup if not its exact flavour. Today, displayed on American supermarket shelves are many inexpensive varieties of imitation syrups with the appearance and somewhat similar flavour of genuine maple syrup, with labels such as "Mrs. Butterworth's", "Hungry Jack's", "Aunt Jemima's", "Log Cabin All Natural Table Syrup", or "Walden Farms Calorie Free Pancake Syrup".

Maple syrup producers are required to be licenced by their state governments, and to meet state inspection standards. Laws also govern labelling: the bottle label must specify the percentage of the contents actually derived from maple sap. The label may also list a grade but that is optional. The four or five grades now in use are based primarily on colour and flavour rather than quality. A consumer must read labels carefully to distinguish genuine maple syrup from the imitations labelled "pancake syrup" or simply "syrup". In an interview with Marie Carter, of a long-time Wisconsin sugaring family, she pointed out that some of the imitations are even preferred by consumers, particularly children, who have become accustomed to the artificial flavours. Today almost all maple products are produced by non-Indians: that is, small farmers who harvest and sell syrup from their own trees, as well as big commercial manufacturers. Fortunately, enough consumers still seem to prefer the real thing to support continuing production of genuine maple syrup.

In contrast with what has happened in maple syrup production during the past three centuries, wild rice has had a quite different history. Despite its early popularity with European explorers and fur traders, by the end of the Treaty Period of the 1800s, it was relatively unknown to non-Indians. The treaties forged between the U.S. government and the various Indian tribes during that tumultuous era were not advantageous to the Indians, whose resultant confinement to reserved lands considered undesirable by the dominant society frequently cut off their access to their former ricing areas and sugar bushes. If they did have any access, of necessity they concentrated on producing what was needed for their own use throughout the year.

It is important to realize that, at the time of European arrival, Native Americans had no concept of private ownership and use of land or water. Instead, they believed that everyone had the right to freely hunt, fish, and forage for the food and other necessities that nature provided, without claiming ownership of the land or water itself. There was recognition of the rights of others to lay claim to certain productive areas such as wild rice stands in lakes, or sugar maple groves, but those claims were based on the claimants' involvement in the processing of the harvested foods to provide for their own sustenance (Vennum 1988, p. 265). To avoid disputes among claimants, ricing chiefs were designated by Indian tribes or families to determine when ricing could begin and to make other decisions and settle arguments.

Wild rice, as a staple of the Indians' subsistence diet, was harvested in late summer, processed and stored carefully, and eaten throughout the year, along with venison and fish in the winter months, maple sugar and syrup in the early spring, fish and small game in the early summer, garden vegetables and wild berries in late summer, before the "ricing moon" in the early fall. Wild rice was especially relied upon as a highly nutritious source of food, and there were many varieties with somewhat differing characteristics, depending on the location of the lake or river, and the water quality and mineral content as well as its purity.

Because its harvesting and processing are so labour intensive, wild rice was very expensive compared with the many other cereal grains, such as wheat, corn, barley, and rye, grown by settlers in the same areas of the U.S. All of those were much more easily and rapidly harvested as well as being already familiar to Europeans before their arrival in North America.

True wild rice is not a perennial but an annual plant that tends to re-seed itself when its ripe and heavy seed heads drop into the water, or are knocked off by feeding birds, ducks, and geese, or by human harvesters who are careful to provide for re-seeding as they harvest. When the seeds are released, they sink to the bottom just where they fall rather than floating away on the surface of the water or wafting off in the breeze.

In the spring, the rice plants first send out shoots below the water surface, then long, narrow leaves emerge above the surface, and then the stalks that bear the seed shoot up several feet into the air. It is primarily pollinated by the wind. A delicate plant, it can be destroyed at any of its stages (ibid., p. 20). Besides slowly-circulating, well-balanced, mineral-rich water, it needs a stable water level. If the water level gets too high; the plant may drown before it reaches sun and air. In earlier times, if drought or too much rain changed the water level and the rice crop failed or could not be harvested, the Native Americans starved unless they could find other foods to replace it.

Although wild rice once was plentiful over a large, climatically diverse area of the U.S. and Canada, resulting in varying genetic characteristics, that area has now been reduced dramatically due to population pressure, recreational use of public waters, farming, and changes in water quality, and it is only being traditionally harvested today in parts of the northern two-thirds of Wisconsin, the part of Minnesota east of the Mississippi River, and immediately adjacent Canada.

State laws have replaced the earlier informal ricing rules of the Ojibways. Except for those Indians who are ricing within reservation boundaries, anyone who now intends to participate in the harvest must purchase a state ricing licence which is available wherever hunting and fishing licences are sold. In addition, to protect the wild rice areas, the Wisconsin and Minnesota Departments of Natural Resources, in concert with the Great Lakes Indian Fish and Wildlife Commission and the tribes, determine the date and hour when ricing may begin, and publicize and enforce the laws.

Fig. 3: Traditional harvesting of wild rice (Courtesy of the Wisconsin Historical Society).

Originally wild rice was harvested during the "ricing moon" (late summer) by Indian canoes passing through the wild rice beds. The long, narrow watercraft each were occupied by two Indian harvesters, one standing in the stern and slowly moving the canoe through the shallow water by using a long pole, forked at its lower end to avoid damage to the rice roots. The other ricer sat facing the prow and flailed, on alternate sides, the tall rice stalks with two short, slender, very lightweight wands called "knocking sticks". One stick was used to pull a clump of heavily loaded rice stalks over the center of the canoe, and the other stick was employed to strike the stalks gently so that the heavy seeds fell into the canoe, the bottom of which was lined with an animal skin or a blanket. When the canoe was heavy with rice, the ricers returned to shore where other members of the ricing party carefully removed the seeds and spread them on a smooth surface to begin drying in the sun. Because the rice ripens over a period of days, the ricers might need to return to knock in the same area several times until most of the seeds were collected. This traditional method of harvest persists today among some Ojibways as well as among some non-Indians who wish to follow the old ways.

The original way of processing wild rice was very labour intensive. After being dried in the sunshine until a large part of the moisture had evaporated, which was an important step to keep the moist rice from developing mould, it was parched in large vessels over a slow, steady fire. After metal kettles became available through trade with the Europeans, those were used, while stirring the rice continuously with wooden paddles so it would dry thoroughly but not burn. The next step was to thresh it by placing it in a large, shallow pit that had been scooped out of the earth and lined with an animal skin or blanket. This was entirely a men's task. In clean moccasins, men and boys began what is called "dancing the rice" or "jigging". They trod the rice while hanging onto stakes sunk in the earth around the pit, until the hulls had been completely loosened from the long, cylindrical seeds. Then the rice was transferred to wide shallow trays and winnowed by being repeatedly tossed in the air, preferably on a breezy day. The heavy seeds fell back onto the tray and the loosened hulls were carried off by the wind. Finally the rice was ready to be cooked, or stored for future use throughout the year. As all of this processing was time consuming and somewhat tedious, it was carried on by entire Indian families who shared in all the work.

In the early 20th century, first attempts to harvest mechanically were given up because of the danger of destruction of the natural rice beds, and use of heavy machinery was prohibited by state laws. At the same time, both Indians and non-Indians began to devise ingenious homemade methods of mechanically drying, parching, threshing, and winnowing the rice.

In midcentury, the University of Minnesota, in cooperation with the State of Minnesota Department of Agriculture, started a concerted effort to find more efficient ways to cultivate, harvest, and process the rice. This effort was stimulated by serious concerns that mechanical harvesting in Canada, where it was not prohibited, would completely overwhelm Minnesota's efforts to make wild rice a better source of income for Indians living in the state, and the state itself. First several basic problems had to be solved, including how to develop a genetic variety of rice with seed heads that would not "explode" spontaneously when ripe, scattering seed everywhere before it could be harvested. But the seed heads also needed to ripen simultaneously rather than requiring several passes through the watery rice fields, because the combine sheared off the entire seed head in one pass. Other problems revolved around how to control the water levels and the quality of the water. The solution arrived at was to shift the rice plants from lakes or rivers to artificially-created peat- or clay-lined paddies, so that water levels could be controlled by dikes or ditches and mechanized harvesting equipment could move over muddy fields without getting bogged down (Sokolov 1981, pp. 36–43; Vennum 1988, pp. 239–240). Hybrid seeds were developed, and pesticides and herbicides are now employed (Iseminger 2000, pp. 23–40), often dispersed over the paddies by airplane. Commercially-sized mechanical dryers, parchers, and winnowers also were developed. The Minnesota Department of Agriculture undertook a massive and successful advertising campaign to expand the market to absorb the big increase in rice production. This included enlisting the cooperation of food manufacturers to incorporate wild rice into their products and the development and wide distribution of free recipe booklets for home cooks and restaurants, using wild rice as an ingredient.

This mechanized rice crop is now known as "paddy rice". Despite attempts by Minnesota state law to label it so it can be distinguished from traditionally harvested wild rice, California does not observe that rule in packaging and labelling its enormous annual crop, so most consumers remain unaware of the difference.

Today much of the wild rice for sale in supermarkets is "paddy rice", grown in Minnesota, less so in Wisconsin, and introduced into California from Minnesota. It is much less costly than what is known as "canoe-harvested rice". Although a relatively small number of the Ojibways continue to harvest in their traditional way, actually re-seeding as they knock from their aluminum or fiberglass watercraft, they are primarily supplying themselves, not treating it like a cash crop. Others still harvest in canoes but sell the unprocessed rice to commercial firms to be finished for sale. And many more, with or without access to ricing lakes, are no longer ricing at all, evidently preferring the ease and convenience of purchasing their foods from local supermarkets as most other Americans do.

The state governments' treatment of wild rice as a marketable commodity is very different from the value the Ojibways have given it as a traditional and ceremonial part of their culture (Vennum 1988, p. 80). There are other differences, too. The debate continues as to whether paddy rice is genetically the same or different from canoe rice, and whether it differs in flavour, colour, or cooking time. Some Indian connoisseurs claim to be able to distinguish between canoe and paddy rice (ibid., p. 54). However, unlike in the production of maple syrup, completely artificial wild rice has not yet been successfully created.

Cheap imitations of maple syrup and mechanization of wild rice already have had very deleterious effects. Native Americans are justifiably fearful of further attempts at genetic engineering of wild rice, including the possible granting of patents in California for strains developed that would change its genetic composition even more and eliminate true wild rice by possible cross-pollination. By resorting to courts of law to defend their rights, they have won small victories but the battle continues (LaDuke 2007, retrieved 27.11.2016 from http://orionmagazine.org).

Indians in Northern Wisconsin have been engaged in a struggle to prevent copper mining that they fear will contaminate water in the ricing lakes there. The same concerns have provoked Indians in Minnesota in their fight to prevent tar sands oil from being piped across their tribal lands (Edrich 2013, p. 48).

Causing even more apprehension is their realization that they are on the front lines of another battle: climate change. Two serious harvest failures within the past ten years are suspected to have been caused by the negative effects of global warming (Pember 2012, p. 15, retrieved 27.11. 2016 from http://indiancountrytodaymedianetwork.com). Climate change can adversely affect any food crop that is dependent on certain ecological conditions to thrive, especially the cold winters that may be moving northward. Thus, there is the very real danger that ricing and sugaring may become lost traditions in the very region where they have been recognized as iconic.

List of References

Printed

Erdrich, Heid E.: *Original Local: Indigenous Foods, Stories and Recipes from the Upper Midwes*t. Minnesota Historical Society Press: St. Paul, MN 2013.

Iseminger, Jeff: "wild ricing reverie". *Wisconsin Trails,* September / October 2000, pp. 24–30.

Lewis, Chelsea: "Day Out: Weather could put chill on maple syrup-making clinics". *Milwaukee Journal Sentinel,* Sunday, March 2, 2014, p. 9E.

Sokolov, Raymond: "The Taming of the Grain: Minnesota Wild Rice." *Fading Feast: A Compendium of Disappearing American Foods.* Farrar Straus Giroux: New York 1981.

Vennum, Thomas, Jr.: *Wild Rice and the Ojibway People.* Minnesota Historical Society Press: St. Paul, MN 1988.

Internet

LaDuke, Winona: "Ricekeepers: A Struggle to Protect Biodiversity and a Native American Way of Life", *Orion Magazine* 26(4), July /August 2007, retrieved 27.11.2016 from http://orionmagazine.org.

Pember, Mary Annette: "Climate Change Threatens the Ojibwe's Rice Harvest". *Indian Country Today Media Network,* November 2, 2012, p. 15, retrieved 27.11.2016 from http://indiancountrytoday medianetwork.com.

Adelia Hanson[1]

Farm, Family, and Friedemanns

Abstract: *This paper tells about the history and culture of a group of Germans from Russia (Ukraine) who came to Oklahoma starting in 1892 and formed a community near Stillwater, Oklahoma they called Marena, before eventually moving their church into Stillwater where it became the nucleus of Salem Lutheran Church.*

"Frieden Kirche" is the name of the Lutheran church that the Germans from Russia (hereinafter referred to as GFR) founded in Oklahoma in 1892 in a community they called Marena, located west of Stillwater, Oklahoma. Oklahoma (formerly Indian territory) was then open to settlement by non-Indians. By statehood in 1907 there were approximately 4,000 GFR living in Oklahoma. Just as they had been in the Ukraine, they remained an agricultural and German speaking people (Douglas 1980, p. 2).

The Germans from Russia in the 1800s were invited to the Ukraine by Catherine the Great, herself German, because of their good agricultural practices. They were given promises of autonomy of religion and language, which were Lutheran and German. They adopted a strain of wheat called "hard red" and soon turned the Ukraine into a breadbasket for Europe (ibid., p. 8).

In the 1870s, these privileges were revoked as Russia wanted to exert its autonomy in the region. Paul Friedemann, the oldest son of Gustav and Augusta Friedemann, was drafted, sent to medical school, and assigned to a Russian military division. Shortly thereafter, the GFR began immigrating to the United States where they settled in Great Plains states which had similar conditions to the Ukraine. They brought with them the seeds of the hard red wheat sewn into their clothes (ibid., pp. 8–9). As in the Ukraine, GFR retained their traditional culture of farm, faith, and family, which was the inspiration for the title of my paper (ibid.).

1 The author, Adelia Hanson (b. 25 September 1941) passed away on Thanksgiving Day, 24 November 2016. Adelia attended the International Ethnological Food Research Conferences in Sweden (1998), Switzerland (2002), Croatia (2004), Norway (2008), Finland (2010) and Sweden (2012), and her papers were published in the conference proceedings. Due to ill-health, Adelia was unable to attend the Heidelberg Conference (2016) to deliver her scheduled paper, which, happily, was available for inclusion here. *Ar dheis Dé go raibh a h-anam dílis.* May she rest in peace (Eds.).

Fig. 1: Friedemann Family

The attachment that the GFR have to their land and religion is illustrated by Florence Friedemann, still living at the age of 86 years. She and her husband, gave their daughter Susan and her husband, land to build a house on the original Oklahoma Friedemann homestead, so that the property would remain in the family.[2]

The one Russian recipe that she and other local Germans from Russia make is *borscht*. In addition, many of them make variations on a dish they call *Halupscher*, a pudding-like dish containing sauerkraut, onion, oatmeal, grated potato, and ham, all baked together as a casserole. Our Seif Russian colleague, Tatiana Veronica, told me that the actual meaning of this Russian dish is stuffed cabbage. Undoubtedly, the GFR version was good for feeding their large families. Also popular with local GFR families were variations on noodle dishes both sweet and savory – *pierogi* with cottage cheese filling, for example.

Gustav and Augusta Friedemann immigrated with their three sons, Adolph, Rudolph, and Robert. They had more descendants in the U. S. than other GFR families. This led a local historian to write, "within 25 years in Stillwater there was a cultural landscape in which Bieberdorfs married Bergstrassers, Kleins married Bieberdorfs, Voises married Bergstrassers, and Friedemanns married everybody" (Friedemann 1987, pp. 108–109).

2 Conversation on July 12, 2016, with his wife Florence Friedemann who is still living, and who, a few years ago, hand-wrote for me many recipes from both sides (she is a Voise).

Fig. 2: Many of the original GFRs at the Less-Bergstrasser wedding in 1910. Gustav and Augusta are seated beside the bridal party.

Fig. 3. The pointed arch windows were reminiscent of those found in Ukrainian churches.

The GFR settlers moved their congregation to Stillwater. The pointed arch windows (Fig. 3) were Dr. Paul Friedemann's wish to recreate the appearance of the Ukrainian churches. The language of the Friedens (or Salem, both meaning peace) church remained German until World War II, when the synod told them they could no longer supply a German-speaking pastor.[3] Thereafter Salem has celebrated its German-speaking heritage with a German-language service. Stillwater is a university town, so this service and the party afterward attract many visitors.[4]

On Mother's Day, the Stillwater newspaper published a photo of the then 78-year-old, last-surviving foreign-born GFR, Mrs. Robert Friedemann with her spinning wheel.[5]

In recent years interesting new information, "Bach in America", has been published by Christoph Wolff (professor of music and former dean of Arts and Sciences at Harvard University, along with a German colleague), linking the Stillwater Friedemann's lineage with Johann Sebastian Bach's eldest son, Wilhelm Friedemann Bach. Solid evidence documenting a link to Bach has been difficult to come by, but one thing we can say is that all the Salem Friedemanns have been musically gifted as pianists and choir directors.

List of References

Printed

Hale, Douglas: *Germans from Russia in Oklahoma*. University of Oklahoma Press: Norman OK 1980.

Friedemann, Jene: *Bread for the Third Generation: An Early History of Salem Lutheran Church, Stillwater, Oklahoma*. Western Publications: Stillwater OK, 1987.

---

3 According to the Salem's Friedemann file.

4 Based on my own experience.

5 Article dated May 5 but no year given.

Johanna Maria van Winter

Medieval Dutch Identity in Two Early Sixteenth-Century Calendars about Lifestyle: *Dat Regiment der ghesontheyt* and *Der Scaepherders Kalengier*. Food Prescriptions and Health Rules by Month and by Season

Abstract: *These two early printed Dutch calendars contain advice for a healthy life by month and by season. Both kinds belong to general lifestyle patterns of Greek, Arabic and Latin origin that were translated into vernacular verses. In these Dutch adaptations both the universal trends and some typical Low Countries characteristics are visible.*

These two Middle Dutch booklets from the beginnings of the art of printing, are different in composition, but both are directed at the same general audience, which is eager to receive instructions about how to behave, in order to maintain a long and healthy life. Both texts have survived in one copy only, and are currently being kept at the Library of Congress in Washington D.C. and at the Central University Library of Ghent, Belgium, respectively.

No modern text edition exists with a description and commentary of *Dat Regiment der ghesontheyt* ("The Regimen of Health"). The text was printed around 1510 by Jan van Doesborch in Antwerp. When it became part of a private collection, the Royal Library of Belgium in Brussels made a photocopy of the original (signature L.P. 508C). Eventually, this whole private collection was auctioned and dispersed in different parts of the world, with this Middle Dutch booklet finding its way to the USA.

Der Scaepherders Kalengier ("The Shepherds' Calendar"), printed in Antwerp in 1513 by Willem Vorsterman, is available in a modern text edition with commentary, including several remarks on the characteristics of calendars and almanacs (Braekman 1985). When compared with a similar French booklet, *Compost et Calendrier des Bergers*, it becomes clear that the Dutch version is not a literal translation of the French text, but rather an original adaptation with abbreviations and additions, and its own series of woodcuts (ibid., pp. 8–13).

Whereas the *Scaepherders Kalengier* has been composed as a real calendar with a page for each month, the *Regiment* looks more like an almanac containing all kinds of good advice.[1] There are no calendar pages per month, but it starts with short mottoes in Latin with a health prescription per month. At the end of the whole treatise we find another section with health rules for each month, this time in Latin verse followed by a Middle Dutch translation. A comparison between the health prescriptions stated at the beginning of each month of the *Regiment*, and the prescriptions formulated as a separate section at the end, shows that the information in these two sets of health rules does not always correspond. In the following section I will discuss the differences between them in more detail. For convenience sake I shall refer to the health prescriptions at the beginning of each month as the "Start" text and the prescriptions given at the end of the almanac as the "End" text.

While the "End" text mentions that warm food and drinks should be taken in January, but that one should refrain from taking mead (honey wine), and states that it is safe to go to baths and to undergo blood-letting, the "Start" text merely states: *Ante cibum vina tum sumas pro medicina*, "Before the meal take wine as a medicine". It does not mention anything about bathing and blood-letting, two activities that play an important role in maintaining good health.

In February, according to the "Start" text, you should neither go bathing nor undergo blood-letting; the "End" text for this month states that you could catch all kinds of illnesses and fevers in this month and that you should let blood from the thumb.

In March, according to the "Start" text, hot bathing is good, but the "End" text advises differently. March is stated to generate much pain; no blood-letting is allowed during this month, carrots should be eaten, and lettuce is good for one.

In April, according to the "End" text, nature renews itself, the blood flows again and blood-letting is allowed, but not from the middle vein (*venam medianam*), according to the "Start" text).

The "Start" text only advises that in May, the meat of young, rather than of old, animals, should be eaten, and that green herbs are good for one; just as blood-letting and bathing are, according to the "End" text.

In June, the "Start" text states, one could keep healthy by drinking spring water, but not on an empty stomach, and neither should one drink mead or new beer. Lettuce, though, is good for one when eaten during this month, according to the "End" text.

1 This booklet lacks page or folio numbers, so that you can only refer to its content by barely visible quire indications. I, therefore, refrain from providing references to the work in this article.

In July the "Start" text advises that one should not avoid bathing. But, according to the "End" text, one should sleep but little, avoid bathing and blood-letting, and drink in moderation.

In August, according to the "Start" text, blood-letting causes one to be quiet but it warns that taking a laxative beverage is harmful to one's health. Both the "End" and the "Start" texts agree on this point: in August, laxatives should be avoided. The "End" text states that in August one should not sleep too much, and one should also avoid heat, sexual intercourse, over-eating, and blood-letting.

In September, the herb agrimony is good for the body, according to the "Start" text. The "End" text says that all fruits are ripe then. Bread with goat's milk and pears with wine are good for one, as well as venison, goose and duck, and no blood-letting should be performed; but one should make a good potion of nettles *(de urtica)*. This last prescription derives from an interesting Dutch translation error of the original Latin text. I will come back to this later.

In October, grape must should be drunk, according to the "Start" text, and new wine becomes available. Venison, goose and fowl, are good for eating then, but one should do so in moderation according to the "End" text.

In November, the "Start" text states that the taking of a medicinal potion is healthy (*potio sana*) and that blood-letting is beneficial against rheumatism, while the "End" text advises that one should follow a moderate diet with little potion (*potio sit rara vana*), and refrain from sexual intercourse in the bath-tub.

In December, according to the "Start" text, warm things (cloth) are good for the body and a lukewarm beverage is good against the cold, while the "End" text advises that one must perform bleeding from the vein in the head, and not wash one's body too much.

According to my hypothesis, these rules are the small remnants of an elaborate system of cleansing prescriptions from the early Christian church in the East-Roman Empire, which have been translated from Greek into Latin and subsequently rendered into several vernaculars, often in rhyming verses (van Winter 2014, pp. 151–159). They eventually lost their original context and gained enormous popularity in medieval Europe by being combined with similar verses from quite a different system that is not Greek-Christian, but Arabic-Muslim, in origin, one which was not organised by month, but by season – the so-called "six non-naturals" (*sex res non naturales*) system. These are the things that are necessary for staying alive, but which do not come or happen naturally, in contrast to the natural things like gender, skin colour, body build, and innate temperament, over which one has no control. The six non-naturals – weather and climate, eating and drinking, moving and resting, sleeping and waking, intake and elimination, and last but not least, the moods of the mind – on the other hand, need the attention and care of the individual (Weiss Adamson 1995, pp. 39–49). Two Arabic-Muslim philosophers, Hunain Ibn-Ishaq or Johannitius (ninth century), and Haly Abbas (tenth century) invented this system as a synthesis of the Greek theories of Hippocrates of Kos (fifth century BC) and Galen of Pergamon (second century AD). Via Syrian translations, this system was rendered into Arabic. According to this theory, known as the Greek humoral pathology, man is regarded as a microcosm in the centre of the macrocosm, with four elements, qualities, seasons, humours and temperaments.

This synthesis of the six non-naturals already existed in an Arabic "Monarch's Mirror" (*Fürstenspiegel*) of the tenth or eleventh century, called *Sirr al Asrar*, or in Latin, *Secretum Secretorum*, "Secret of Secrets" (ibid., pp. 50–56). In this encyclopaedic text, prescriptions were given to a monarch about the best way to care for the prosperity of his country and the well-being of his people. In this context, eating and drinking and other means for preserving health played an important role. This "Monarch's Mirror" came into Christian hands with the conquest of the Muslim city of Toledo in Spain (1085), was translated into Latin, and was subsequently rendered into many vernacular languages from the twelfth century onwards.

The system of the six non-naturals as such, including the Greek humoral pathology, was systematised in the eleventh century, by the Christian Arabic philosopher Ibn Butlan, in a clearly-structured "Chess-board of Health", that was thereafter translated into Latin as *Tacuinum Sanitatis* in the thirteenth century (ibid., pp. 83–91).

Together with the Latin translations of the Greek humoral pathology, produced in South Italy in the School of Salerno since the end of the eleventh century, these theories by month and by season formed the starting point for manifold translations into all sorts of vernaculars, preferably in rhyming verses. The brief month rules of our *Regiment der ghesontheyt* actually are no more than a shallow extract from the complex treatises from Toledo, Salerno, and other centres of translation.

The composition of *Der Scaepherders Kalengier*, is, on the other hand, far more structured and devotes more verses on lifestyle per month, placed below a woodcut on the left page, while featuring a month calendar with saints and a Roman calendar on the right-hand page. Above the month calendar, the number of days of that month, the number of its lunar days, and the number of hours of the night, are mentioned. January has 31 days, 30 lunar days, and the night contains 16 hours. The verses on the left-hand page start with the sign of the zodiac entered by the sun in the course of that month, and visualised in a round woodcut in the corner, left and right in turn, and sometimes in the middle. For January this is Aquarius, the Waterman.

The signs of the zodiac are important in both booklets, because the system of blood-letting is inextricably linked to them. Before the separate month prescriptions at the end of the treatise ("End" text), the *Regiment* also has a treatise about blood-letting for each sign of the zodiac, beginning with Aries (halfway through March), followed by Taurus, Gemini, Cancer, Leo, Virgo, Libra, Scorpio, Sagittarius, Capricornus, Aquarius and Pisces. A Latin prescription is given each time, followed by a Middle Dutch translation, all in verse. A little round woodcut gives a picture of the sign. The prescriptions warn against blood-letting from certain body parts when the moon stays in that sign. For instance, when the moon is in Aries, blood-letting from the head, touching your ears, or shaving your beard, are not allowed. However, no explanation for these pieces of negative advice is given.

Unlike the *Regiment*, the *Scaepherders Kalengier* contains an Zodiac Man indicating which part of the human body is reigned over by which sign of the zodiac. There, it is explained, that you may not let blood from a specific part of the body, if the sun or the moon is in that sign (Braekman 1985, p. 13, facsimile D4 verso). Because Aries reigns over the head, one should not perform blood-letting from the head or the ears in that month.

In the *Scaepherders Kalengier*, a rule of life by season for the shepherds is given after the blood-letting prescriptions, starting with the spring season, that falls in the months February, March and April. This season is hot and wet by nature and belongs to a sanguine temperament. Therefore, the shepherds dress themselves so as not to be too warm or too cool, and they live moderately in all respects. They eat light cooling dishes like bream and several other kinds of scaly fish, drink tempered wine, and refrain from eating things that are too sweet. In this season, blood-letting is a good way to get rid of the bad humours of the winter, and a medicinal potion is good against coarse humours. The shepherds eat whenever they have an appetite, but not too much, and not until the stomach is full. Meat and fish are better baked than boiled, and cooked dishes make better nutrition if they are roasted afterwards on a grill. For the other seasons, similar rules are valid, in order to counterbalance the extreme qualities of that season.

This system of dietary rules by season is based on the antique Greek humoral pathology comprising the four elements, qualities, humours and temperaments. Its pieces of advice are practical and aimed at daily use in the kitchen and for the meal. Whereas the rules by month mention several medicinal and purgative herbs, this is not the case with the rules by season. The system of the six non-naturals has borrowed more elements from the rules by season than from the rules by month.

In the *Regiment*, the six non-naturals are given primary attention, albeit without a clear rule by season, but by practical prescriptions scattered throughout the treatise. In this respect, the *Regiment* follows its own order by not starting with the climate and measures against the weather, but with the moods of the mind, which traditionally feature in the last category.

Fig. 1: Dat Regiment der Ghesontheyt, first pages with woodcut (Brussels, Royal Library, LP 508 C.).

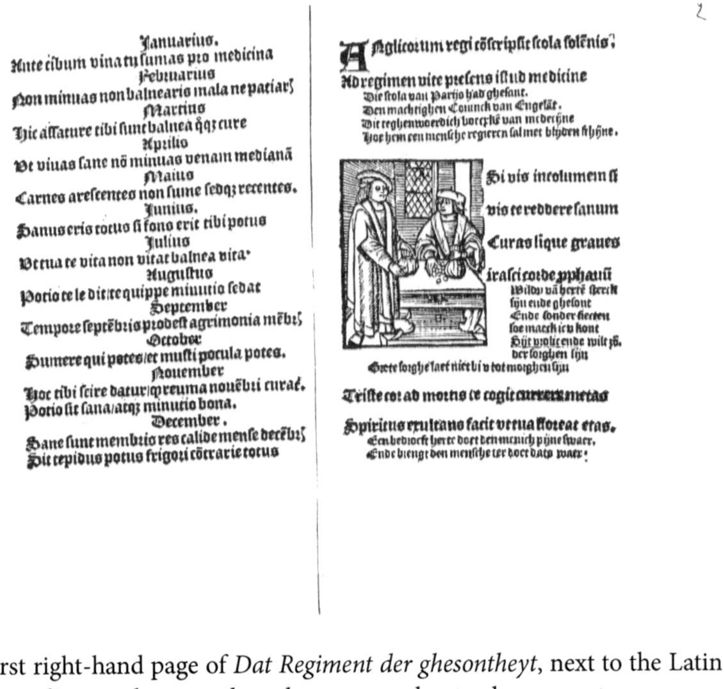

Januarius.
Ante cibum vina tu sumas pro medicina
Februarius
Non minuas non balnearis mala ne patiaris
Martius
Hic assature tibi sunt balnea quoque cure
Aprilis
Ut vivas sane nõ minuas venam medianã
Maius
Carnes arescentes non sume sedque recentes.
Junius.
Sanus eris totus si sonos erit tibi potus
Julius
Ut tua te vita non vitat balnea vita.
Augustus
Potio te le dit: te quippe minutio sedat
September
Tempore septẽbris prodest agrimonia mẽbris
October
Sumere qui potes/et musti pocula potes.
November
Hoc tibi scire datur/quia reuma novẽbri curatur.
Potio sit sana/atque minutio bona.
December.
Sane sunt membris res calide mense decẽbris
Sit tepidus potus frigori cõtrarie totus

Anglicorum regi cõscripsit scola solẽnis:
Ad regimen vite presens istud medicine
Die scola van Parijs heeft ghesant.
Den machtighen Coninck van Engelãt.
Dit reghenwoerdich boecxkẽ van medecijne
Hoe hem een mensche regieren sal met blyden schijne.

Si vis incolumem si
vis te reddere sanum
Curas lingue graves
irasci corde prophanum
Wildy vã herte sterck
sijn ende ghesont
Ende sonder siecten
soe macht icu kont
Sijt vrolic ende wilt zõ.
der sorghen sijn
Grote sorghe laet niet bi u tot morghen sijn

Triste cor ad mortis te cogit [illegible] metas
Spiritus exultans facit ut tua floreat etas.
Een bedroeft herte doet den menich pijne swaer.
Ende brengt den mensche ter doot dats waer.

On the first right-hand page of *Dat Regiment der ghesontheyt*, next to the Latin prescriptions by month, a woodcut shows a merchant, who comes to a money-changer to pay his debt, with a sack of money in his hands. It is accompanied by Latin and Middle Dutch rhyming verses stating the moral that to keep healthy you should neither take rage nor great worry with you through the night: "Sijt vrolic ende wilt zonder sorghen sijn, Grote sorghe laet niet bi u tot morghen sijn", "Be merry and without worries. Do not let great worry stay with you till the morning."

This is a general rule, which, however, can be interpreted in different ways. In some beautifully-illustrated manuscripts of the *Tacuinum Sanitatis* or "Checkboard of Health" from the fourteenth century, that contain the six non-naturals, this rule is divided into *Ira* (Rage) and *Gaudia* (Joy), and is depicted by a woman who tears a veil between her teeth on the one hand, and by people who entertain themselves with music and dance on the other (Arano, 1975, p. 109, nr. 66 (*Sonare et balare*), p. 132, nrs. 175, 176 (*Ira*). The text of the Middle Dutch treatise express a quite different moral: pay your debts before the night falls, in order to keep healthy. This reflects the feeling that, already by that time, the inhabitants of the Low Countries are neither hotheads nor merry-makers, but rather merchants.

I promised to come back to another Middle Dutch characteristic in these treatises, namely a translation error in the verse for September. Of all the Middle Dutch and Middle German texts of this kind which I have collected, only these two Middle Dutch booklets show this error (Van Winter 2012, pp. 169–218). It concerns a Latin verse from the School of Salerno that states: *Atque diuretica tibi potio fertur amoena*, "And it has said that a diuretic potion is good for you." Because the Dutch author did not know the word "diuretic", "urine-abstergent", he divided it into *de urtica*. The whole sentence was then mutilated into *Atque de urtica tibi potio fertur amica*, which he translated as: "And drink it over nettles". With "nettles" he may be referring to the stinging nettle, a plant which, in alternative medicine, still has the reputation of being a healthy kind of nourishment.

In this way, these two early printed booklets, *Dat Regiment der ghesontheyt* and *Der Scaepherders kalengier*, fit into a general European trend of care for a healthy lifestyle, against a background of Greek-Arabic-Latin science. At the same time, however, they have retained some characteristics of their own origin, as attested by the composition, translation, and illustrations that have been added.

List of References

Printed

Arano, Luisa Cogliati: *Tacuinum Sanitatis, Middeleeuwse gezondheidsleer*. Het Spectrum: Utrecht / Antwerpen 1975. Also in other languages.

Braekman, W. L. (ed.): *Der Scaepherders Kalengier*. Een Vlaams volksboek, naar het unieke exemplaar van de Antwerpse druk door Willem Vorsterman van 1513, bezorgd en ingeleid door W. L. Braekman. Marc Van de Wiele: Brugge 1985.

Weiss Adamson, Melitta: *Medieval Dietetics*. Food and Drink in *Regimen Sanitatis* Literature from 800 to 1400. Peter Lang: Frankfurt am Main 1995, pp. 39–49.

van Winter, Johanna Maria: "Sind die *Regimina duodecim mensium* als 'Mönchmedizin' zu betrachten?". In Hofmeister-Winter, Andrea / Klug, Helmut W. / Kranich, Karin (eds.): *Der Koch ist der bessere Arzt. Zum Verhältnis von Diätetik und Kulinarik im Mittelalter und in der frühen Neuzeit*. Peter Lang: Frankfurt am Main 2014, pp. 151–159.

van Winter, Johanna Maria: "Middelnederlandse voedings- en gezondheidsregels per maand en per seizoen: geleerde raadgevingen voor een ongeleerd publiek". In *Geneeskunde in Nederlandstalige teksten tot 1600*. Handelingen van het zesde symposium "Geschiedenis der geneeskundige wetenschappen", ingericht door de Koninklijke Academie voor Geneeskunde van België op 20 maart 2004. Koninklijke Academie voor Geneeskunde van Belgie: Brussel 2012 (Academia Regia Belgica Medicinae. Dissertationes, Series historica. 12), pp. 169–218.

Part II: Food and the Imagination

Keynote Lecture

Stefan Bongard

Food Logistics: Behind the Curtain

Abstract: *The supply of food from foreign countries available in Germany is mainly based on complex global food supply chains. This paper describes typical structures of global food supply chains focusing on distribution structure, delivery time, transportation costs and proportional transport costs at the point-of-sale, and points out some certain logistic peculiarities with selected cases.*

Introduction

The food retail sector in Germany is able to supply a huge amount of different products. Customers can choose from a variety of market types, ranging from discounters to superstores. Generally speaking, the average customer has an eye on prices and levels of quality of groceries or beverages, rather than on the logistics challenges that occur in the supply chain of the products on their shopping lists. Moreover, consumers have become increasingly used to buying produce out of season, such as apples that nowadays can be bought throughout the year. In order to enable delivery of such a wide range of foodstuffs to be made, a plethora of different global food-supply chains are in place, most of which are acting invisibly to the customers' eyes. These food supply chains have many interesting features which make it worthwhile to take a closer look behind the scenes. Since 2009, continuous research has been carried out by logistics students at the University of Applied Sciences Ludwigshafen am Rhein in order to find out more about global food supply chains within the scope of a logistics class. The project is supported by the "Institut für Alltagskultur und Gesundheit", represented by Professor Dr. Silke Bartsch (University of Education, Karlsruhe), who has been coordinating the selection of foodstuffs since 2014. This paper will explore some interesting examples of food supply chains with regard to specific logistic aspects associated with them.

Class

Firstly, the students are assigned the task of carrying out an analysis of the food supply chain of a selected food product, focusing on four features:

- distribution structure
- delivery time
- transportation costs, and
- proportional transport costs at the point-of-sale

Ideally, a group of four students works on one assignment, consisting primarily of field research. Subsequently, the students prepare a presentation as well as a seminar paper of about 30 to 40 pages. Over the last few years, more than 40 food products from all over the world have been examined in the course of such assignments. For the purposes of this paper, a few examples have been selected in order to highlight specific logistics aspects of food supply chains. It needs to be said that neither the author nor the lecturer has carried out any cross-checks regarding the results presented here.

Basics

The selection of food products is based on the expectation of finding interesting logistic details in the supply chains of these products, on the one hand, and of sourcing countries of origin far away from Germany on the other. A positive side effect that can be observed is that students receive detailed information about certain products and learn about particularities of foreign countries. The assignment itself consists of tasking the students to explore the supply chain for the products in questions from place of origin all the way downstream to point-of-sale (the latter being a supermarket or wholesaler in most cases).

Distribution Structure

In general, the students find the most typical logistics distribution structures for the products, which can be described as follows. During the first stage, the products are harvested, collected and brought to harbours or, though less frequently, to airports. This process, in which products are sent from a consignor to a transfer site, is commonly referred to as the "preliminary leg" in transportation (also referred to as "pre-leg" or "pre-carriage"). The next stage is called the "main leg", in which long distances need to be covered by using appropriate means of transportation, including large container vessels, which can load up to almost 20,000 TEU.[1] The main leg is followed by the so-called "subsequent-leg" (or "on-carriage"), where products are finally shipped to customers.

Pineapples from the Ivory Coast are a good example for a typical logistic distribution structure. The pineapple farms are located within a radius of 35 to 180 km around the country's economic capital, Abidjan. The pineapples are shipped to the port of Abidjan by truck (pre-leg) and subsequently loaded into reefers (refrigerated containers), which are transferred to a container ship. The destination of the

1 Abbreviation for "Twenty-foot Equivalent Unit", the standard container size in worldwide trade.

main leg is Antwerp, Belgium. Thus, the pineapples travel nearly 7,000 km across the Atlantic Ocean. In Antwerp, the pineapples are trans-shipped to trucks, which take the products to their points of delivery throughout Europe.

Fig. 1: The Distribution Structure of pineapples from the Ivory Coast to Europe.

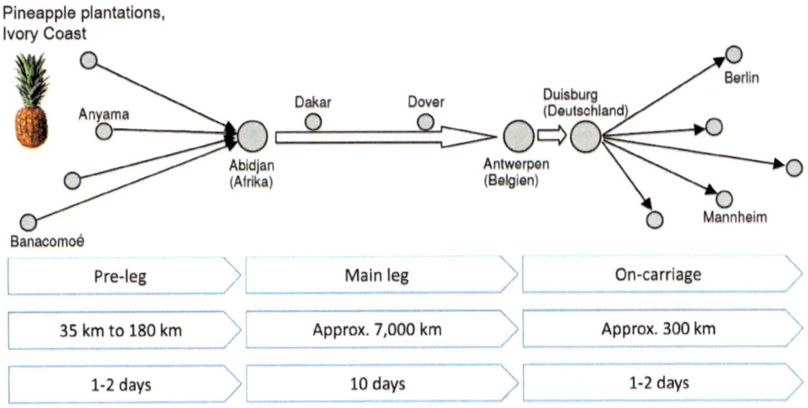

Delivery Time

All in all, the pineapples have travelled a total distance of about 7,400 km, with a total delivery time of approximately 14 days, until they arrive at the warehouses of the supermarket chains. Customers are usually only aware of the fact that the pineapple they want to buy was grown and harvested in the Ivory Coast or in Costa Rica. What they are not aware of is the extended delivery time for the product within the supply chain. Furthermore, pineapples are not usually delivered directly to the supermarkets, but rather to retailer warehouses where they spend additional time waiting for delivery to a certain POS (Points-of-Sale). Here, the prospect of deterioration plays a vital role in the delivery element of the supply chain: the longer pineapples are stored in the warehouse, the higher the risk that they will go bad; and customers would most certainly have good reason to complain in that event.

Transportation Costs and Proportional Transport Costs at the Point-of-Sale

The calculation scheme for transportation costs contains several variables, e.g. the Bunker Adjustment Factor (BAF), which refers to surcharges due to oil prices or container rates, which, in turn, depend on supply and demand or exchange rates for currencies. Therefore, the results of the calculation of transport costs can vary. Typically, transportation costs are calculated for each sequence in the supply chain. Due to the long haul and the length of the main leg, the share of total transportation costs is often significantly higher than 50 %. However, it is crucial that the relation between the retail price at the POS, and the transportation costs per unit, remain highly efficient. The following table shows surprising results. For the transport of ginger from China, the portion of transport costs associated with the main leg amounts to only slightly more than 1 % of the retail price as a whole. On the other hand, the portion of transport costs arising during the main leg adds up to as much as 94 % of the total transport costs.

Fig. 2: Calculation Scheme for Transport Costs.

Products		Pineapple	Ginger	Organic Potatoes	Organic Carrots
Origin		Ivory Coast	Shaanxi, China	Egypt	Israel
Unit		piece	kg	kg	kg
Pre-leg	Distance in km	100	150	164	78
	Transportation Costs in €	100	100	209	250
	As Percentage of the Total Costs	9%	5%	6%	8%
	Quantity	2,304	21,000	25,000	24,000
	Transportation Costs per unit	0.04	0.00	0.01	0.01
	As Percentage of the Retail Price	2.2%	0.1%	0.7%	0.4%
	Costs per km	1.00	0.67	1.27	3.21
Main leg	Distance in km	7,000	20,000	6,945	7,340
	Transportation Costs in €	600	1,800	2,430	2,495
	As Percentage of the Total Costs	**57%**	**94%**	**67%**	**81%**
	Quantity	2,304	21,000	25,000	24,000
	Transportation Costs per unit	0.26	0.09	0.10	0.10
	As Percentage of the Retail Price	**13.1%**	**1.3%**	**8.1%**	**4.3%**
	Costs per km	0.09	0.09	0.35	0.34
On-carriage 1	Distance in km	200	100	883	565
	Transportation Costs in €	300	20	1000	328
	As Percentage of the Total Costs	28%	1%	27%	11%
	Quantity	2,304	39	25,000	2,400
	Transportation Costs per unit	0.13	0.51	0.04	0.14
	As Percentage of the Retail Price	6.5%	8.0%	3.3%	5.7%
	Costs per km	1.50	0.20	1.13	0.58
On-carriage 2	Distance in km	300			13
	Transportation Costs in €	60			0.5
	As Percentage of the Total Costs	6%	0%	0%	0%
	Quantity	288			12
	Transportation Costs per unit	0.21	0.00	0.00	0.04
	As Percentage of the Retail Price	10.5%	0.0%	0.0%	1.7%
	Costs per km	0.20	0.00	0.00	0.04
Totals	Distance in km	7,600	20,250	7,992	7,996
	Transportation Costs in €	1,060	1,920	3,639	3,074
	Transportation Costs per unit	0.64	0.60	0.15	0.29
Proportional Costs	Retail price at POS in €/unit	1.99	6.42	1.20	2.39
	Transportation Costs per unit	0.64	0.60	0.15	0.29
	in %	32%	9%	12%	12%

The above efficiency analysis demonstrates the fact that the importation of food products from all around the globe can be realized in a profitable manner. The costs that can be attributed to the main runs between the continents are so low per single item, that they can be ignored for the purposes of any decision making in relation to costs as a whole.

What is much more important concerning costs is the design of an efficient on-carriage distribution system, which is far more challenging along downstream processes, since quantities are broken down into ever smaller units before they arrive at their destination, which, in turn, causes the relation of transport costs to the quantity of transported goods to become less efficient. The increasing trend of buying food online (Krüger / Warschun / Vogelpohl 2015, p. 3) makes the design of on-carriage distribution systems even more complicated: the more food is sent directly to end-consumers, the fewer the products that are shipped to existing outlets.

Selected Cases

The following explanations will concentrate on certain peculiarities in food supply chains which had been researched by logistics students at the University of Applied Sciences Ludwigshafen.

Orange Juice from Brazil

While most goods are transported in standardized containers, liquid products require some alternative modes of transportation. Orange juice from Brazil is partially transported in tank ships that have been designed especially for such purposes. One of these ships is the "Premium do Brasil". She is 205 m in length, 32.2 m in width, with a draft of 11.4 m, and a total capacity of 37,000 t. Orange juice can be loaded into 16 tanks, each with a capacity of approximately 2,300 t. The separation of tanks is necessary because these ships transport concentrate as well as NFC[2] orange juice. The typical ratio per consignment is 80 % concentrate and 20 % NFC orange juice. It is obvious that it is much more efficient to transport concentrate, as one can reduce one litre of direct orange juice to 0.2 litres of concentrate. However, as consumer demand for NFC orange juice is currently rising, NFC orange juice's share of the load has been steadily increasing. As these ships are customized for orange juice transport, they return empty to Brazil.

2 Abbreviation for "Not from Concentrate".

Fish Sticks, Alaska Coalfish, and the Bering Sea

Leaving aside the aspect of taste, fish sticks (*Fischstäbchen*; also known as "fish fingers") seem full of superlatives. In 2011, about 60,000 t of fish sticks were sold in Germany alone, which equals 24 pieces per capita (O.V. 2012, p. 1, retrieved 16.7.2016 from http://www.oekotest.de/cgi/index.cgi?artnr=100829&bernr=04). For fish sticks made from the Alaska coalfish (whose origin is in the Bering Sea), the main leg to Bremerhaven (Germany) by ship adds up to about 20,000 km, a distance that stretches almost over half of the globe. Another peculiarity of the use of the Alaska coalfish for fish sticks is the storage time involved: After fishing and filleting, the coalfish is frozen into fillet blocks weighing approximately 7.5 kg each. In Dutch Harbour (Unalaska, Alaska), a centre of the fish trade, these blocks are stored for up to three months at a time, before they make their journey to Europe. It may take three more months of storage before these fish fillet blocks are cut, fried, and brought to the retailer outlets. From a food safety point of view, there may be no risks attached to eating fish that has been frozen for six months, but one must realize that fish sticks are anything but "fresh fish".

Apple Juice from China

According to a EU Commission report, China accounted for 61 % of global apple juice exports in 2006 (EU Commission 2008, p. 9). One centre of apple plantations is Shaanxi, a province in central China. From here, harvested apples are trucked over a distance of more than 1,000 km to Tianjin, where a company called Tianjin Kunyu International Co. Ltd., processes concentrate in a factory employing more than 500 workers. The apple juice is stored in steel drums, each containing 275 l of concentrate in aseptic bags made of plastic. These steel drums are loaded into standard 20-foot containers (TEU), each one holding 80 drums. After loading the apple juice concentrate into containers, they are transported via truck over 538 km to the city of Qingdao, which runs one of the biggest harbours in China. From Qingdao the apple juice continues on its way to European harbours, which adds a distance of more than 20,000 km and between 30 and 35 days of transportation time to the concentrate. The buyers of this concentrate are the manufacturers of apply juice, who simply add water to the concentrate.

It is nearly impossible for consumers of apple juice to find out the origin of the apples that have been used for the product, since, thanks to current declaration regulations, suppliers of apple juice are not obliged to reveal such data on the packaging of the product. However, if consumers had background knowledge about the logistical effort involved in the supplying of apple juice, it might cause them to rethink their buying decisions concerning the product, thereby bringing local suppliers of apple juice in their relevant set.

Apples from South Tyrol

While global supply chains impress because of the transportation distances and long delivery times involved, European supply chains have, in some cases, impressive characteristics, also. In South Tyrol, for example, more than 7,000 companies harvest almost 950,000 t of apples each year, from mid-August until the end of November ("Südtirol – Zahlen", 2016, retrieved 16.7.2016 from http://www.suedtirolerapfel.com/de/unser-land/zahlen.html). After the harvest, these apples are stored in specialized cold stores, where they can be stocked for up to one year. This is possible thanks to the concept of Dynamic Controlled Atmosphere storage (DCA), which "involves the reduction of the oxygen level in the storage atmosphere to near the lowest level tolerated by the fruit, the so-called anaerobic compensation point (ACP)" (Gasser et al. 2010, p. 39). This method allows for the delivery of apples throughout the year and may, therefore, provide an explanation as to why it is possible to buy apples in any season. The main leg to Germany is relatively short, so that for the central market of Mannheim, Germany, a next-day-delivery situation can be guaranteed.

Apples from New Zealand

Another explanation for the high availability of apples is the off-season importation of apples from countries like Chile or New Zealand. In the case of New Zealand, the apples travel more than 23,000 km, in about 35 days, before they reach Europe. Until the month of May, they can be transported using standard reefers without a Controlled Atmosphere (CA) system, but in June they need specialized containers with CA systems in place. At first sight, this sounds like an ecological "nightmare" because of the vast main-leg distance involved, but the eco-balance comparison to local apples shows, that "apples from Germany are not per se any more eco-friendly than apples from Chile or New Zealand" (Ehrenfried 2013, retrieved 15.7.2016 from http://www.wiwo.de/technologie/green/living/frage-der-woche-sind-aepfel-aus-neuseeland-klimakiller/13546620.html). In springtime particularly, the eco-balance of imported apples can be better than that of local apples, due to the energy consumption required for local storage over several months.[3]

3 For a deeper discussion of the topic, cf. Ehrenfried (2013), retrieved 15.7.2016 from http://www.wiwo.de/technologie/green/living/frage-der-woche-sind-aepfel-aus-neuseeland-klimakiller/13546620.html.

Conclusion and Outlook

For most consumers of food products, the hidden logistics activities that take place in the background of the supply chain are obviously not visible and, therefore, have no influence on buying-decision processes.[4] Based on the findings of our research in over 40 food supply chains during logistics classes at our university, the assumption is that if more of that background information were available, more people would incorporate this knowledge into their decisions about whether or not to buy food from around the globe or to give preference to local food. The logistics classes at the University of Applied Sciences Ludwigshafen will continue to examine global food supply chains, and the participants are looking forward to finding a way in which to publish their results online so that public access to the information is possible.

List of References

Printed

Dani, Samir: *Food Supply Chain Management and Logistics*. KoganPage: London 2015.

EU Commission: "China: Out of the Dragon's Den?". Directorate-General for Agriculture and Rural Development, Monitoring Agritrade Policy, May 2008.

Gasser, F. / Eppler, T. / Naunheim, W. / Gabioud, S. / Bozzi, Nising A.: "Dynamic CA Storage of Apples: Monitoring of the Critical Oxygen Concentration and Adjustment of Optimum Conditions during Oxygen Reduction". In Erkan M. / Aksoy, U. (eds.): Proceedings of 10th International Controlled and Modified Atmosphere Research Conference. *Acta Horticulturae* 876, 2010, pp. 39–46.

Krüger, L. / Warschun, M. / Vogelpohl, N.: Online Food Retailing: Der Markt wächst, A.T. Kearney, Düsseldorf, 2015.

Internet

Ehrenfried, F.: "Sind Äpfel aus Neuseeland Klimakiller?", 2013, retrieved 15.7.2016 from http://www.wiwo.de/technologie/green/living/frage-der-woche-sind-aepfel-aus-neuseeland-klimakiller/13546620.html.

O.V., "Fischstäbchen", 2012, retrieved 16.7.2016 from http://www.oekotest.de/cgi/index.cgi?artnr=100829&bernr=04.

"Südtirol – Zahlen", 2016, retrieved 16.7.2016 from http://www.suedtirolerapfel.com/de/unser-land/zahlen.html.

4 For more information regarding food supply chains cf. Dani 2015.

Marcus Richter

Imagination and Beyond: Assembling "Good Food" in Biodynamic Agriculture[1]

Abstract: *The article results from ongoing research into the creation of value in biodynamic agriculture, which is an organic farming method drawing on anthroposophical cosmology. It starts from the premise that "good food" exists, albeit not in terms of essence or (fraudulent) imagination, but as something in the making and, therefore, traces biodynamic practices.*

Visiting the Countryside

A crowd of some 30 people was gathering in the courtyard of the "Dottenfelderhof" on a late Saturday morning in mid-September 2015. The townspeople, of whom I was one, had come to participate in one of three guided tours offered on this sunny weekend by the biodynamic farm, which is located in the northern outskirts of Frankfurt, Germany's financial centre.[2] Facing the so-called "Präparaterührstand" (preparation stir stand, Fig. 1), it did not take long until we gained a first impression of what distinguishes the agricultural practices of the farmers jointly working the land of the "Dottenfelderhof"[3] from those of their organic farming colleagues and, even more so, from those of conventional farmers.[4] The farmer, who was our guide during the following 90 minutes, emphasised

1 I am grateful to my colleagues at the Institute for European Ethnology / Cultural Studies of Philipps University of Marburg for the generous support which allowed me to contribute to the conference that preceded this volume.

2 The vignette given in the following paragraphs draws on my handwritten and photographic field notes of the farm tour, 12 September 2015.

3 The "Dottenfelderhof", which enables about 100 persons to make a living, is run cooperatively by several families and employees living on the farm.

4 According to the latest data provided by the Demeter association (http://www.demeter.net/statistics, retrieved 20.7.2016), which is the certification organisation of biodynamic products and owner of the eponymous trademark since 1928, there are 1,476 farms working land to the extent of 72,588 hectares in Germany, which not only follow biodynamic principles, what is at anybody's discretion, but which are also certified to do so. While this is only 0.5 per cent of both Germany's total number of farms and

that conveying an impression of this difference was the concern of the tour, for, he stated, "we go by tractor, muck out the cattle shed, manage accounting and online banking, and yet there is something more happening".

Fig. 1: The preparation stir stand in the courtyard of the "Dottenfelderhof" (Photo: Marcus Richter, 12 September 2015).

Our guide explained that biodynamic farming, devised by the anthroposophical mastermind Rudolf Steiner in 1924,[5] was about working with preparations. He introduced the two spray preparations and outlined briefly how they were made: We got to know that cow horns stuffed either with fresh cow manure (Fig. 2.2) or with a "porridge" made of powdered quartz (Fig. 2.1) were buried for six months in autumn, respectively in spring, in order to expose them to winter or summer forces. We learned how a handful of the decomposed horn

agricultural area (cf. data of the German Federal Statistical Office, accessible on https://www.destatis.de, retrieved 20.7.2016), Germany is in the vanguard of the global biodynamic movement, which counts 4,956 certified biodynamic farms with an agricultural area of 164,323 hectares.

5 Rudolf Steiner, mastermind of anthroposophy and founder of the Waldorf School, gave a lecture in 1924 in response to a request from farmers who had observed the "degeneration" of soil, seeds, and agricultural products in the course of the rise of industrialized agriculture. This lecture, which offered a way out of this process of decay caused by materialistic reductionism, marked the birth of biodynamic farming. (See Steiner 2004.)

manure and a teaspoon of horn silica were dynamized by rhythmical stirring each in 100 litres of water for one hour. We were told that the solutions gained from this stirring procedure were sprayed onto an area under crops of around 20 hectares in order to make the soil alive. This vitalisation – the farmer clarified the homeopathic doses not without giving rise to incredulous laughter among some of the visitors – did not work as a substantial effect but as an effect of the forces: "We work with the forces, with the life forces. That is what makes the difference in biodynamic farming."

Figs. 2.1 and 2.2.: Making spray preparations during the so-called preparations day, organised by the "Forschungsring für biologisch-dynamische Landwirtschaft", Darmstadt (Photo: Marcus Richter, 11 April 2015 / 11 October 2014).

After a stopover in a small room, where both the spray preparations and six more compost preparations[6] were stored in a wooden box filled with peat for lagging, and where some horn manure was passed around among the visitors so that they could convince themselves of its humus-like quality, the tour continued "in the heart of the farm", as the farmer put it, that is, in the cattle shed. There, we encountered 55 dairy cows eating freshly-cut grass after having been milked, and we listened to the farmer talking about the importance of cows within the "farm organism". He emphasised that the keeping of cattle

6 For a brief introduction to how to make and use the compost preparations, see Via, Wali: "Biodynamic Compost Preparations", on the website of the Biodynamic Association (USA) (https://www.biodynamics.com/content/biodynamic-compost-preparations, retrieved 20.7.2016).

was mandatory in biodynamic farming, not because of their milk production, but due to the need for a source of rich manure. Since the cows spent 18 hours a day feeding and ruminating what the farm's pastures yield, they moreover would know the farm and its soil the best. The farmer went on to compare the average annual milk production of one of the farm's cows (4,000 litre) with that of an "industrialized cow" (7,000 litre), and he talked about the so-called "lifetime-achievement". This concept, he explained, involves how cows are kept in terms of species appropriateness, wellbeing, and long-term productivity, instead of raising them for "high performance" in the short term as if they were "milk machines". Pointing to the fact that each of the cows in front of us had a pair of horns that crowned their heads, he spoke about the dehorning of cows and the procedure involved. Although this "mutilation" was contrary to the significance of the horns for the cattle, it was a common practice in conventional and, to some degree, even in organic farming. Finally, he touched upon natural mating, which, as he stressed, was anything but a matter of course in contemporary cattle husbandry at large, but the only proper way for the farmers of the "Dottenfelderhof" to maintain their herd. To this end, two bulls were among the dairy cows.

While listening to our guide speaking about mother-raised (suckling) calves and glancing at a cow with its recently-born calf, I recognised a stockman who was bending down in front of another cow, stroking her neck, and quite obviously whispering to her (Fig. 3.1). The cow's name was Bulivia, according to a plate hanging over the stall, which also gave her date of birth, information about the last time she had calved, and identified her parents. Since I had already learned about the rather idiosyncratic way in which biodynamic farmers relate to their cows when I had spent four days on another biodynamic farm four months earlier, an idea came to mind about what was occurring on the opposite side of the stall. Soon afterwards, this idea was confirmed, firstly, by a trailer which we passed the moment we left the cattle shed and, secondly, by the farmer-guide's answer to my question regarding what his colleague was doing. He informed me that the stockman on duty that morning was saying goodbye to Bulivia. Together with a young bull, which had already been loaded onto the trailer, she was to be brought to another biodynamic farm nearby in order to be slaughtered. "We always inform our cows when the time has come for them to leave", the farmer explained.

Figs. 3.1 and 3.2: Whispering with cows and vine tendrils (Photo: Marcus Richter, 12 September 2016).

Tracing "Good Food" in the Making

What I want to draw attention to with this vignette is not the fact of townspeople coming from Frankfurt and its suburbs to the countryside in order to get to know where and how the "good food" is produced which they can buy either in the farm's grocery store or in their neighbourhood supermarket as indicated by the quality label "Demeter".[7] Following Tobias Scheidegger's deliberations on the recent boom of the rural in urban life-worlds, as it is manifesting itself in contemporary images of farmers in advertising, in commodities' aesthetics, and in farmers' self-portrayal, one could surely interpret this thirst for knowledge "as an indication of an identity crisis of urban and industrial society" (Scheidegger 2009, p. 197; author's translation). However, my concern is not this need, which is catered for by the several events which the farmers of the "Dottenfelderhof" have on offer throughout the year, including chicken feeding and potato harvesting. Nor am I at all eager to adapt the critical approach which is deployed by Scheidegger as he sets out to uncover what "really" hides behind "the pervasive labelling of food as authentic" and "narrational food additives" (ibid., 206), in

7 Cf. note 4 and Fig. 4.

order to relate myself to the rural idyll of the "Dottenfelderhof" and, in general, to any biodynamic utterance of quality (Fig. 4). For entering on this beaten path, I argue, cannot but result in a defeatist form of reasoning which asserts that there is no such thing as "good food" at all, just as "there is no right life in the wrong one" (Adorno 1951, p. 59; after Dennis Redmond's translation). This turns out to be true not only when it comes to industrial food production, but also for any kind of food production (even for those that explicitly pursue alternatives to conventional mass production) once the "critical intelligence" (Latour 1999, p. 281) is mobilised to reveal continuing contradictions, displaced injustices, and obvious shortcomings. Leaving all of this aside, the purpose of my introductory vignette is, therefore, to do as the farmer was trying to do on the tour, namely, to give outsiders an idea of a biodynamic socio-material setting in which "good food" is assembled, and to touch on some of the construction site's hotspots.

Fig. 4. "Good raw milk" and eggs in the shop of a biodynamic farm in Saxony (Photo by Marcus Richter, 19 August 2014).

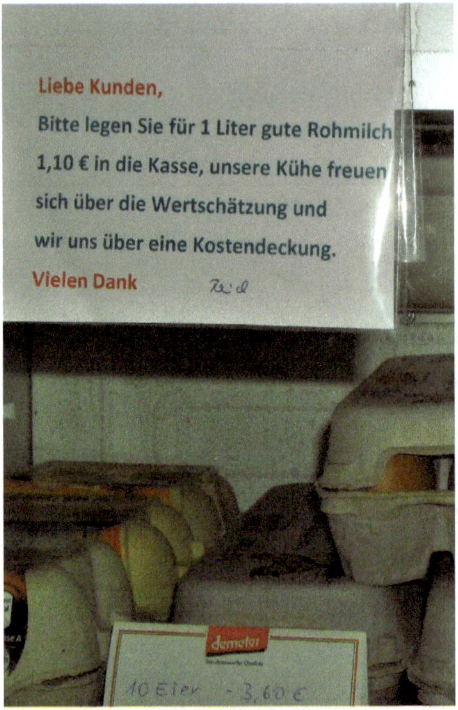

This goes along with what I am concerned with in my ongoing dissertation project on the creation of value in biodynamic agriculture, which is an ethnographic study of the production processes of "good food". Picking up on post-constructivist contributions to social and cultural theory that reject both modern and postmodern styles of reasoning, I attempt to reformulate the former interest in agricultural food production, which was one of the leading interests in early studies on work undertaken by German-speaking cultural anthropologists (Peukert / Lauffer 1951, p. 36), but is not an issue of ethnographic research on "work" as it is defined currently by the disciplinary subfield of "work and labour studies".[8] Just as we have gained insight into the fabrication of scientific (arte)facts (Latour 1987), into the production of creativity in advertising agencies (Krämer 2014), and into the enacting of "The Body Multiple" in medical practice (Mol 2002) by following "things as well as words, hands as well as eyes, technologies as well as organizational features" (ibid., p. 53) – to name just a few of the fields of inquiry in which Bruno Latour's call to "modify our anthropology of creation" (Latour 1999, p. 283) has been echoed – now as I (re)turn to the countryside in order to learn about the creation of value in biodynamic agriculture, the "goodness" of food that I am interested in is the quality which biodynamic food possesses as it is processed.[9]

With this approach, I attempt to contribute to the development of "bringing ANT inspired concepts [...] to bear on ethnographic concerns that seemed to fall outside the scope of science and technology" (Jensen 2012, p. 13), the primary arena of rethinking social and cultural scientists' understanding of (im)materialities and practice. I am especially trying to surmount an understanding of the creation of value as it is applied by Sidney Mintz in his "Notes Toward a Cultural Construction of Modern Foods", in which he adheres to the distinction drawn between "inherent characteristics of the product" and "the way those characteristics are conceptualised in marketing" (Mintz 2009, p. 211). Instead, my point of departure is that the construction of "good food" is not merely a matter of representation, imagination, perception or marketing, but a matter of practice that is spreading over "heterogeneous ingredients" (Mol 2002, p. 53). In this way, I too relate to the statement of an English biodynamic farmer in a documentary film on the anthroposophical stimuli given by Rudolf Steiner – to agriculture and beyond. Standing in a raspberry field and speaking

8 See the website of the committee of "Work and Labour Studies" of Deutsche Gesellschaft für Volkskunde ("German Society of Folkore Studies") (http://www.dgv-arbeitskulturen.de/english/committee/, retrieved 20.8.2016).

9 For this approach, see also Mol / Heuts 2013, pp. 125–146.

about the application of the spray preparations as well as about the multiple forces involved in growing the raspberries that surround her, the farmer states: "I don't understand the minutia of it, and I don't need to understand. But what I need to really know and believe is that I'm not alone in this garden working to grow all this" (Stedall 2012, 11:31).[10]

Acknowledging the "Weight of Being"

Instead of immersing deeper into the assembling of "good food" in biodynamic farming, which is, anyway, a matter for further research in the course of my dissertation project, I would like to dwell on some consequences of my approach and yet stay in touch with the practices outlined above and their ingredients. Considering what is happening besides going by tractor, milking, slaughtering, and all of the things even conventional farmers are doing, I, therefore, want to ask for what Bruno Latour calls the "weight of being" in his "Anthropology of the Moderns" (Latour 2014, p. 201).

In that regard, it makes sense to recall two rather well-established approaches that have already been deployed to biodynamic agriculture. There is, for example, an explanation of biodynamic practices provided by those detached observers who do not limit their commentaries to just accusing the biodynamic movement of its "mystical trimming" and "vague phraseology" (Merkenschlager 1933, p. 124; author's translation). Following this explanation, which had already become common soon after horns stuffed with cow manure had been buried for the first time, the work with horns, fermented stinging-nettle brew, cosmic forces, and other means, which are rather beyond the scope of modern rationalism, can be signified as an expression of a "crisis of faith" in modernity (ibid.). Apart from this approach, which is all too familiar to cultural anthropologists, it is conceivable that one takes biodynamic farming into account as a market enterprise that is esoteric on the surface, but still subject to the constraints and contradictions of capitalism. This political economy approach is suggested by "critical intelligence", probably just as much with regard to the 200 hectares "Dottenfelderhof" as it is busy running a bakery, a café, and a grocery store on its premises, as considering an Austrian farm of 2,000 hectares on the Austrian-Hungarian border:[11] In addition to direct marketing, this biodynamic farm promotes some of its products at

10 Stedall, Jonathan: *The Challenge of Rudolf Steiner*. Cupola Production: UK, 2012, 11:31. Documentary Film.

11 The farm I am referring to here has been visited by me for farm tours in 2009, 2010, and 2015.

international fairs and also sells them via the Internet. Manpower is, furthermore, mainly recruited in Hungary due to lower labour costs on that side of the border.

What leaves me unsatisfied with these two approaches is that there is always something which carries more weight when it comes to the biodynamic creation of value, whether it is the logic of the market, economical interests and constraints, uncertainties, moments of crises, or, in general, the consequences of modernity. Consequently, everything that takes place beyond these "heavy weights" is assessed to be subsidiary and compensatory in nature and its existence is, thus, disregarded. This is not because anthropologists, who are basically driven by "the small, the simple, the elementary, the face-to-face" (Appadurai 1986, p. 357), do not cherish the somehow exotic and esoteric bagatelle involved, but due to the fact that we are also informed by ideas such as that of Siegfried Giedion, according to which it is "the sun [which] is mirrored even in a coffee spoon" (Giedion 1970, p. 3). With that said, however, nothing less than a pivotal point is premised, that is, something around which everything is revolving.

In order to make the point of my argument against this "insipid monocentricity" (Deleuze 2004, p. 332) more comprehensible, we better return to the "Dottenfelderhof"; not, however, to the rural idyll of the courtyard, where we jumped into biodynamic farming just as the townspeople did on their tour last September, but to the moment Bulivia's life was drawing to an end. In doing so, we turn particularly towards the question of what "weight of being" do the ingredients of biodynamic agricultural practice, idiosyncratic though they may be, carry. Conceived of in this manner, the saying of goodbye to a cow, which is not (only) a cow with a number, but the cow Bulivia, thanking her for the manure and the milk she has produced during her lifetime of eleven years, and encouraging her for her last walk in life, does not amount to anything more than being a (hopeless) attempt by the farmer to cope with a guilty conscience. But let there be no misunderstanding about the following: Stockpersons feel sorrow about sending cows to the slaughter and they are aware of the double binds which accompany their work. This became especially clear to me on a later farm tour (March 2016), which was dedicated to questions of biodynamic cattle-husbandry, when the stockman-guide talked about the delicate issue of not yet having found a proper way of dealing with male calves which, therefore, remained a rather worthless "by-product" of dairy farming – even in biodynamic agriculture. And yet, the relationship with the cattle does not pose an inevitable contradiction in terms as it is both caring and utilizing, not to say fatal. Nor is this relationship reducible to anything like the naked truth of animal husbandry, that is, the fact that humans exploit animals, as critics committed to veganism might put it, and actually did on the farm tour by intervening that, eventually, even a lovingly slaughtered cow is still a slaughtered cow.

Similarly, it would be a cheap shot if one approaches the "original quote" of an Austrian biodynamic vintner – which is printed on his wine boxes (Fig. 3.2) and which states that he enjoys having conversations with the tendrils of the grapevine, and even receives "good ideas" in response – as being nothing more than a funny advertising stunt, let alone if one deals with it in terms of fetishism. For farmers do not needlessly introduce something like "hogwash"[12] "into a chain of operations molded out of a combination of know-how, effective knowledge, and confirmed automatic reflexes" by whispering with cows and vine tendrils (Descola 2013, p. 83). Nor are they "suddenly switching from [the weightier] rationality" that all agricultural practitioners ought to follow in order to receive milk from cows and grapes from grapevines, "into irrationality and from instrumentalized knowledge into a fantasy" (ibid.). Drawing on Philippe Descola, who has reflected on the dualism of the real and the imagined by taking the example of the Achuar people singing magic songs shortly before shooting their prey, IT IS MUCH MORE SO that both actions – as, for instance, whispering to and slaughtering cows – are "part of the issue of relations that [biodynamic farmers] establish with [cows (and grapevines)], and each has a role to play" (ibid.) in the assembling of "good food" in biodynamic agriculture.

List of References

Printed

Adorno, Theodor W.: *Minima Moralia: Reflexionen aus dem beschädigten Leben* ("Minima Moralia: Reflections on a Damaged Life"). Suhrkamp: Berlin and Frankfurt 1951.

Appadurai, Arjun: "Theory in Anthropology: Centre and Periphery". *Comparative Studies in Society and History* 28, 1986, pp. 356–361.

Deleuze, Gilles: *Difference and Repetition*. Continuum: London / New York 2004.

Descola, Philipp: *Beyond Nature and Culture*. The University of Chicago Press: Chicago 2013.

Giedion, Siegfried: *Mechanization Takes Command: A Contribution to Anonymous History*. Oxford University Press: New York 1970.

12 Cf. Via, Wali: "Biodynamic Compost Preparations", on the website of the Biodynamic Association (USA) (https://www.biodynamics.com/content/biodynamic-compost-preparations, retrieved 20.7.2016).

Jensen, Casper Bruun: "Anthropology as a Following Science: Humanity and Sociality in Continuous Variation". *NatureCulture* 1(1), 2012, pp. 1–24.

Krämer, Hannes: *Die Praxis der Kreativität: Eine Ethnografie kreativer Arbeit* ("The Practice of Creativity: An Ethnography of Creative Work"). Transcript Verlag: Bielefeld 2014.

Latour, Bruno: *Modes of Existence: An Anthropology of the Moderns*. Harvard University Press: Cambridge MA / London 2014.

Latour, Bruno: *Pandora's Hope: Essays on the Reality of Science Studies*. Harvard University Press: Cambridge MA / London 1999.

Latour, Bruno: *Science in Action: How to Follow Scientists and Engineers Through Society*. Harvard University Press: Cambridge MA 1987.

Merkenschlager, Friedrich: "Zeitkrise und die sogenannte 'Biologisch-dynamische Düngung'" ("Time Crisis and the So-called Biological Dynamic Fertilisation"). *Natur und Kultur: Monatsschrift für Naturwissenschaft und ihre Grenzgebiete* 30(4), 1933, pp. 121–125.

Mintz, Sidney W.: "Notes Toward a Cultural Construction of Modern Foods". *Social Anthropology / Anthropologie Sociale* 17(2), 2009, pp. 209–216.

Mol, Annemarie / Heuts, Frank: "What Is a Good Tomato? A Case of Valuing in Practice". *Valuation Studies* 1(2), 2013, pp. 125–146.

Mol, Annemarie: *The Body Multiple: Ontology in Medical Practice*. Duke University Press: Durham and London 2002.

Peuckert, Will-Erich / Lauffer, Otto: *Volkskunde: Quellen und Forschungen seit 1930* ("Folklore Studies: Sources and Studies Since 1930"). A. Francke Verlag: Bern 1951.

Scheidegger, Tobias: "Der Boom des Bäuerlichen: Neue Bauern-Bilder in Werbung, Warenästhetik und bäuerlicher Selbstdarstellung" ("The Boom of the Rural: New Images of Farmers in Advertising, in Commodities Aesthetics, and in Farmers' Self-portrayals"). *Schweizerisches Archiv für Volkskunde* 105, 2009, pp. 193–219.

Steiner, Rudolf: *Agriculture Course: The Birth of the Biodynamic Method*. Rudolf Steiner Press: Forest Row, UK 2004.

Internet

Demeter Association: http://www.demeter.net/statistics, retrieved 20.7.2016.

German Federal Statistical Office: https://www.destatis.de, retrieved 20.7.2016.

Via, Wali, "Biodynamic Compost Preparations", Biodynamic Association (USA), retrieved 20.7.2016 from https://www.biodynamics.com/content/biodynamic-compost-preparations.

"Work and Labour Studies", Deutsche Gesellschaft für Volkskunde ("German Society of Folkore Studies"), retrieved 20.8.2016 from http://www.dgv-arbeitskulturen.de/english/committee/.

Leen Beyers

Food and the City: The Invisible Food Chain of an Industrialised City

Abstract: *Today's invisibility of food, and the consequent mistrust engendered thereby, is not just a matter of the invisible origin of ingredients. It is also a consequence of the hidden geography of food. Major technological and cultural shifts arising from 19th century industrialization have moved the supply and sale of food, and food waste, to the invisible periphery of cities. This essay illustrates this situation with a spatial history of the city of Antwerp (Belgium).*

The Hungriness of Cities

Cities all over the world depend on the countryside for their continued existence, and are shaped by food. Like monsters, cities devour crops from the countryside near and far. Cities are also the places where, for centuries, agricultural crops have been processed into culinary specialities, thereby gaining added value. Their connectedness to rural lands allows cities to specialize in activities other than agriculture, or, in other words, to become "cities". Food supply and processing, and the sale, preparation and consumption of food, and also food waste, form the basic fabric of cities, and link them inextricably to the countryside.[1] Prior to industrialization, cities with a productive hinterland, or port cities importing food, had the opportunity to develop into large cities, because they could count on the existence of a large-scale food supply system. Antwerp, which, in the middle of the sixteenth century, numbered 100,000 inhabitants, is a good example of this. New transport facilities since industrialization, such as trains, and later on trucks and planes, allowed existing cities to expand immensely, and created the possibility for the development of cities anywhere on the globe.

Assigning such a prominent role to food as a mechanism by which to understand the city and the urbanization process, is a notion that seems to run counter

1 The pace of global urbanization has prompted both urban planners, food specialists and historians to look at the city from the food angle. See, for example: Scholliers / van den Eeckhout 2013, pp. 69–81; Atkins / Lummel / Oddy 2007; Cronon 1991; Kaika 2005; Hubbard 2006; Steel 2008; Radeff 2012, pp. 29–46.

to our intuitive understanding of the world at large. Is this because cities have become dense masses of people, the majority of which tend to work in non-food or subsistence-related sectors, such as industry, banking and finance? And is farming still the exclusive preserve of the countryside? Whoever maintains such an artificial dichotomy between town and country, ignores the shared and intertwined history of the two, and disregards what is perhaps the greatest challenge of our time: the exponential increase in the world's population, and the fact that, in the future, an ever-greater number of people is likely to be concentrated in cities and metropolitan areas, which will need to be fed in a way that is socially, ecologically and economically viable. In 1900, an estimated 10 % of the population worldwide lived in and around urban conurbations, while the most recent forecast suggests that this ratio will have risen to as much as 75 % by the year 2050.[2]

Local and Global: From Visible to Invisible Flows

The survival of a metropolis like Antwerp has always been dependent on an extensive local and global hinterland. Hence, the globalisation process of the food chain in and around Antwerp was a gradual one, growing from an initial limited set of foodstuffs to every type of perishable food today. Globalisation shapes the daily urban experience, but the impact of the industralization of spaces of transhipment and food supply, on daily urban life, must have been deeper still. Since the second half of the 19th century, the food-supply operation has moved from the centre to the invisible periphery of the city.

While urban and local agriculture had existed in and around Antwerp for centuries, and had taken on a different guise with every passing century, it had never fully covered all of the city's nutritional requirements. Early on, imported food arrived at the docks from overseas. An initial stage of the globalisation of the food chain in and around Antwerp took place in the 16th century. By the end of the 15th century Antwerp had acquired a central position in the Western European trade in luxury goods, including cane sugar from slave plantations in the Canary Islands and Madeira. The resultant economic success caused the population to grow explosively, and the city had to rely for about 20 % of its corn, for life-essential bread and beer, on overseas imports, coming in large part from the

2 Since the turn of the new millennium, the Food and Agriculture Organization (FAO) of the United Nations has placed the challenge firmly on the world stage: www.fao.org/in-action/food-for-cities-programme/en, retrieved 14.7.2016.

Baltic region. Hence, from early on, overseas food imports consisted not only of exotic crops, but also included cheap imports of well-known local crops.

A second major phase in the globalisation of the food chain in the Antwerp region started in the 19th century. After the so-called fall of Antwerp, that is, its re-conquest by the Spanish Habsburg powers in 1585 and the secession of the northern Netherlands, the city became a regional centre. In the 19th century, political conditions improved, and the port of Antwerp once again acquired a major position in the Western European trade sector. In the second half of the 19th century, industrial innovations such as trains, steamships, trucks and containers, and political conditions, such as overseas colonisation, resulted in a vast expansion in the variety of goods imported into Antwerp.[3]

Together, the industrial transport technologies and cultural trends in relation to hygiene had, since the end of the 19th century, drastically changed the visibility of the food supply in the city. In order to give a more detailed description of this transition and its impact on the daily experience of city dwellers, I would like to focus on the way meat arrived in Antwerp in the 16th and 20th centuries, respectively. The classic model of the German geographer, Johann Heinrich von Thünen (1826), of the provisioning of cities, in the pre-industrial context, argues that while fruit and vegetables generally came from a first provision zone, close to the city, cattle could be raised on pastures a few hundred kilometres away, since they could walk to the city to be sold and then slaughtered there. A lot of new versions of this model have been made, in particular for cities with a river, but it explains quite well why cattle could be brought from as far away as Denmark, Holstein and Friesland to the Antwerp region from the 16th century onwards. The cattle were bought in the spring and fattened in Holland or, even closer, on the polders north of the city, and in neighbouring Borgerhout. Transportation of the cattle was partly by ship and partly by means of the cattle themselves walking to the city. Both local farmers and butchers raised cattle on the polders since these lands were ideal for doing so.

On market days cattle, mainly oxen, were sold at the two cattle markets, which were both close to the city walls, and directly connected to the polders surrounding the city. Once slaughtered, beef and pork were sold in the Butcher's Hall, a covered market-hall close to the oldest cattle market. Slaughtering was carried out in that area also, in and around the workhouses of the butchers, who all lived

---

3 For an overview of this first and second phase of global food importation in the 16th and 19th centuries, see Segers / Parmentier / Vrelust 2016, pp. 18–59.

in this neighbourhood. Offal often ended up on the streets or in the city canals. Due to the growth of the population in the 16th century, most of the pastures for cattle breeding disappeared. People, however, continued to fatten their own pigs and poultry in and around their homes in the city up until the 19th century. In other words, whether the cattle originated locally or overseas, every citizen saw and smelled the sale and the slaughtering of animals.[4]

Fig. 1: Antwerp's old Ox Market. Peter van Bredael. Antwerp, c. 1650. Oil on canvas. Royal Museum of Fine Arts of Antwerp, inv. nr. 784. © www.lukasweb.be, photo Hugo Maertens.

For a long time, meat was a luxury food, and thus fish, both locally-caught and imported salted varieties, such as herring, was much more important than flesh for the daily diet of the average inhabitant of Antwerp. It is, therefore, quite surprising that subsequently in Antwerp, a port city with a good connection

4 On the pre-industrial cattle trade, see Limberger 2008, pp. 79, 217; and Gijsbers 1999. On slaughtering and cattle in the pre-industrial city, see Willems 2009, pp. 183–184, 189; and Poulussen 1987.

to the sea, fish was completely displaced by meat in the diet of the people, in the course of the 20th century. This happened for the following reasons. Firstly, at the end of the 19th century, the price of meat dropped significantly thanks to the possibility of importing live cattle, by steamship, from as far away as Argentina, in South America, to be followed by the importation of frozen meat not much later from the same region. In 1884, steamers brought the first cargoes of frozen meat from Argentina to Antwerp. Policy makers were convinced that the working classes needed cheap corn and meat in order to remain productive, and this opened up the market for those American imported goods. Secondly, in the course of the 20th century, many local farmers in Flanders started to specialize in cattle breeding, themselves. They profited from the importation of cheap fodder, often soya from Brazil handled via the port of Antwerp. At the same time, the meat they produced in their large-scale farms was, of necessity, cheap, because they had to compete at the European and global market levels, especially since the liberalisation of the international food trade in the 1980s. The visibility of cattle-breeding in the landscape is relatively limited nowadays, since the cattle are raised in sheds and no longer go out to graze in fields.[5]

Street names still remind us of the many places in Antwerp where cattle and meat were sold, but cattle are no longer present in the city. In 1877, the city opened a public slaughterhouse for cattle and pigs. Because of the cholera plague and more general hygiene concerns, Antwerp moved slaughtering to the city periphery, following the example of other European cities. Not much later, the cattle market also moved to the same site. In 2006, the slaughterhouse had to close down because it could no longer meet the new hygiene standards required by European legislation, and also because of financial reasons. Since then, slaughtering, even of small animals, has completely left the city environs and is carried out in several slaughterhouses in the countryside. Today, trucks unobtrusively transport the slaughtered carcasses into the city to butcher shops and supermarkets.[6]

---

5 On the importation of meat and corn to fight hunger in the 19th century, and on agriculture in Flanders, see Segers / Parmentier / Vrelust 2016, pp. 46–49, 51–54; Segers et al. 2013, pp. 225–257.

6 See further, Linters 1988.

Fig. 2: Meat delivery in the city. Antwerp, 2015. © Gilles Scheijnen for Karel de Grote Hogeschool.

While most of the food provisioning moved to the city periphery in the 19th century, the food industry itself settled in the centre of the city. After 1800, this industry flourished, due to the importation of new foodstuffs from overseas, such as coffee, cocoa and meat. It was also the result of new technology, such as the availability of steam-powered machinery and greater export opportunities. Companies preferred the city centre location as it was close to the railway station and the docks. Bouillon producer, Liebig, for instance, opened its distribution centre right in the middle of Meir, the main shopping street. The story of the Liebig company demonstrates how global, as well as how invisible, the food chain became in the 19th century. The meat extract was made from cattle grazing in Fray Bentos, Uruguay. The barrels with bouillon were transported to Antwerp, where they were packed in smaller units, and distributed all over the world. Like other food companies, Liebig was looking for more space and left the city of Antwerp in the 1960s for an invisible site on the periphery. The inhabitants of Antwerp no longer wake up to the fragrance of bouillon, chocolate or coffee.[7]

7 See: Judel 2003, pp. 6–17; Landuyt 1984, pp. 87–103.

Shopping: From Social and Sensual to Restrained Experience

Since the second half of the 19th century shopping for food in Antwerp has turned gradually into a restrained experience, in which contact with food, and contact between buyers and sellers of food, has diminished greatly. The perspective of urban history helps us to understand how this happened. Antwerp had been a renowned *coopstadt*, "merchant city", since the Middle Ages, and the names of streets and squares, which often refer to food markets – for example, Ossenmarkt, Eiermarkt and Melkmarkt ("Ox Market", "Egg Market" and "Milk Market") – respectively, bear witness to this. These open-air markets, like the city itself, were rural in origin. Antwerp itself probably developed from the activities of a local rural community selling its own surplus goods, as well as those from overseas brought in by ships. Thanks to its weekly food markets, and its twice-yearly great luxury-goods' markets – those of Pentecost and Bamis (the latter in October) – the city flourished.

Up until the end of the 18th century, open-air markets were essential for the sale of fruit and vegetables, dairy goods and fish, and were situated in the centre of the city. Expensive meat, mainly beef and pork, was sold in the covered Butcher's Hall. Shops have an equally long history in Antwerp. The medieval markets for luxury goods, such as sheets, jewels and spices, evolved into more permanent shops and covered market-places in the 16th century, when Antwerp became the commercial capital of northwestern Europe. In the following centuries, two types of food shops existed in Antwerp: bakery shops and groceries selling the more expensive overseas goods, such as spices, and later on coffee, tea and tobacco.

Whether doing so at the markets, in shops, or in dealing with peddlers, extensive social and sensual skills were required in order to sell and buy food, as standardization requirements in terms of prices, packaging, or quality levels were unknown at the time. Hence, discussions concerning quality, bargaining about the price, and buying on credit, were much in evidence. A manual on how to handle these matters at the Antwerp markets was printed in the city in 1649. Since food could not be kept for a long time, shopping for small quantities was almost a daily affair, most of all for housewives and for the household personnel of the wealthy city dwellers. Food was presented in bulk in the markets and in shops, and in order to assess the quality of the goods, sellers could smell and touch it. The manual encouraged people to enquire about the origin of food, from the merchants.[8]

---

8 *Antwerpse merckten, waer in den handel van-de vismerckt, vleesch-huys ende andere, claer ende duydelijck wordt uytgebeldt. Seer vermackelijk om te lesen voor alle jonckheyt*

Fig. 3: Poultry Market, possibly on the Meir. Philips Galle (publisher) and Hans Bol (designer), Antwerp, 1582. Engraving. © Museum Plantin-Moretus, Printing Room, Antwerp, PK.OP.07601.

From the 18th century onwards, concerns grew about the rubbish and the stench emanating from the markets, as this was considered to be causing illnesses.[9] New hygiene standards resulted in small shops becoming popular. In addition, the cheaper prices for glass, and the steadily-increasing purchasing power of the burgeoning population, stimulated the advent of small shops selling many types of fresh produce, including meat, fish, and vegetables, in the course of the 19th century. Members of the former merchants' guild changed from their market stalls to more respectably-regarded shop premises. Markets did not disappear, however, though they gradually moved to the edge of town, away from the "clean" city centre. Farmers started to dominate the fruit and vegetables markets, but by the 1950s they were replaced by market stall-holders dependent on a wholesale sector. The city also constructed more hygienic, covered market-halls, for the sale of meat and fish. In the 1930s, all of these markets, except for one, were already closed down.

The greatest spatial and social changes in Antwerp took place from 1958 onwards, with the arrival of supermarkets with adjacent car parks. Today, in Belgium, the market share of supermarkets vis-à-vis that of independent grocers is 95 %. The predecessor of the first self-service supermarket was the luxury warehouse Grand Bazar, which opened in 1885 in the centre of Antwerp. It was a store with luxury merchandize, such as clothes and household goods, sweets and biscuits. From 1920 onwards, the Grand Bazar also offered fresh food. In

1649. For an overview of pre-industrial shopping spaces and practices in Antwerp, see Van Damme 2007, pp. 63–72; Van Damme / Teughels, 2016, pp. 64–82.

9 See also: Corbin 1986.

1958, the Grand Bazar turned its luxury warehouse into a self-service supermarket and opened a second, brand-new supermarket in Antwerp, based on the American model – with pre-packaged food, trolleys, and a car park. In the 1950s, Grand Bazar was convinced that shopping by car was the future of the industry. Grand Bazar was right, at least until the 1990s. Large supermarkets are on the decline today because of traffic problems. Supermarket chains are opening increasing numbers of small stores on street corners. In 2013–2014, Antwerp boasted about having 486 supermarkets, of which about 112 were larger than 400 m^2.[10]

Fig. 4: Grocer Geeraerts, Antwerp, c. 1900. The windows in glass did not immediately change the old habit of putting the goods on the pavement. © Frans Lauwers, Merksem-Antwerp.

10 For an overview of shopping spaces and practices since 1800, see Van Damme / Teughels 2016, pp. 82–96; Van Damme 2014, pp. 78–103; Université Libre de Bruxelles, Archives Grand Bazar, nr. 520 (2), nr. 324–325, nr. 880–883 (Localisations), nr. 1178 (Luchtbal). On the market share of supermarkets, see *Nielsen Grocery Universe 2014* (http://www.nielsen.com/be/en/insights/reports/2014/nielsen-grocery-universe-2014.html, retrieved 9.8.2016). For the number of supermarkets in Antwerp, in 2013–2014, see City of Antwerp Research Department; Locatus.

Whether functioning as mini-supermarkets or hyper-markets, the social and sensual experience of shopping in a supermarket is very different from shopping for food at the 16th century open air market, or in the 19th century grocery shop full of bulk goods. The spatial shifts within the Grand Bazar itself, as it evolved from being a luxury warehouse to a self-service supermarket, are telling in this regard. In the 1920s and 1930s, the Grand Bazar started to sell fresh food, in a way very similar to what was happening in respectable small shops at the time. A picture of the butchers' department in the Grand Bazar of this period, shows butchers, and the carcasses with meat. The butchers were there to cut the meat at the request of clients. Since 1958, the personnel in the shops have no longer prepared food. The cash desks became the most important meeting point between clients and staff. Simultaneously, the number of personnel in the distribution centre of Grand Bazar in the periphery of Antwerp increased. Here, behind the scences, the butchers' department and the packing department were extended from the 1950s onwards.

Fig. 5: The meat department and personnel in the Grand Bazar, Antwerp, c. 1920–1944. © Fondation Bernheim Brussels, Collection: Archives Grand Bazar, Université Libre de Bruxelles, nr. 324–325.

Fig. 6: Packaging meat in the distribution centre of the Grand Bazar, Kontich, c. 1960.© Fondation Bernheim Brussels, Collection: Archives Grand Bazar, Université Libre de Bruxelles, nr. 880–883.

Today, in mainstream supermarkets, the distance between clients, food, and personnel preparing the food, is even greater than it was in the 1950s, with trends like online shoppng, cash and carry outlets, and digital cash desks without personnel, on the increase. There are two exceptions to this trend. Firstly, the traditional independent grocers of diverse cultural origins, who package and present food in a variety of different ways. Secondly, luxury food shops which showcase raw food in order to distinguish themselves in this regard from the supermarket experience. In these perfectly climatised shopping spaces, the expensive management of authenticity also includes the management of smell to a degree considered acceptable. This scenario does not automatically imply that correct information about the origin of the food on display will necessarily be provided. Thus, mainstream supermarkets could easily adopt this visual strategy without changing their invisible wholesale practices.

Fig. 7: Grocer Man Fat, Dambruggestraat. Antwerp, 2015. © MAS, photo: Sanne De Wilde.

Fig. 8: The "window fridge" of Ateliers Mille Vaches, a new luxury butcher in Antwerp, trading since June 2016. © Atelier Mille Vaches, Antwerp.

Food Waste: From Recycling to Covering

Since the 1970s engineers and ecologists, and, from the 1990s, historians, have started to conceive of the city as a living metabolism, which consumes energy, water, air and materials, and produces waste in return. They use the contrasting model of the two-way city and one-way city. Two-way cities recycle their waste products and reuse them in their mostly-local food-chain. One-way cities consume in a more global fashion and throw away most of their waste products. Historians have criticised this too-linear analysis as if industrial cities evolved straight away into one-way cities.[11] In the following lines, two-way and one-way practices in Antwerp are described, not to fully confirm the linear analysis, but to understand how and why food waste has been covered and hidden in a more drastic fashion since the 19th century.

In Antwerp, the 18th century, as well as the more industrial 19th century, were the heydays of the recycling of city waste and its re-use in local agriculture. The age-old practice of collecting waste from the streets and cesspits, and of selling it on as a fertilizer in the countryside, was modernized and adapted to industrial technological advancements at the turn of the 19th century. One the one hand, the demand for city waste in Flemish agriculture increased in the 18th century. In addition to those engaged in subsistence farming, a greater number of farmers decided in favour of growing crops, such as flax, for profit, and realized successful harvests thanks to city waste which they had used as a fertilizer. On the other hand, the growth of the city population, and new concerns about hygiene, led to a demand for new waste policies. Steam pumps to collect sewage, and new sweeping machines to collect street waste, were adopted. In addition, the city of Antwerp's hygiene department acquired rural land in 1893 to create a sewage farm. But the farming stopped around 1929, because the urban sewage had become too thin to be useful as a fertilizer, due to the popularity of the flushing toilet. And the city's rubbish had come to contain too much metal, paper and plastic, and so the content of the city dump was no longer suitable for agricultural purposes.[12]

---

11 For further discussion see: Vermoesen et al. 2016, pp. 170–171.

12 Ibid., pp. 173–184. See also Dienst Openbare Reiniging 1962; De Graef / Soens 2014, pp. 9–40.

Fig. 9: A sludge cart with a tipping barrel releasing its load into a barge. The barge then sailed from Antwerp to the countryside of Brecht, north of Antwerp, where the sludge was used as fertiliser, c. 1890. Egide Linnig. Antwerp City Archives, PHOTO-GF #1676.

While these practices of waste recycling continued through the industrial age until the 1930s, a simultaneous long history of covering and hiding waste also shaped the city of Antwerp from pre-industrial times. The shape of toilet furniture and its connection to the city's sewage system is revealing in this regard. The first type of pre-industrial toilet was the dry toilet connected to a cesspit, which was emptied out by an emptier of cesspools, who then transported the waste in a barge to the countryside, where it was used as a fertilizer. In the less than ideal case, the toilet was connected to the city's canals and the waste was released into the water. A second, simpler type, was the toilet bowl, which was ideally emptied into a cesspit, but otherwise into the city's canals or onto the city's streets. Making these toilets less visible, by, for example, hiding them in a piece of furniture, became a trend in rich house interiors in the 18th century. Up until the 19th century, excrement was covered over in different ways. Due to the covering, at least part of the city's human excrement ended up in the canals and was, therfore, not re-used. Because of the waste- and stench-problem of the city canals, people living close to them were asked to cover them over, that is, to hide the waste.

Fig. 10: The "book" toilet. This toilet room, constructed in Antwerp in 1772, was designed in order to look like a small library. It was connected to a cesspit. © Stefan Dewickere for Herita.

The next step in the covering of human waste was the introduction of flushing toilets. The modern flushing toilet with the siphon preventing the escape of foul air from the sewer, which was created at the end of the 18th century, was introduced into Antwerp at the end of the 19th century. Via the water toilet, which was odourless thanks to the water and the siphon, human waste was washed away together with the water. It was no longer obligatory to connect the water toilets to cesspits, as farmers were no longer interested in the thin sewage from these toilets. From around 1900 until 1995, the sewage of almost 70,000 houses in Antwerp ended up in the city's canals. It flowed from these underground canals directly into the Scheldt. The pollution of the Scheldt, which then became invisible, continued for an entire century – in fact, right up until the Aquafin company began purifying Antwerp's sewage in 1995.[13]

13 On the history of toilets and sewers (in Antwerp and beyond), see Maclot 1988, pp. 121–152; Billen / Decroly 2003; Poulussen 1987.

In the same way, street waste and waste from the city's canals were, for centuries, collected by a street-sweeping company and sold in the countryside as fertilizer. Not all of the waste was reused, but until the end of the 19th century, waste actually remained an economic good. A liberal politician advocating sewage farming in 1899, criticized the burning of waste by calling it a barbarian crime in a densely populated city, surrounded by moorland in need of fertilizers.[14] He lost the argument, because from the 1920s onwards, Antwerp's street and household waste was transported to landfill areas and dumps and, finally, in 1975, an incinerator was built on the periphery of the city. The dumps and incinerator turned waste into a highly visible issue in the 1990s, due to protests about air pollution and resultant health consequences. Interestingly, the prevention of food waste itself was not yet a strong argument back then. Today, waste prevention and the recycling of waste into energy, are elements central to the arguments of both critics and advocates of the oven.[15]

Conclusion: A Hidden Geography

As the short description above reveals, the visibility of the urban food chain has shifted over the centuries. Today, the city is shaped by a highly-visible restaurant culture, which only looks set to expand. The supply of food to the city and the removal of waste, by contrast, are far less discernible in the post-industrialized era. In this day and age, the link between producers and consumers of food has been largely severed, mainly as a result of the broader range of industrial production, transport and packaging options. Yet, cultural norms related to hygiene have also played a part, resulting in the fact that the characteristic aroma (and stench!) of food has become far less desirable in densely-populated cities such as Antwerp.

This essay on spatial patterns does not address in detail how today's invisibility of the food chain adds to the mistrust surrounding food and agriculture. In-depth research of food discourses and practices is highly relevant in this regard. In order to stimulate this kind of research, I would like to end with a reference to the work of photographer Henk Wildschut.[16] As he finished his FOOD project, he argued

---

14 De Beuckelaer 1899.

15 Dienst Openbare Reiniging (http://www.isvag.be/nl/werkwijze, http://kathleenvanbrempt.be/antwerpen/gemeenteraad/verbrandingsoven-isvag-in-wilrijk-moet-dicht-elders-anders-en-beter/, retrieved 9.8.2016).

16 "Food, Background – Henk Wildschut" (http://www.henkwildschut.com/work/food/background-food/, retrieved 14.7.2016). For a similar argument, see Fresco 2012.

in the following way about the blindness of (urban) consumers with regard to the food chain, for instance, with regard to the scale of food production:

> The fact that current solutions to many food-related issues often have consumers up in arms can be blamed in part on the food industry itself. Thinking of profits, they paint a romanticized picture of the way things are. These are the images we love to see: cows in the meadow, farmers on tractors bringing vegetables to the supermarket. At the same time critics are alerting us to the flipside of intensive and industrial food production with soundbites like "plofkip" (literally, a chicken fit to burst) and "pig towers".
> Given our unprecedented interest these days in how our food is produced, such conflicting reports only sow confusion. However aware we are of seductive sales techniques and marketing strategies, we still prefer, against our better judgement, that romanticized picture than to see the situation as it really is.

List of References

Printed

Antwerpse merckten, waer in den handel van-de vismerckt, vleesch-huys ende andere, claer ende duydelijck wordt uytgebeldt. Seer vermackelijk om te lesen voor alle jonckheyt ("Antwerp Markets, a Depiction of the Sale at the Fish Market, in the Butcher's Hall, and Others. An Entertaining Manual for All Youngsters"). Jacob van Gheelen: Antwerp 1649.

Atkins, Peter / Lummel, Peter / Oddy, Dereck (eds.): *Food and the City in Europe since* 1800. Ashgate: Aldershot 2007.

Billen, Claire / Decroly, Jean-Michel: *De kleinste kamertjes in de grootstad. Openbaar sanitair in Brussel van de middeleeuwen tot vandaag* ("The Smallest Rooms of the Metropolis. Public Sanitary Facilities in Brussels since the Middle Ages"). Musea van de Stad Brussel: Brussel 2003.

Corbin, Alain: *Le miasme et la jonquille. L'odorat et l'imaginaire sociale, XVIIIe-XIXe siècles*, 3rd ed. Flammarion: Paris 1986.

Cronon, William: *Nature's Metropolis: Chicago and the Great West*. W. W. Norton: New York 1991.

De Beuckelaer, François Xavier: *Ontginning der heiden in de Kempen* ("Exploitation of the Moorlands in the Kempen Region"). drukk. De Backer: Antwerpen 1899.

De Graef, Peter / Soens, Tim: "Boer en burger ecologisch verenigd? Een microperspectief op het gebruik van stedelijk afval als meststof in de vroegmoderne Vlaamse landbouw" ("An Ecological Bond between Farmer and Citizen? A Micro-perspective on the Use of Urban Waste as Fertilizer in the Premodern Flemish Husbandry"). *Jaarboek voor ecologische geschiedenis* 2014, pp. 9–40.

Dienst Openbare Reiniging: *Uit de geschiedenis van de Antwerpse stadsreiniging* ("History of the Urban Sanitation Department of the City of Antwerp"). Dienst Openbare Reiniging: Antwerpen, 1962.

Fresco, Louise: *Hamburgers in het paradijs. Voedsel in tijden van schaarste en overvloed* ("A Hamburger in Paradise. Food in Times of Scarcity and Abundance"). Bert Bakker: Amsterdam 2012.

Gijsbers, Wilhelmina: *Kapitale ossen. De internationale handel in slachtvee in Noordwest-Europa 1300–1750* ("Capital Oxen. The International Trade in Beef Cattle in Northwestern Europe 1300–1750"). Uitgeverij Verloren: Hilversum 1999.

Hubbard, Phil: *Key Concepts in Geography. The City.* Routledge: London / New York: 2006.

Judel, Günther: "Die Geschichte von Liebigs Fleischextrakt". *Spiegel der Forschung* 20, 2003, pp. 6–17.

Kaika, Maria: *City of Flows: Modernity, Nature and the City*. Routledge: London / New York 2005.

Landuyt, Guido: "De voedingsnijverheid" ("The Food Industry"). In Baeten, Roland (ed.): *Industriële revoluties in de provincie* Antwerpen. Standaard: Antwerpen 1984, pp. 87–103.

Limberger, Michael: *Sixteenth Century Antwerp and Its Rural Surroundings. Social and Economic Changes in the Hinterland of a Commercial Metropolis (ca. 1450 – ca. 1570)*. Brepols: Turnhout 2008.

Linters, Adriaan: *Jubileumuitgave van de Antwerpse verenigingen van vee en vlees* ("Jubilee Publication on the History of the Antwerp Associations of Cattle and Meat"). Stad Antwerpen: Antwerpen 1988.

Maclot, Petra: "De afvoer van het vast afval en van de gebruikswaters binnen het traditionele Antwerpse woonhuis (1500–1800)" ("The Management of Waste and Water in the Traditional Antwerp Dwelling, 1500–1800"). In Maclot, Petra / Pottier, Werner (eds.): *'n Propere tijd!? (On)leefbaar Antwerpen thuis en op straat (1500–1800)*. Antwerpse vereniging voor Bodem- en Grotonderzoek, Antwerpen 1988), pp. 121–152.

Poulussen, Peter: *Van burenlast tot milieuhinder. Het stedelijk leefmilieu 1500–1800* ("From Neighbour's Dispute to Environmental Nuisance. The Urban Environment 1500–1800"). DNB / Uitgeverij Pelckmans: Kapellen 1987.

Radeff, Anne: "Food Systems: Central Decentral Networks". In Kümin, Beat (ed.): *A Cultural History of Food in the Early Modern* Age. Berg Publishers: London / New York 2012), pp. 29–46.

Scholliers, Peter / van den Eeckhout, Patricia: "Feeding Growing Cities in the Nineteenth and Twentieth Centuries: Problems, Innovations and Reputations". In Murcott, Anne / Belasco, Warren / Jackson, Peter (eds.): *The Handbook of Food* Research. Bloomsbury Academic Press: London 2013, pp. 69–81.

Segers, Yves / Parmentier, Jan / Vrelust, Jef: "Naar de stad. Productie- en aanvoercircuits van voedsel en drank" ("Into the City. Production and Supply of Food and Drinks"). In Beyers, Leen / Damme, Ilja Van (eds.): *Antwerpen à la carte. Eten en de stad, van de middeleeuwen tot vandaag*. BAI: Antwerp 2016, pp. 18–59.

Segers, Yves / Van Molle, Leen / Kooij, P. / Bieleman, J.: "The Low Countries, 1750–2000". In Segersand, Yves / Van Molle, Leen (eds.): *The Agro-food Market: Production, Distribution and Consumption*. Brepols: Turnhout 2013, pp. 225–257.

Steel, Carolyn: *Hungry City: How Food Shapes Our Lives*. Verso: London 2008.

Université Libre de Bruxelles, Archives Grand Bazar, nr. 520 (2), nr. 324–325, nr. 880–883 (Localisations), nr. 1178 (Luchtbal).

Van Damme, Ilja: "Antwerp goes shopping! Continuity and Change in Retail Space and Shopping Interactions from the Sixteenth to the Nineteenth Century". In Furnée, Jan Hein (ed.): *The Landscape of Consumption: Shopping Streets and Cultures in Western Europe, 1200–1900*. Palgrave Macmillan: London 2014, pp. 78–103.

Van Damme, Ilja: *Verleiden en verkopen. Antwerpse kleinhandelaars en hun klanten in tijden van crisis (ca. 1648–1748)* ("Attracting and Selling. Antwerp Retailers and their Clients in Times of Crisis, ca. 1648–1748"). Aksant: Amsterdam 2007, pp. 63–72.

Van Damme, Ilja / Teughels, Nelleke: "Boodschappen doen. Over markten, winkels en supermarkten" ("Shopping. On Markets, Shops and Supermarkets"). In Beyers, Leen / Van Damme, Ilja: *Antwerpen à la carte. Eten en de stad, van de middeleeuwen tot vandaag*. BAI: Antwerp 2016, pp. 64–82.

Vermoesen, Reinoud / Soens, Tim / Graef, Pieter De / van Vaerenberg, Jeroen: "Uit de stad. Verwerking en hergebruik van stedelijk voedselafval" ("Out of the City. The Recycling of Urban Food Waste"). In Beyers, Leen / Van Damme, Ilja (eds.): *Eten en de stad, van de middeleeuwen tot vandaag*. BAI: Antwerp 2016, pp. 166–197.

Willems, Bart: *Leven op de pof. Krediet bij de Antwerpse middenstand in de achttiende eeuw* ("Credit Relations among the Antwerp Middle Class in the 18th Century"). Aksant: Amsterdam 2009.

Internet

Dienst Openbare Reiniging, *Uit de geschiedenis* ("History of the Urban Sanitation Department"), retrieved 14.7.2016 from http://www.isvag.be/nl/werkwijze, and also http://kathleenvanbrempt.be/antwerpen/gemeenteraad/verbrandingsoven-isvag-in-wilrijk-moet-dicht-elders-anders-en-beter/, retrieved 14.7.2016.

"Food, Background – Henk Wildschut", retrieved 14.7.2016 from Wildhttp://www.henkwildschut.com/work/food/background-food/.

Nielsen Grocery Universe 2014, retrieved 9.8.2016 from http://www.nielsen.com/be/en/insights/reports/2014/nielsen-grocery-universe-2014.html.

United Nations: Food and Agriculture Organization (FAO), retrieved 14.7.2016 from www.fao.org/in-action/food-for-cities-programme/en.

Anna Rydz-Żbikowska

The Future of The Common Agricultural Policy and Organic Agriculture in the European Union

Abstract: *The aim of the article is to determine what the main factors framing The Common Agricultural Policy are, and also to ascertain the direction of its current goals and action priorities. Furthermore, this paper is an attempt to assess the impact of The Common Agricultural Policy on the development of organic farming in the European Union. The research methods used in the article include an analysis of available documentary and literature sources on the topics in question, the development of relevant statistical surveys, and the use of a deductive approach in order to draw some conclusions from the stated agricultural policy of the European Union.*

Introduction

The proper functioning of the economy of any country is firmly associated with the efficient operation of its agricultural sector as this helps to ensure food security for its citizens. This sector is thus perceived as being a strategic economic one because economic growth, improved quality of life and health, are all associated with an increased demand for healthy food, produced with the utmost care and commonly accepted methods. As an integral part of economies, agriculture and its development is dependent on the specific geographical and economic conditions of the country in question. The agricultural sector, as well as rural areas, are strictly subject to the intervention of the state and local authorities, as their knowledge and experience allows them to customize political tools to specific indigenous conditions. Exceptionally large-scale intervention and the provision of favourable conditions for the implementation of the principles of the sustainable development concept, are undoubtedly characteristic for European Union countries. With regard to the development of sustainable agriculture and rural areas – a major concern existing side by side with environmental policy programmes – the Common Agricultural Policy of the EU and the sphere of action concerning organic farming, are of major importance (Piworowicz 2015, pp. 9–11), especially since the significance of organic farming worldwide is increasing every year. Undoubtedly, this phenomenon is noticeable mainly in European Union countries, where organic farming is seen as a strategic element of the reform of The Common Agricultural Policy. It should also be noted, that the aspired-for future shape of The Common Agricultural Policy is one in which a compromise between the objectives concerning the economy, environment and social aspects, is achieved (Maciejczak 2007, p. 3). In its commitments set out by The Common Agricultural Policy over the last twenty years, the importance of protecting the environment because of its impact on future food security, and of preserving plant and animal welfare as well as the sustainable management of natural resources, was clearly stated (Król 2013, p. 408). It is also worth noting that organic farming is an agricultural system, that involves not only the environmental element, but also one that impacts positively on social and cultural aspects of life, while contributing to higher food-production standards and food quality. Moreover, organic agriculture, in line with the paradigm of the modern village, involves the public good, such as contributing to the increasing of employment in rural areas and the improvement of quality of life. Organic farming practices can contribute to the creation of the public good by enhancing the quality of the air, soil and water, by contibuting towards the achievement of a stable climatic situation and the improvement of the resilience of land to natural disasters, such as fires and floods. Agriculture, however, also plays a significant role in ensuring food security and the vitality of rural areas. What is more, it contributes in economic, social and cultural terms to quality of life in rural areas and, in broader terms, to the whole rural-economy sector (Baldock / Hart 2011, p. 4). An important objective of organic farming, emphasized in the regulations of the EU, is that of responding to consumer needs. Therefore, the further development of, and the financial support for organic farming in Europe, would reflect trends already observable in global agricultural markets, and, at the same time, meet the expectations of today's consumers about food quality. It is worth underscoring here that the driving force behind the intensive market development of organic farming in the European Union was the introduction of subsidies for organic farming. The organic market is now one of the most dynamically-developing sectors of the market for food products in the European Union (Hamm / Gronefeld 2004, p. 23).

The Common Agricultural Policy 2014–2020 and its Implications for Organic Farming

Although it has undergone a number of reforms, and new priority areas have already been designated, The Common Agricultural Policy is still evolving. While key amendments to the current CAP date back to 2013, new proposals regarding its future shape are already in existence. The European Commission, in its

Communication to the European Parliament in November 2010 presented new challenges for CAP for the years 2014–2020. These are as follows:

- more efficient use of natural resources such as water, air, and ensuring biodiversity
- ensuring food security in the EU and globally
- reducing the impact of agricultural and greenhouse gas emissions on climate change
- strengthening the role of local governments in order to actively participate in environmental protection and energy supply from renewable energy sources
- strengthening territorial and social cohesion in the rural areas of the European Union
- putting emphasis on the structural diversity of farms in the European Union and the diversity of production systems
- ensuring equitable and sustainable distribution of support under the CAP between Member States and farmers (The European Commission 2010).

Reform of the Common Agricultural Policy dating from 2013 was the final phase of the process of change which had been proposed in 2010, with the aim of ensuring food security, sustainable rural development, and environmental protection. The main objective of the reform was to enable farmers to adapt to instantly-changing market conditions, and to guarantee consumer access to high-quality nutritional food.[1] All the changes brought about by the reform of The Common Agricultural Policy in 2013, have contributed to a more efficient use of funds by encouraging farmers to become more competitive in the market area. It is also worth emphasizing that the CAP reform of 2013 introduced a new structure of direct payments to farmers according to CAP priorities thus ensuring a more equitable distribution of such funds, and that it also stressed the role of green investment, the development of food security networks, and the strengthening of rural progress. The challenges likely to impede the realization of the goals set out by the new agricultural policy after 2013 have been determined according to specific characteristics and areas of agricultural markets, as follows:

- "economic challenges (food security, decrease of crop yields, fluctuations in prices of agricultural products, high costs of sustainable agricultural production),

1 See in this regard: "Krajowa Sieć Obszarów Wiejskich, 2009, retrieved 18.4.2016 from http://ksow.pl/wpr-po-2013-roku/propozycje-legislacyjne-ke/ekologizacja-wspolnej-polityki-rolnej-po-2013-r.html.

- environmental challenges (the problem of depletion of natural resources, including water resources and soil, which is a threat to the extinction of some plant and animal species and loss of biodiversity)
- territorial challenges (rural development problems resulting from the structure of demographic changes, economic and social development, including depopulation, and the relocation of investment and business centers)".[2]

The Common Agricultural Policy in order to tackle these challenges aimed to contribute to the implementation of the "Europe 2020 Strategy" by using:

- "smart growth – improving resource efficiency and competitiveness with technical knowledge and innovation,
- intelligent and sustainable development by securing renewable bases for food and foodstuff production, ensuring sustainable land management and combating the loss of biodiversity, the promotion of research and development,
- the development of a social-inclusion policy by increasing the economic potential of rural areas and the stimulation of employment".[3]

Achieving green growth in the agricultural sector and in the rural economy, means striving for economic development, in order to prevent environmental degradation, as a way of improving the quality of life (The European Commission 2010).

The objectives of the reformed Common Agricultural Policy, are:

- "profitable food production (supporting farm income-activities, improving the competitiveness of the agricultural sector, financial support for farms with hard and naturally-limited conditions)
- sustainable management of natural resources and climate action (ensuring sustainable production activities, green growth and innovation, mitigation of climate change)
- balanced territorial development (support for rural employment and maintaining the social structure of suburban areas, improving the economy of the countryside)".[4]

---

2 Ministerstwo Rolnictwa i Rozwoju Wsi, 2009, retrieved 23.4.2016 from file:///C:/Documents%20and%20Settings/Anna/Moje%20dokumenty/Downloads/Przysz%C5%82o%C5%9B%C4%87%20WPR%20po%202013%20roku.pdf.

3 "Parlament Europejski 2013", retrieved 18.4.2016 from http://www.europarl.europa.eu/news/pl/news-room/20131118IPR25538/Polityka-rolna-UE-na-lata-2014-2020-zielona-i-sprawiedliwa.

4 Ibid.

Organic Farming: Clarifying the Concept

The concept of organic farming can be explained under the provisions of EU Council Regulation No 20192/91 of 24 June 1991, dealing with organic agriculture and the labelling of its products and foodstuffs (Council Regulation no. 20192/91). It should be emphasized, however, that this regulation – although it is perceived as being the most important, internationally-accepted act in terms of organic agriculture – does not contain an explicit definition of "organic farming" – although it does clarify and define practices that are regarded as falling within its scope (Żelezik 2009, pp. 156–157). A commonly-used principle with regard to organic farming is, that "the only method that is permitted, is what the criteria allow us to use. Therefore, only such means of production are acceptable as have been mentioned in these criteria" (Tyburski / Żakowska-Biemans 2007, pp. 7–13).

The European Commission, in turn, defines organic agriculture as follows: "Organic farming is a way of producing food that respects natural life cycles. It minimizes the human impact on the environment and operates as naturally as possible…".[5] Traditional practices for organic farming, included by the Commission are:

- the use of long-term crop rotation
- a radical movement against the use of chemical pesticides and synthetic fertilizers
- a total prohibition of genetically modified organisms
- the use of own management resources
- the breeding of animals in a free-stall system
- the use of appropriate and suitable animal husbandry practices for the particular type of breeding in operation.[6]

According to the International Federation of Organic Agricultural Movements (IFOAM), organic agriculture is a collection of various, detailed concepts of farming, compatible with the requirements of soil, plants and animals, and its ultimate goal is the production of food with high quality standards, while simultaneously maintaining biological balance in the environment. It is assumed, with regard to organic farming, that the relationship between agriculture, the environment, and social and economic issues, should be considered.

---

5 See: The European Commission, 2014, Agriculture and Rural Development, Organic Farming, *Producing Organic*, retrieved 7.4.2016 from http://ec.europa.eu/agriculture/organic/organic-farming/what-is-organic-farming/producing-organic/index_en.htm.

6 Ibid.

Basic principles of ecological agriculture as adopted by IFOAM during its 2005 congress in Adelaide, Australia, are:

- "health (intensifying the health of soil, plants, animals, humans and the Earth, as part of an indivisible unity)
- ecology (organic farming operates on the model of ecological systems, whereas the circulation of matter and energy-flow in nature, is part of these processes, and helps to sustain them)
- justice (organic farming is shaped by relations that guarantee a decent life for people in a common environment)
- care (organic farming is carried out prudently, in the sense of responsibility for the health and well-being of present and future generations, and the natural balance in the environment)".[7]

Statistics on Organic Farming in the European Union

More than 11.6 million hectares of agricultural land in Europe (with 10.3 million ha representing European Union countries) were cultivated in an organic manner by more than 340,000 agricultural producers (in the European Union the number of agricultural processors amounted to 260,000) at the end of 2014. It is estimated that approximately 2.4 % of all cropland usage in Europe in 2014, involved organic farming methods. Data published by FiBL and IFOAM in the report "The World of Organic Agriculture 2016" indicate that over 27 % of all organic farmland in the world belongs to EU member states. Compared to 2013, there was an increase in the total land-area cultivated organically in the EU by approximately 0.3 million ha, in 2014. It is worth emphasizing here that during the last decade, a significant annual increase in organically-cultivated land in Europe and in the European Union, has been observed. Most important, however, is the fact that, since 2004, the total area of organically-cultivated land has doubled.[8]

---

7 Ibid., retrieved 20.4.2016.

8 See: Willer / Lernoud 2016, retrieved 26.4.2016 from https://shop.fibl.org/fileadmin/documents/shop/1698-organic-world-2016.pdf.

Fig. 1: Development of the organic area in Europe 1985–2013 (in million hectares).

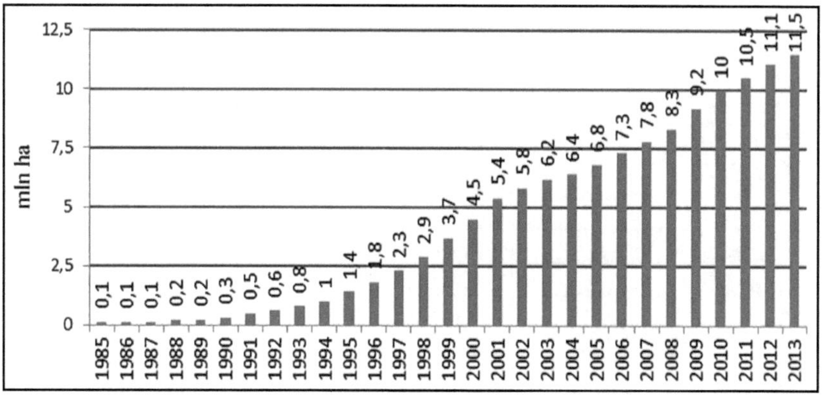

Source : Author's elaboration on the basis of Willer / Lernoud 2016; retrieved 26.4.2016 from https://shop.fibl.org/fileadmin/documents/shop/1698-organic-world-2016.pdf.

The countries with the largest area of land cultivated organically in 2014 were: Spain (1.2 million hectares), Italy (1.4 million ha) and France (1.1 million ha).

Fig. 2: The ten countries with the largest area of organic land in Europe in 2013 (in million ha).

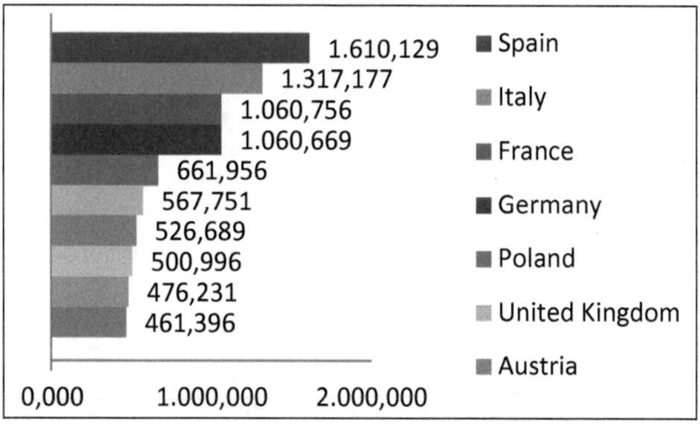

Source : Author's elaboration on the basis of Willer / Lernoud 2016; retrieved 26.4.2016 from https://shop.fibl.org/fileadmin/documents/shop/1698-organic-world-2016.pdf.

Eight European countries stand out in that the share of organically-cultivated land is more than 10 % of all cultivated land. These countries include: Lichtenstein (more than 31 %), Austria (19.5 %), and Sweden (16.3 %). Retail sales of organic products in Europe amounted to 26.2 billion Euro in 2014 (23.9 billion in the European Union as a whole), an increase of 7.6 % compared to the figure for 2013.[9]

Fig. 3: Shares in organic agricultural land in Europe in 2014 (in %).

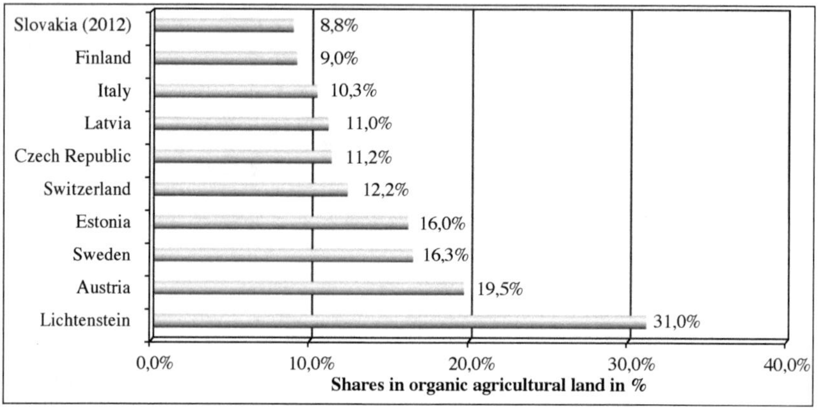

Source : Author's elaboration on the basis of Willer / Lernoud 2016; retrieved 26.4.2016 from https://shop.fibl.org/fileadmin/documents/shop/1698-organic-world-2016.pdf.

The largest market for organic products and organic farming in 2014 was Germany, where retail sales of organic products amounted to 7.9 billion Euro. Another country with great potential in the context of the sales of organic products was France (retail sales amounting to 4.8 billion Euro), as well as the United Kingdom, where sales of organic products have yielded 2.3 billion Euro. The biggest surprise in 2014 and 2015 proved to be Sweden, where the market for organic products had increased by more than 40 %. This is even more surprising due to the fact that the Swedish market is perceived as being an already well-developed and well-established one. In a world perspective, European countries are characterized by a very high market-share of organic products (they are in the very top-rank), as well as by a very high consumption of organic products per capita. The three European countries which had more than a 5 % share of the global market for organic products in 2011 were: Denmark 7.6 %, Switzerland 7.1 %, and Austria 6.5 %. These countries achieved an even higher market-

9 Willer / Lernoud 2016, retrieved 26.4.2016 from https://shop.fibl.org/fileadmin/documents/shop/1698-organic-world-2016.pdf.

share for individual products or product groups (e.g. egg market) in 2014. Six European countries reported that, within their borders, the consumption of organic products exceeded 100 Euro per capita. Switzerland, however, leads the way in this regard with a per capita consumtion of organic products exceding 221 Euro in value.

Conclusions

The analysis shows the growing importance of the European Union's Common Agricultural Policy and the implementation of its main objectives, in particular under the provisions of the last reform dating to 2013. This includes the increasing of financial support for active farmers and the simplifying of procedure for farmers who use environmental-friendly farming methods (including organic farming), when applying for funds. Furthermore, actions under The Common Agricultural Policy are targeted towards investment in research and development, the use of modern technologies and machinery in the cultivation of agriculture, the promotion of employment and entrepreneurship in rural areas, and the supporting of young farmers. These objectives are regarded as a priority by member countries, especially regarding the upgrading and modernization of agricultural markets. An analysis of the current state of the European Union's organic farming situation confirmed that the implementation of measures arising from the reform of The Common Agricultural Policy after 2013, not only determines the formation process, but also enhances the development of organic farming strategies. Progress in organic farming is particularly important from the point of view of food security, environmental protection, the conservation of natural resources, the revitalization of agriculture, technological infrastructure development, and the professional activation of farmers. It should be noted, however, that the future of the European market, including organic farming, is a complex process, that involves not only adjusting to the requirements posed by organic farming itself, but also one that necessitates the construction of institutional support and adequate preparation for this kind of agricultural production.

List of References

Printed

Baldock, David / Hart, Kaley (eds.): *Dobra Publiczne i Interwencja Publiczna w Rolnictwie* ("Public Goods and Public Intervention in Agriculture"). Urząd Publikacji Komisji Europejskiej: Brussels 2011.

Hamm, Ulrich / Gronefeld, Friederike / Halpin, Darren (eds.): *The European Market for Organic Food: Revised and Updated Analysis*. School of Management and Business. The University of Wales, Aberystwyth: Aberystwyth 2004.

Król, Monika A.: *Ekologizacja Wspólnej Polityki Rolnej – zagadnienia prawne* ("Greening of the Common Agricultural Policy – Legal Issues"). Wydział Prawa i Administracji. *Polityki Europejskie, Finanse i Marketing* 10(59), 2013, pp. 402–421.

Maciejczak, Mariusz: *Zasada Wzajemnej Zgodności-Działanie Służące Poprawie Jakości w Unii Europejskiej* ("Cross Compliance – The Measure Challenging Improvement of Quality in European Union"), Postzrównoważony Rozwój: Przestrzeń, Natura, Kultura i Jakość, Wydawnictwo Uniwersytet Sorbona IV, Paryż 2007.

Piworowicz, Jowita: *Wspólna Polityka Rolna i jej wpływ na rozwój rolnictwa w Polsce* ("The Common Agricultural Policy and its Impact on the Evolution of Agriculture in Poland"). Uniwersytet Warmińsko-Mazurski w Olsztynie: Olsztyn 2015.

The European Commission. "Communication from the Commission to the European Parliament, the Council, the European Economic and Social Committee and the Committee of the Regions: The CAP towards 2020: Meeting the challenges of the future of food, natural resources and territorial challenges". European Commission: Brussels 2010.

Tyburski, Józef / Żakowska-Biemans, Sylwia: *Wprowadzenie do rolnictwa ekologicznego* ("Introduction to Organic Agriculture"). Wydawnictwo SGGW: Warszawa 2007.

Żelezik, Monika: *Dlaczego rolnictwo ekologiczne?* ("Why Organic Agriculture?"), Rocznik Świętokrzyski. Ser. B – Nauki Przyr. 30: 155–166, Polska Akademia Nauk – Oddział w Krakowie, Kieleckie Towarzystwo Naukowe, Samodzielny Zakład Ochrony i Kształtowania Środowiska Uniwersytetu Humanistyczno-Przyrodniczego Jana Kochanowskiego w Kielcach, Wydawnictwo Polskiej Akademii Nauk: Kielce 2009.

Internet

"International Federation for Organic Agriculture Movement, 2006", retrieved 20.4.2016 from *The IFOAM Norms For Organic Production and Processing*, Germany http://www.ifoam.bio/en/ifoam-norms.

"International Federation for Organic Agriculture Movements, 2005", *Principles of Organic Agriculture*, Adelaide, retrieved 20 April 2016 from https://shop.fibl.org/fileadmin/documents/shop/1698-organic-world-2016.pdf.

"Krajowa Sieć Obszarów Wiejskich, 2009", *Ekologizacja" Wspólnej Polityki Rolnej po 2013 roku* ("Greening of the Common Agricultural Policy after 2013"), retrieved 18.4.2016 from http://ksow.pl/wpr-po-2013-roku/propozycje-legislacyjne-ke/ekologizacja-wspolnej-polityki-rolnej-po-2013-r.html.

"Ministerstwo Rolnictwa i Rozwoju Wsi, 2009", *Wspólna Polityka Rolna po 2013 roku*" ("Greening of The Common Agricultural Policy"), Warszawa (2009), retrieved 23.4.2016 from file: ///C:/Documents%20and%20Settings/Anna/Moje%20dokumenty/Downloads/Przysz%C5%82o%C5%9B%C4%87%20WPR%20po%202013%20roku.pdf.

"Parlament Europejski, 2013, Komunikat Prasowy" *Polityka rolna UE na lata 2014–2020: zielona i sprawiedliwa*" ("EU Agricultural Policy for 2014–2020: Green and Fair"), retrieved 18.4.2016 from http://www.europarl.europa.eu/news/pl/news-room/20131118IPR25538/Polityka-rolna-UE-na-lata-2014-2020-zielona-i-sprawiedliwa.

"The European Commission, 2014, Agriculture and Rural Development, Organic Farming", *Producing Organic,* retrieved 7.4.2016 from http://ec.europa.eu/agriculture/organic/organic-farming/what-is-organic-farming/producing-organic/index_en.html.

Willer, H. / Lernoud, J., 2016: *The World of Organic Agriculture. Statistics and Emerging Trends 2016*, Research Institute for Organic Agriculture (FiBL), Frick and IFOAM-Organics International, Bonn, retrieved 26.4.2016 from https://shop.fibl.org/fileadmin/documents/shop/1698-organic-world-2016.pdf.

Eszter Kisbán*

Choose Local, Try Organic, Think Ecological – Actions and Ideas in the Recent Hungarian Food Realm

Abstract: *After earlier "traditional", local, healthy, and ecological are the current keywords linked to the promotion and choice of food in Hungary. Such a shift of focus has been widespread, and still continues, in much of Europe. Here, two phenomena are used to characterize the state of affairs in this regard in this country. The first is the changing concept, form and actors of the food market. The other recalls three decades of organic farming and organic food use.*

Symbolically, the year 1970 is widely seen as marking the birth of the modern environmental movement.[1] The food realm is an important segment of it. The keywords *Choose Local, Try Organic, Think Ecological,* indicate widespread actions and intentions in much of Europe. In the case of Hungary, I shall discuss two phenomena in this context, highlighting just the milestones of their regional development. The first is the return of farmers' markets since the year 2006. The other is the introduction of organic farming and organic food in the period from 1983 to the present day. I intend to present the timeline of events for comparison within the European context. Emphasis will be placed on hard data, that is, less on ideas and more on actions.

Food Market in Changing Times

In the three recent urban generations there are three different concepts of a food market. All the three variants have been experienced in action by the oldest generation only. Looking back from today, the types of these markets can be called the traditional, the conventional, and the recently-arrived new form of the "farmers' market". Preceding these forms were the now historical markets, known only by descriptions and pictures. The first transitional period, that from the historical to the traditional, began in the 1890s. From traditional

* Eszter Kisbán is emeritus professor (European ethnology) of the University of Pécs, Hungary.

1 The first observance of the "Earth Day", USA, 1970. Ausubel / Victor / Wernick 1995, pp. 2–15.

to conventional, i.e. the next period of change unfolded in the 1960s, and the addition of the farmers' market followed in the early 21st century.

Industrialization in Hungary, followed by the rapid urbanization of the country, began in the second half of the 19th century and accelerated very quickly in its last two decades. In the food realm, this development brought with it, e.g., the specialization of villages in vegetable growing concentrated around urban centres. In 1873, neighbouring cities were merged to form the capital city with the present name, Budapest, with the river Danube dividing the Buda and the Pest sides. Farmers and small first-hand retailers informally ran the "historical" food-markets on the streets and small squares of the old town centre, sitting one by one under their own market-umbrellas without any stalls. The city authorities decided to change this situation and to concentrate the exchange of goods in special buildings – that is, to open a new period of markets, the one we now call the "traditional" food markets. Seven market halls were planned, five on the Pest side and two on the Buda side of the city. The markets in Pest, the busier and more densely-populated part, should had been opened all at the same time, preferably in the millennium year of the country. In fact, they were opened one year later, in 1897.[2] With the status of ancient monuments, the elegant market-hall buildings still function as food markets today. The halls were built different in size but intentionally to the same design. With undivided airspace they are like three-nave churches, built with or without balconies. Prestigious cast-iron columns support the roof, the balconies, and divide the interior. The front and back doors are wide enough for the horse-drawn wagons of their first decades of operation. Farmers, retailers and wholesalers were all obliged to use the halls, and here even auctions were held in their early years. Later, the auctions and wholesalers left the halls, the number of retailers began to increase, but farmers ruled the scene and were characteristic of the market halls up to the late 1950s. The retailer also dealt with products of the country. That composition of sales, sellers and products is seen as the old "traditional" form of the market. Today, the type of the food markets is, by and large, the "conventional" one for the customer, and it is a place of small and large retailers with goods representing both national and global products, and with unprocessed and industrially-processed foods. Farmers are in the minority nowadays.

2 See further: Balázs 2009/4, retrieved 8.11.2016 from http://mult-kor.hu/20091215_vasarcsarnokok_szuletese.

The social structure of the traditional system changed dramatically when farmers left the food markets en masse because they had lost command of the agricultural products. With the forced collectivization in the early socialist era, most of the farmers lost the private ownership of their land. It was only later in this period that co-owner members of the large collective farms were themselves allowed to use a small holding once again. As a result, their products, such as vegetables, fruit, eggs, milk, poultry, and processed meat in small quantities, could come to the urban markets once more. Private farming returned after the change of the political and economic regime in 1989 and, while some of the few small farmers and smallholders again visit the conventional markets, they do not dominate them.[3]

During the 20th century further market halls were built in Budapest and in some other cities, all in the style of their time. Nevertheless, most of the domestic food markets or part of a market were run in the open air. The presence or absence of farmers and retailers at these markets developed in a manner similar to that stated above. Nevertheless, all recent generations have had some experience of direct producers like those of former markets when the farmers' market par excellence appeared as a novelty during recent years, as an alternative to the conventional food markets.

Farmers' Markets of Local, Seasonal Products

Compared with the broader neighbourhood in Middle Europe but also with the wider European scene, recent farmers' markets appeared quite late in Hungary. In Munich, the capital city of Bavaria in Germany, for example, the first such markets opened in May and October 1989. By their 25th anniversary in 2014, eleven farmers' markets were operating for over 1.5 million inhabitants in that city. In the UK, the farmers' market, which opened in the historic city of Bath, South West England, in 1997, is presented as the first such market in the country. Referring expressis verbis to the UN Agenda 21, an action plan for the 21st century on sustainability, the local government initiated, and a farmers' association organized, and still operates, the large Bath market. This has remained the only one in the city which has a population of nearly 90 thousand people.[4]

---

3 For more about the political and socio-economic changes in the period, with turning points in 1989 and 2004, see Báti in this volume.

4 For information about the Munich market, see: https://www.muenchner-bauernmaerkte.de/; and for the Bath Farmer's Market, UK, see http://www.bathfarmersmarket.co.uk, retrieved 18.8.2016.

The Beginnings

The first two Hungarian farmers' markets opened in 2006 and 2007, respectively, with the third pioneering as recently as 2010. All three were based on private initiatives. The first was the only one started in an urban context, in the capital city Budapest. There the market place was chosen in a green suburban area (Máriaremete), next to a historic pilgrimage church, 14 km distant from the city centre, in the vicinity of a small, incorporated village. The initiator in this case was an electrical engineer with inherited concern about the countryside, its farmers, and fair market opportunities. Until its dissolution after WW II., his father had been an executive officer of *Hangya* ("The Ant"), the national Co-operative for joint purchase and sales of the members, including a farmer's department. The two other early markets were run in rural areas, in the type of villages where urban folk regularly turn up for shorter or longer periods as a matter of course. Both markets operated in nice, quiet areas, one in the vicinity of Lake Balaton (Káptalantóti 2007) and the other at the Danube Bend (Nagymaros 2010). The young initiators in these cases were, respectively, a lady with a degree in bioengineering, who ran a garden there herself, and a male psychologist, with a second degree in environmental policy. Both invited the local farmers to support the markets with their products, and both opened the markets in their own villages with, more or less, the support, of the local authorities. Neither of them expected to make a living from the enterprise. Beyond the immediate goals of enabling farmers to make a fair income, and of giving consumers the pleasure of having fresh, healthy and tasty food available, both of these initiators were familiar with, and serious about the philosophy and concerns regarding sustainability, fair trade and rural development. All of these three farmers' markets have flourished and are well known to the present day.

A Metropolitan Scene

The capital city Budapest with its 1.8 million inhabitants is located in the middle of the country. In the city, the distance from the centre to the edges is between 13 and 26 km as the crow flies. After the incorporation of 23 surrounding small cities and villages in 1930, the capital, today, is divided into 23 districts. The districts numbered 1 to 14 cover the former city area and are surrounded by the nine new ones.

In order to look at the recent food markets, a certain house in district 8 will be used as an observation point, for illustration purposes. This address is in the inner city, in the urban band next to the medieval nucleus, in a zone which was developed during the 19th century.

From this point of departure, there are 10 food markets within walking distance, that is within a few steps and a distance of 1.8 km, or, in other words, between a 3 and a 23-minute walk away The markets are situated like a chain in a band involving four older municipal districts, numbered as 6, 7, 8, and 9 today. 4 of the 10 markets run inside market halls. These are 4 of the 5 representative halls of the Pest side of the city, opened in 1897, and already mentioned above. Each of these districts have their own hall. The largest building, in district 9 on the banks of the river Danube, with its 10,000 m^2 floor area, has always been the Main Market Hall of the city of Budapest. Retailers in these halls operate every weekday. Farmers, with their own products, have never been excluded from these halls, but they commonly avoid the overwhelming competition of the retailers today. Having noticed that farmers' markets are becoming trendy, one of the market halls installed a prominent farmers' section, with stalls inside its walls, after recent renovation of the building. There are 5 further farmers' markets in the area. All of them operate outdoors under shelters, with stands, stalls and tables, and between 10 and 50 of them typically operate from one to two days each week. Unique amongst them is the *Simple Garden* farmers' market in district 7, as will be discussed below. Such density of markets in general, and of farmer's markets in particular, is exceptional both in the capital city and in the countryside. An organic market in District 12, now the largest in the country, is 4.7 km away by car from the same point of departure mentioned above, and will be discussed later in this paper.

Agrarian and Rural Development Policy

It was during the years 2011 and 2012 that the National Central Direction first took action to promote the introduction of farmers' markets, consisting of local products of the country. Urged on by home as well as international developments, the Ministry of Agriculture and Rural Development, step by step, developed and produced legislation and regulations for farmers' markets, catering for small and medium sized family farms, and their local products. The completed regulation came into force in June 2012 and enabled farmers' markets to start and operate with remarkable ease.[5]

The basic rules discussed the points that were already elaborated in former international regulations. The core criteria included: the definition of small and medium sized farms, the concept of local product and producer, as well as primary and

---

5 See National Food Chain Safety Office (*NÉBIH*) on the farmers' markets: legislation and regulations, http://portal.nebih.gov.hu/-/a-helyi-termeloi-piacok-uzemelteteserol, retrieved 18.8.2016.

processed produce, certification of food safety, the presence of somebody from the farm at the stall, and the availability of information about the whole business for the consumer. I only mention, that "local" was defined as being within a radius of 40 kilometres around the farm, or within the county boundary, but using the markets in the capital city open to everybody. Why was it decided to choose the local? Reflecting the argumentation put forward for the wide public it was mentioned, as a first level, the immediate interest of the consumer in health, the freshness and safety of the food, and the personal meeting with the producer. At the next level, the countryside and the national economy were emphasized. This included taking responsibility for the environment with its nature, cultivation, and people, and especially for the small farmers, and their income and living conditions. The common consumer would not, as yet, be familar with the concept of sustainable development.

During the preparations, the first farmers' market of the new regime had already opened in Budapest to model and demonstrate the co-operation of the Ministry of Agriculture, the farmers' representatives, and the local council. The personal opening address by the minister confirmed the expectation that favourable legislation was on the way. The extensive media coverage that ensued, was the primary aim of the occasion. The place for the market was chosen in a hurry and was not as yet either friendly or exemplary (on the edge of District 10). As part of a quick nationwide investigation on food markets for the Ministry of Agriculture, 41 operating markets had, by the end of 2011, responded, and had stated that they could be seen as farmers' market or as moving in the suggested direction.[6]

In October 2011, a small company of young independent initiators started a Saturday evening farmer's market in the entertainment area of District 7 of Budapest. While waiting for the expected favourable legislation, the event was stated to be an experiment which would take place once a month. The market's location in Budapest was in the small inner yard of a three-storeyed late-19th century, downtown dwelling-house. Under the name "*The Simple*" or the "*Simple-garden*", the whole run-down unit was already famous as an iconic postmodern youth nightspot with appropriate music, temporary exhibitions, and amusing decoration. There were manifold daylight programmes as well. One of the operators brought personal experience from the above-mentioned farmers' market at the Danube Bend. In early June of the following year (2012), that is immediately after the new market-regulation came in force, *The Simple's* farmer's market legitimized itself as a permanent institution, operating every Sunday morning. With the maximum

6 In this connection see: Juhász / Szabó 2011–2012, retrieved 25.7.2016 from https://www.aki.gov.hu/Piacok.

number of 50 stalls, it is a top-quality market, a unique institution, and is well-frequented by young and elderly consumers alike.

The rather new wholesale flower-market in Budapest District 13 was also quick to start a Saturday morning farmers' market in May 2012, on the day off from its main business.

On the last Friday of June, the month when the Market Law Act came into force, the Ministry of Agriculture opened a farmers' market under the arcades of its own building. Called the "*Rural Sample*", it operated with 50 stalls every Friday morning. The market was on the nation's main square, just across from the Parliament building, and got rather loud press coverage. It worked for ten month there, until the whole square was closed for construction works in 2013. The square reopened, but without the food market, which never returned to that high profile location.

As a result of successful co-operation, the local council of District 7 and the "Hungarian Market Co-operative" opened the farmers' market along the green garden of the church on the "Square of the Roses" in August 2012. The Co-operative itself was set up at the very end of 2011 for the purpose of building contacts between farmers and consumers.[7]

Fig 1: Farmers' market on the Roses' Square, Budapest 7 (Photo: Hungarian Market Co-operative, 2012).

7 Here I thank the Magyar Piac Szövetség ("Hungarian Market Co-operative") for the photo of the Rózsák tere (the "Roses' Square" market).

The ministry expected that a good hundred working farmers' markets would be operating nationwide by the end of that year. Unfortunately, there are no expert statistics about them to date. In Budapest alone, the number fluctuates between 35 and 40.[8] The most-frequented market days for farmers and consumers are Saturday, Friday and Thursday, in that order. The ruling vision for the location of a farmers' market is open air in green surroundings. Even in the densely built-up areas of the capital city, most organizers found spots next to small green parks or just some large trees. There is a striking opposition between this trend and the still-appreciated spectacular market halls from the 19th century.

The Actors

The institution of the modern farmers' market penetrated the country after quite a late start. The pioneering innovators were committed individuals with different intentions but neither of them came from among the farmers or from the ranks of the agricultural intelligentsia. Thus the adoption of the farmers' markets progressed rather slowly. The process accelerated only when the relevant institutional actors realised their duty towards progressing the markets and the opportunity to be gained from doing so. First in the 2010s, central government, local and regional authorities, as well as farmer organizations, and local and professional associations, supported the development wholeheartedly. The changing approach was followed by major positive media coverage. Using the farmers' markets is already trendy, and public figures and other well-known people are happy to be seen there.

The farmers take care that the prices should not be higher than those at good quality retailers in the conventional market. Using these new markets makes the consumers think more about the advantages of seasonality, the development of the region, and even in some cases about the wider sustainability concept. All in all, farmers' markets are firmly integrated into the country by now. They are reasonably priced, well known by the public, increasingly supported by all the involved parties, and still in a period of continuous growth.

Some small organic farmers also use the farmers' markets regularly or on an occasional basis. Their sign-boards announce their organic specialization and whether or not it is certified for the period in question. The specialized organic market preceded the new general farmers' markets by decades. According to wide-

---

8 For discussion of the number of farmers' markets see: *Local Product Online Magazine* 2014.11.24, retrieved 28.8.2016 from http://www.helyitermekmagazin.hu/2014/, and National Agrarian Chamber, interactive list, 9.10.2016 from http://nak.hu/termeloipiac-kereso.

spread consumers' interpretation, the organic market is often seen as a special variant of the farmers' market. The similarities are mostly seen in traits such as fresh, local, healthy, and the presence of the farmer at the market stall. However, a large proportion of households are not yet familiar with either the full concept of organic food and farming or the operation of the few organic markets in the country.

Fig 2: Eco-Market, BioCulture Federation, Budapest 12 (Photo Máté Barabás 2016).

Organic Food

In a survey of the operating food markets carried out for the government in 2011–2012, 16 organic markets were listed. 14 operated in cities and 2 in holiday-resort villages of the Balaton area. This list included the capital city, but only 8 of the country's total of 19 county seats.[9]

After three decades of early experience with organic farming, consumption of organic food is still very low, countrywide. Where does the process of reshaping the meals stand? What kinds of attitudes do people have to organic food? How

9 In this connection see: Juhász / Szabó 2011–2012, retrieved 25.7.2016 from https://www.aki.gov.hu/Piacok.

large are the groups of consumers? What is the volume of consumption? What are the favourite organic products on the market? What are the information nets like?

A few representative surveys help with a review of the sitution. These include the following aspects, although unfortunately not all of them are to be found in the same data collections: the size of the consumer group: the buyers, non-buyers, and self-sufficient households; the organic products' share of the total market in food; the average value of the consumption of organic products on a national scale; and the buyers' supply sources. Where international surveys, including Hungarian data, provide comparison, I shall refer to the English-language versions.

The first representative national survey of organic food, enquiring about consumer attitudes to and frequency of purchase of this kind of food, was carried out by the market research institute GfK Hungaria, in 2006. At the opposite ends of the scale were the 3.1 % of the households who bought organic food on a weekly basis, and the 76 % who never bought such food. Further segments between the two groups were the bi-weekly, once a month, and less than once a month, purchasers – and the over 13 % "casual" buyers.[10] For the same year, the IFOAM survey indicated a 2-Euro average consumption-rate of organic food, and a market share of 0.2 % of the total food market for Hungary (Padel / Schaac / Willer 2009, Table 36, p. 162).

The next representative survey is from 2012 (Szente 2014, pp. 26–27). It seems that a wider group of the frequent consumers might stand at 10 % today, including a nearly 4 % strong hard-core group of the most dedicated, and most frequent consumers, and the group of the committed, regular, but less-frequent consumers. At the opposite end, there is still the large non-consumer group of 60–70 %. This includes people who do not know about organic food, who do not see it as being important, who firmly reject it, and many who cannot afford it. In between, there are the people with a positive attitude towards organic food, a strong group of about 30 %, who know about such food, who consider purchasing it, and who buy it now and then. This is what the following Table 1 would tell about attitudes towards organic food.

---

10 For attitudes to, and frequency of, purchase of organic food see: GfK Hungaria, and Conscious Shopper, GfK Hungaria 2007. Summary in Conscious Shopper Tudatosvásárló-online 1 February 2007, retrieved 18.8.2016 from http://tudatosvasarlo.hu/cikk/biokorkep-magyarok-tobbsege-egyaltalan-nem-vasarol-bioelelmiszert.

Table 1: Purchase of organic food: the gap between attitudes and behavior, 2012.

Attitudes to organic origin of food				
attention to planning to purchase	%		Attention to the buying decision	%
important	10.5		yes	3.7
partial interest	28.2		partial	26.2
not important	59.8		no attention	70.1
cannot answer	1.8			

(Source: Szente 2014, Figs. 1–2. Diagrams)

Quite a substantial difference is evident, between those who considered organic food important (10.5 %), and those who would/could choose organic at the actual food-purchase stage (3.7 %) – that is between attitudes and behaviour in relation to organic food. With the whole Hungarian population of 10 millions, the 3.7 % regular buyers of organic food would amount to 370,000 people, with household, nationwide.

For the same period, the 2014 international survey gave the organic share of the total food retail sales in Hungary as being still far below 1 %: it recalled the figure 0.3 % from 2009, and the value of average consumption as amounting to 2.5 Euro – no better figures have been published subsequently. The recent domestic estimate of the share is between 0.5 and 1 per cent at best. The ten leading countries in terms of organic food consumption reported figures between 2.2 % – in both Croatia and Italy at the bottom of the group – and 7.6 % – in Switzerland – at the top of that group, in 2014. In the same year, the average spending for organic food was 35.5 Euro in Europe, while the same was between 221 and 54 Euro at the two ends of the group of the ten countries leading in this respect, Switzerland and Norway, respectively (Willer et al. 2016, Table 1 (p. 21); Fig. 3 (p. 26); Fig. 6 (p. 29).[11]

Asking consumers about the sources of organic food supply instead of asking about retail sales only, brought self-sufficiency into the picture in the 2006 survey. An estimate about the use of sales channels for 2012 was presented at a high

11 For the 2009 consumption data for Hungary see Dezsény / Drexler 2014, pp. 137–139.

profile research conference by one of the best experts. It indicates the increase in supermarket sales and the use of specialized shops in this context.[12]

Table 2: Source of supply of organic foods, relative importance.

marketing channels and own product	**representative, multiple choice, % 2006**	**expert estimate, % 2012**
supermarket, hypermarkets	43	60
smaller general retailers	18	
specialized shop	15	20
online		6–7
direct from the farm		2–3
organic market	25	
organic market, fairs, occasional events		6–10
own products	17	not included

(Source: GfK Hungaria 2007; Frühwald 2012)

With multiple choice in the 2006 survey, consumers mentioned vegetables and fruit (42 %), fresh bread (30 %), fruit and vegetable juices (25 %), followed by muesli and yoghurt (25 %) as the most popular organic products purchased.[13] Organic muesli and yoghurt were just novelties in the supermarkets from abroad, such as Tesco and several others present in Hungary at that time, while the other preferred foods were bought fresh directly from the farmer at the market, or from a small-scale processor. Quite remarkable is the prominent place of fresh bread in the list as there was only one fully-specialized organic bakery in the country at that time.

A decade later, local produce is still the most popular of all the organic foods on sale, with milk products added to the previous groups. Successful products of direct sales are also jellies and pickles, dry noodles, fresh bakery goods, eggs,

12 See: GfK Hungaria, and Conscious Shopper, GfK Hungaria 2007). Summary in Conscious Shopper Tudatosvásárló-online 1 February 2007, retrieved 18.8.2016 from http://tudatosvasarlo.hu/cikk/biokorkep-magyarok-tobbsege-egyaltalan-nem-vasarol-bioelelmiszert); also Frühwald 2012, pp. 10–13.

13 See further: GfK Hungaria, and Conscious Shopper, GfK Hungaria 2007, retrieved 18.8.2016 from http://tudatosvasarlo.hu/cikk/biokorkep-magyarok-tobbsege-egyaltalan-nem-vasarol-bioelelmiszert.

and long-life meat products. Supermarkets are the main channels for easily-stored produce, such as the grain-mill products including flour, meal, muesli and groats, industrially-processed organic noodles, long-life meat products and fresh milk, all mainly from abroad, only partly from domestic processors. It was only in the mid-2010s that supermarkets dared to fill double pages of advertising weeklies with organic produce. Foods on offfer from many small "health stores" also include genuine long-life organic foods. Marketing experts estimate that organic sales of all the product groups and marketing channels together would, at this stage, include several hundred kinds of organic foods.

Organic food is not included in school meals, and only one hospital is reported to have ordered a regular delivery of organic vegetables for its kitchen. The only restaurant with a dominant organic choice operates in a county seat city and is run by one of the most important organic farmers in the country. Organic is not a topic of far-reaching advertisements, and no trendy opinion leader ever mentions organic food publicly.

Important sources of information and inspiration about organic food for the wider public, are the visible presence of the farms, and the institutions of the organic world.

Fig 3: Eco-Market, BioCulture Federation, Budapest 12 (Photo Máté Barabás 2016).

Organic Farming

The registration of market-orientated organic farming started in 1988, when there were 15 farms with 1,000 hectares of land between them.[14] The recent 1,672 organic farms are to be found distributed all over the country. Only a few of them are large or medium in size, and many are small farms, amounting to 124,842 hectares in total. Apart from certified organic production, a number of small farmers and home gardeners also produce proper organic food for sale, in small quantities, but it is not always economical for them to pay for inspection and certification, as required of certified organic producers. The share of controlled organic land in the entire agricultural sector was 2.7 % in Hungary in 2014, 2.4 % in Europe, and an average of 5.7 % in the European Community at that time. 80 % to 90 % of total Hungarian organic production, predominantly consisting of the unprocessed cereals and the oil crops of the large farms, is exported. Most of the 257 certified organic processors are small manufacturers of fruit, vegetables, and milk and meat products for the domestic market (Willer / Meredith, 2016, pp. 190–198).[15] With this moderate size, organic farming is far ahead of organic food on tables.

Public discourse about organic agriculture began in the 1980s, i.e. almost a decade after the foundation of IFOAM, the International Federation of Organic Agriculture Movements, in 1972. Overcoming the resistance of official domestic policy, the start of a *BioCulture Club* in Budapest in 1983 was the inaugural event for the movement. Started by a communications expert and two agrarian engineers, early members of the club were weekend gardeners, environmentalists, and health-conscious people looking for natural therapies. Already by 1984, members joined the garden-design engineer and built an organic garden on the permanent ground of the Budapest Fair. Although for demonstration purposes only, it ran very successfully for twelve years. At the time of the first organic experiences on arable land, the not-for-profit organization *BioCulture* Association (*Biokultúra Egyesület*) was officially registered as an "association for organic agriculture, the environment and health", in 1987.[16] Their periodical *Biokultúra* was launched in 1989. Local and regional associations followed, then all joined

14 With rapid growth, 18 and then 49 farms operated on 1500 and 3000 hectares respectively in 1989 and 1990 (Solti 2012, p. 31).

15 See also Willer / Lernoud 2016, Table 49 (p. 200); Fig. 93 (p. 211); Table 55 (p. 223); Willer / Schaack / Lernoud / Meredith 2016, Table 1 (p. 21); Fig. 3 (p. 26); Fig. 6 (p. 29).

16 See Kovács / Frühwald, retrieved 20.8.2016 from http://www.organic-europe.net/country-info/hungary/country-report/2005.html.

in the national *BioCulture Federation* of regional and thematic sections in 2005 (*Biokultúra Szövetség*).

The *BioCulture* Association opened the first Hungarian organic market in Budapest. This was in 1991, and the open-air market on the Buda side of the city, was supported by the vegetables and fruit of 8–10 small organic gardeners, The stalls stood on a small intimate green square in front of a library. The market moved twice as it was in need of more space. The *Federation* proudly points out that the market has always been positioned "next door to culture", including in front of, or alongside, a library, a music school, or a theater.[17]

The Ecological Market

The "Eco-Market of the Hungarian BioCulture Federation", as it is called today, operates with a hundred sales' desks on the crowded 1,200 m^2 of its third location. The Federation opened a second market in 2009, operating on the green ground of a historic mansion house in the outskirts of the Buda side of the city.

The organic discourse started with the term "biological", which shortly became "bio" in this country. "Bio" was not changed in proper names of institutions and periodicals which started under that term, but the broader-focused "ecological" became the attribute in the official language in 2007. When the European Commission first regulated organic production and control in that year, each country chose the term for the official text in the national language. As organic farming is the main type of ecological farming, many of the countries opted for this term.[18] The term "Ecological" was used in the follow-up Hungarian domestic legislation, and turns attention towards the sustainability concept as well – after health and environment, as already pointed out.

Locally-grown organic food is seen as the symbol of eco food and ecological farming. The range of adequate values varies in different groups of consumers, extending from "palatable" to "sustainable", and including the terms fresh, healthy, secure, trustworthy, fair (trade), (socially) responsible, the farm and the farmer, the countryside, rural development, environment, and ecology. Several surveys, using small samples, investigated consumer attitudes towards organic food, of different social groups. Health consciousness seems to be the predominant driving

17 Seléndy 2009, retrieved 20.8.2016 from http://www.biokontroll.hu/cms/index.php?option=com_content&view=article&id=447:oekopiaci-kerdesek&catid=111:biokereskedelem&Itemid=43.

18 Council Regulation (EC) No 834 / 2007, and COMMISSION REGULATION (EC) No 889/2008 (http://eur-lex.europa.eu/legal-content), retrieved 10.8.2016.

force in this context. Looking for the attitudes of the so-called LOHAS (Lifestyles of Health and Sustainability) consumer group, a large representative survey was recently completed in the field of marketing research. Using a method of value segmentation, the author was able to, firstly, sort out the sustainability-committed larger consumer-group in the sample, and the LOHAS part of it as the second step (Rácz 2014). Certainly, at the other end of the sustainability-conscious lifestyle-variants are the ecovillagers, whether buying or growing food, farming towards self-sufficiency, or engaged in market gardening. The ten Hungarian ecovillages are, themselves, quite different in this regard (Farkas 2015, pp. 1–9).

List of References

Printed

Ausubel, Jesse H. / Victor, David G. / Wernick, Iddo K.: "The Environment Since 1970". *The Nature and Implications of Environmental Change* 1(3), 1995, pp. 2–15.

Dezsény, Zoltán / Drexler, Dóra: "Country Report: Hungary". In Meredith, Stephen / Willer, Helga (eds.): *Organic in Europe. Prospects and Development* (IFOAM EU Group: Bruxelles 2014), pp. 137–139.

Frühwald, Ferenc: "A biogazdálkodás és a biotermékek helye a médiában és a kereskedelemben" ("Organic Farming, Organic Products in the Media and on the Market"). In Ökológiai Mezőgazdasági Kutatóintézet (Research Institute of Organic Agricultur) (ed.): *Az ökológiai gazdálkodás hazai helyzete: Trendek és kitörési pontok* ("Organic Farming in Hungary: Trends and Breakout Points"). Szent István Egyetemi Kiadó: Gödöllő 2012, pp. 10–13.

Padel, Susanne / Schaack, Diana / Willer, Helga: "Development of the Organic Market in Europe". In Willer, Helga / Kilcher, Lukas (eds.): *The World of Organic Agriculture. Statistics and Emerging Trends 2009.* FIBL-IFOAM Report. FiBL, Frick and IFOAM-Organics International: Bonn 2009, pp. 155–163. Table 36, p. 162.

Rácz, Georgina: "Az értékek változásának és a fenntartható fejlődés trendjének hatása a hazai élelmiszerfogyasztásra" ("Effects of Value Transformation and Trend of Sustainable Development on Domestic Food Consumption'). Agroinform: Budapest 2014.

Solti, Gábor: "A hazai ökogazdálkodás és a biokultúra válsága, a kilábalás lehetséges útjai", ("Organic Farming in Hungary, Crisis and Possible Ways of Recovery"). In [Ökológiai Mezőgazdasági Kutatóintézet (Research Institute of Organic Agriculture) ed.,] *Az ökológiai gazdálkodás hazai helyzete: Trendek és kitörési pontok* ("Organic Farming in Hungary: Trends and Breakout Points"). Szent István Egyetemi Kiadó: Gödöllő 2012, pp. 29–37.

Szente, Viktoria: "Szeretjük a bioélelmiszereket, de sok a korlát" ("Organic is Attractive, but there are Many Obstacles to Buying"). *Biokultúra* 25 (4), 2014, pp. 26–27.

Willer, Helga / Lernoud, Julia (eds.): *The World of Organic Agriculture: Statistics and Emerging Trends* (Research Institute of Organic Agriculture (FiBL), Frick and IFOAM–Organics International: Bonn 2016 (= *Yearbook, Organics International* 2016).

Willer, Helga / Meredith, Stephen: "Organic Farming in Europe". In Willer, Helga / Lernoud, Julia (eds.): *The World of Organic Agriculture: Statistics and Emerging Trends* (Research Institute of Organic Agriculture (FiBL), Frick and IFOAM–Organics International: Bonn 2016) (= *Yearbook, Organics International* 2016), pp. 190–198.

Willer, Helga / Schaack, Diana / Lernoud, Julia / Meredith, Stephen: "Growth Trends in European Organic Food and Farming". In Meredith, Stephen / Willer, Helga (eds.): *Organic in Europe 2016: Prospects and Developments*. IFOAM EU: Brussels: 2016, pp. 20–58.

Internet

Balázs, Bálint: "Vásárcsarnokok születése" ("Arrival of the Market Halls"). *Mult-Kor e-journal* 2009/4, retrieved 8.11.2016, from http://mult-kor.hu/20091215_vasarcsarnokok_szuletese.

"Bath Farmer's Market", retrieved 18.8.2016 from http://www.bathfarmersmarket.co.uk.

Council Regulation (EC) No 834 / 2007, and COMMISSION REGULATION (EC) No 889/2008, retrieved 10.8.2016 from http://eur-lex.europa.eu/legal-content.

Farkas, Judit: "'Nincsenek receptek'": A magyar ökofalvak táplálkozásantropológiai vizsgálata' ("'There are No Recipes'"). Anthropological Study of Food in Hungarian Eco-villages. *Tabula* 16(1–2), 2015, pp. 1–9. *Online Journal of the Hungarian Ethnographical Museum* retrieved 8.11.2016 from http://tabula.neprajz.hu/neprajz.07.16a.php.

GfK Hungaria, and Conscious Shopper, GfK Hungaria, "A lakosság bioélelmiszer-vásárlási gyakorisága és fogyasztói attitűdök" ("Organic Food: Consumer Attitudes and Frequency of Purchase"). GfK: Budapest 2007. Summary in Conscious Shopper Tudatosvásárló-online 1 February 2007, retrieved 18.8.2016 from http://tudatosvasarlo.hu/cikk/biokorkep-magyarok-tobbsege-egyaltalan-nem-vasarol-bioelelmiszert.

Juhász, Anikó / Szabó, Dorottya: *A piacok, vásárcsarnokok és vásárok elhelyezkedése és jellemzői, a termelői piacok kiemelésével* ("Food Markets, Market Halls, and Fairs in the Country, Farmers' Markets Highlighted"). Research papers (Research Institute of Agricultural Economics: Budapest 2011–2012), retrieved 25.7.2016 from https://www.aki.gov.hu/Piacok.

Kovács, Annamária / Frühwald, Ferenc: "Organic Farming in Hungary 2005", Country report on Organic Europe website, FiBL, retrieved 20.8.2016 from http://www.organic-europe.net/country-info/hungary/country-report/2005.html.

Local Product Online Magazine 24.11.2014, retrieved 28.8.2016 from http://www.helyitermekmagazin.hu/2014/.

Munich Farmers' Markets, retrieved 18.8.201 from https://www.muenchner-bauernmaerkte.de/.

"National Agrarian Chamber, interactive list", retrieved 9.10.2016 from http://nak.hu/termeloipiac-kereso.

"National Food Chain Safety Office (*NÉBIH*) on the farmers' markets: legislation and regulations", retrieved18.8.2016 from http://portal.nebih.gov.hu/-/a-helyi-termeloi-piacok-uzemelteteserol.

Seléndy, Szabolcs: "Ökopiaci kérdések" ("Organic Markets of the BioCulture Federation, Start and Development"), *Biokultúra* 20 (2009/4), retrieved 20.8.2016 from http://www.biokontroll.hu/cms/index.php?option=com_content&view=article&id=447:oekopiaci-kerdesek&catid=111:biokereskedelem&Itemid=43.

Antonia-Leda Matalas, Eirini Bathrellou, Milia Tzoutzou

When Natural Food is Unappealing: Depictions of Children's Perception of Food in Animated Comics' Series

Abstract: *The study focused on analysing animated comics in order to exemplify the way in which children's need for imaginative stories may perpetuate dislike towards healthy foods. Representative episodes from ten popular animated comics' series were reviewed and all food-related scenes and accompanying comments were analysed. Scenes presenting food in its natural form, as vegetables and fruits, were found to be considerably fewer compared to those depicting processed foods. Furthermore, vegetables and fruit were sometimes presented as being unfamiliar and unappealing food items, in contrast to candy, cakes and convenience foods which were depicted as being associated with joyful events.*

Research has shown that messages conveyed to children via food advertisements and other products of media culture, influence their perception of food, as well as their food choices. A few studies have been conducted to examine the way in which particular foods are depicted in films and television series addressed to children. These films and TV series project scenes in which food is presented to youngsters, often in conjunction with verbal and visual comments. The aim of the present study is to gain insight into the stereotypes to which children are exposed, with regard to specific types of food and their qualities, when watching animated comics. Ten animated comic series were selected, based on their high TV audience-viewing ratings in Greece. Two independent raters viewed ten randomly-selected episodes from each of the series, and all food-related scenes, as well as associated verbal and visual comments, were recorded. The recording was accomplished with the aid of a checklist especially developed for the present study. Food items were classified into ten groups: dairy, meat and fish, bakery and cereals, vegetables, fruit, sweets, convenience foods and snacks, sweetened beverages, other, and non-identifiable food. Content analysis revealed that scenes which presented food in its natural form (i.e. meat, fish, vegetables and fruit), were considerably fewer than those which presented food in sweetened form (i.e. sweets, beverages or convenience foods). Furthermore, in some scenes, vegetables and fruit were presented as being unfamiliar and non-appealing in character. A young hero's exclamation, "What are those things?", while staring in fear at some vegetables, is indicative of this situation. In contrast, the consumption of candy, cakes and other convenience foods is associated with positive messages and joyful social events. Positive characteristics are attributed to these items regardless of whether they are consumed or not. The analysis of animated comics' series exemplifies the way in which children's need for imaginative stories may interfere with their food choices and perpetuate dislike towards healthy foods.

The Media as a Means of Food Experiences for Children

Food habits are the result of the interaction of various factors such as immediate family surroundings and the wider social and natural environment of the individual. Food preferences are thus formed through each individual's personal behaviour, and are connected with cultural roots such as family habits and the need for communication and socialization (Birch / Fisher 1998, pp. 539–549). Moreover, young people's desire to create an "identity" for themselves influences their food choices. The results of a study which examined the connection between the consumption of specific food items and social milieu (Stead et al. 2011, pp. 1131–1139), indicated that popular food brands, such as various cola and chocolate-flavoured beverages, were selected by teenagers as foods, the consumption of which was related by them to their being considered popular, cool and modern by their group. Regarding healthy foods, the participants' opinions were remarkable in that they depicted healthy eating as being socially risky and connected with the behaviour of weird, nerdy and untrendy persons. Consequently, adolescents may use food choices in order to support the image they want to project and to enable them to associate with other peer groups.

Children receive various stimuli from a very early age and form eating behaviours under the influence of experiences which penetrate their daily lives in numerous ways. The media convey stereotypes and values which can become behavioural patterns and influence children's food preferences and choices (Birch / Fisher 1998, pp. 539–549). Thus, television programmes, series, and commercials, are the "transmitters" of a massive amount of information culture which provides experiences as well as societal values for children.

Media Culture Emphasizes Unhealthy Food to Young Audiences

Previous research has indicated that messages transmitted to children via food advertisements and other products of media culture have an impact on their perception of food, as well as on their food choices. It has been repeatedly demonstrated that television, the Internet, as well as the press media, advertise mainly processed foods, such as salty snacks, beverages, and various sweet desserts. No et al. (2014, pp. 75–81) compared all food reports for branded (advertised) and non-branded (just depictions) foods appearing in popular magazines addressed to children and adolescents, in terms of their nutritional value based on their recommended frequency of intake. Their findings suggested that the branded food references tended to be more frequent for unhealthy foods – foods with high fat, salt and sugar content – recommended for only occasional consumption. On the contrary, healthy food references – for fruit, vegetables and cereals – accounted for only 3 % of the total food references. In the same context, content analysis of Internet commercials addressed to children from 8 to 9 years of age, showed that the food advertisements were not only frequent and sometimes implicit, but also that they were referring mainly to foods with high sugar or fat content, such as candies, ice cream, chips, hamburgers etc. (Jones / Fabrianesi 2008, pp. 588–595), It is noteworthy that only one advertisement referred to vegetables.

Moreover, it seems that there is some confusion from the youngsters' part regarding the nutritional profile of advertised foods. For example, children seemed to overestimate the nutritional value of some television advertised products (Hart / Bishop / Truby 2002, pp. 129–140), while in another study they appeared to be able to memorize foods with their commercial names, while failing to identify the food category to which the advertised product belonged (Kraak / Pelletier 1998, p. 15).

Much research has now documented the "mimic" effect of advertisements on children's eating behaviour. Children, in response to exposure to an advertised product, increase both their demand for it (Gentil / Walsh 2002, pp. 157–178), and also their actual consumption of it (Borzekowski / Robinson 2001, pp. 42–46), the latter being an effect especially evident in overweight/obese children (Halford et al. 2004, pp. 221–225).

Animated Cartoon Characters in Food Promotion

Animated cartoon characters are used as a tool for the promotion of many kinds of goods to children and adolescents. Research has shown that the animated cartoon characters which are used on television and on the Internet, are easily recognizable by children, as they often refer to their popular heroes, and they are thus very important for the profits of the food industry (Hastings et al. 2006). The characters are used in order to attract children's attention, to present the food product in an imaginative and entertaining way, to provoke an imitation effect, and finally to motivate the young audiences to purchase the advertised food (De Julio 2010, pp. 96–107).

Recent literature on the topic reveals that when adults are engaged in advertising food products to children, such products usually refer to a popular cartoon hero. In addition, it has also been found that the use of animation techniques is closely related to the promotion of food products addressed to children, a finding that applies to a considerably lesser extent when toys are the objects advertised. Actually, a relevant study in Greece, on the content and techniques of television advertisements during children's programmes, recorded that 67 % of the food commercials at that time employed animation techniques, while only 13 % of the non-food commercials did so (Bathrellou et al. 2006, pp. 127–133). Roberto et al. (2010, pp. 88–93) demonstrated a relationship between printed animated cartoon characters and children's preferences for them. In their study, children were asked to choose between two packages of the same product. The only difference between the two packages was the depiction of an animated cartoon character on only one of them. The results of the test showed that half of the children stated that the snack with the hero on the package had a better taste than the one without it.

Images of Food in Stories Addressed to Children

Only a limited amount of research on the food references in various stories addressed to children has been carried out to date, and the little that has been done has mainly examined picture stories for preschool children. One such study recorded the food messages in 114 children's books (Byrne / Nitzke 2000, pp. 359–362). Fruit was the most frequently-depicted food category. The context in which the various foods were presented was, generally speaking, positive, and only very rarely negative. The researchers distinguished the positive attributes of a food item as being either "funny" or "healthy". Interestingly, foods which were depicted in illustrations or described in the text as being "funny", frequently had only a low nutrient profile; food items associated with the fun element were more likely to be cookies, a cake, or an ice cream, rather than a fruit or a juice. In contrast, the latter items were connected with the element of "health". A similar study investigated, firstly, preschool children's reaction to a vegetable unknown to them (kohlrabi) and, secondly, whether the depiction of this vegetable in a book would influence their willingness to taste it (Byrne / Nitzke 2002, pp. 211–214). A book with a suitable subject was selected for the study, and modifications were applied to each page, with the aim of presenting kohlrabi either in a negative or in a positive way. The group of children who read the book with the positive depiction of the vegetable showed more of a willingness to taste it.

In a recent study (Goldman / Descartes 2016, pp. 203–208) it was shown that the images and texts in children's books often referred to healthy foods. From a total of 69 children's popular educational and storytelling books, the majority included a reference to healthy foods, more than half of which (57 %) were for fruit, followed by those for dairy products and vegetables, and then for bread and cereals (one-third). However, additional analysis of the centrality of those healthy foods in the plot of the story served to diminish this projection. Although fruit was the most frequently-reported food category, it was often placed in the background of the story, rather than in the centre of the narrative plot. Moreover, in the majority of cases, its depiction in the story was not a positive one. Similarly, the positive effect of vegetables was lower when compared to that of other food categories. On the other hand, however, nutrient-poor foods, even if they appeared less frequently, were always positively presented and had central positioning in the texts. For example, references to ice cream in the stories were related to moments of euphoria, celebration or happy outcomes.

Another study analysing food and beverage depictions in 97 books targeted to children between 2 and 5 years of age, found that healthy foods were presented in a positive way (England et al. 2015, pp. 1257–1264). The books in question were categorized according to those mentioning nutritious food and those referring to empty calorie foods. Food mentions in the books in question were further characterized as being positive, negative or neutral. For example, any message pointing out the consequences of a bad or empty calorie diet on health was considered to be a positive one. References to nutritious foods were thus considered to be positive messages. Fruit, desserts and protein-foods were the most frequently-mentioned food categories. Overall, references to nutritious food items outnumbered those pertaining to empty-calorie foods. It is noteworthy that negative verbal and visual references were only recorded for empty calorie foods and not for any of the nutritious foods. With regard to the content of stories projected on television, an analysis carried out by Korr (2008, pp. 449–462) showed that in animated programmes, sweets were the food items most frequently referred to, while fruit was the second most frequently-mentioned food. Meat and salty snacks were placed in the third and fourth categories, according to the frequency of their appearance. From the above data we may conclude that, compared to foods advertised on television, both the printed and the animated stories for children which were examined contained more references to nutritious, rather than to empty calorie, foods.

The Concept of Natural Food

The concept "natural" is an ambiguous one, because in the modern world what is usually called "natural" cannot be distinguished from what is regarded as being "cultural". Nevertheless "naturalness" is generally viewed as a positive and attractive attribute, particularly in the domain of food. Thus, the attribute "natural" is often emphasized in advertisements for foods and beverages. The properties of natural food as perceived by lay people have been examined in a few European and American adult populations. In summary, the results of these studies show, that the history and the way of processing a primary food product, seem to be the major influence in determining whether or not it is a natural product. More specifically, Rozin (2005, pp. 652–658) has shown that "naturalness" is substantially compromised when changes in substance are involved and arising, for example, from chemical transformations or as a result of the addition or subtraction of entities, while physical transformations (resulting from freezing or crushing) have much less of an impact on the "naturalness" of the food. Furthermore, less processed food, or food processed in a traditional way without additives, seems to be largely associated with "naturalness"; in contrast, foods, the ingredients of which have undergone multiple stages of processing, and to which chemically-derived entities have been added, are associated with the concept of "unnatural" food (Verhoogh et al. 2003, pp. 29–49). In our study, we applied the above concepts of "natural" and "unnatural" to distinguish foods that are close to being "natural" from foods that are not. Thus, foodstuffs which retain much of their integrity (i.e. fruit, vegetables, meat and fish) were considered to be closest to being "natural" food. At the other end of the spectrum, the various convenience foods, processed snacks and sweets, as well as the various standardized soft beverages, were considered to be the least "natural" foods by virtue of the processing regime that their preparation typically involved.

Goal and Methods of the Study

Film movies and television series addressed to young audiences project scenes in which food is presented in conjunction with verbal and visual comments; however, the way in which particular foods are depicted in these stories has received relatively little attention to date. Thus, the aim of the present study was to gain insight into the messages concerning foods and their qualities to which children are exposed while watching animated comics' series on television or on the Internet.

Ten animated cartoon series from Greek television stations were selected based on their high television audience viewing (all 10 series are also available online).[1] Two independent raters viewed ten randomly-selected episodes from each one of the series. Raters recorded every food item presented in the

1 The 10 series studied were: "Ben 10", "Jewelpet", "Mermaid Melody Pitchi, Pichi, Pitch", "Tutenstein", "Dora the Explorer", "Tom and Jerry", "Penguins of Madagascar", "Teen Days", "LazyTown", and "SpongeBob SquarePants".

episodes, regardless of whether it was consumed or not, as well as any relevant comments expressed either by the main characters or by secondary ones, concerning the food in question. Frequency of food consumption was evaluated based on the range of times it was presented: 1–4, 5–9, or 10 times or more. Recording was accomplished with the aid of a checklist especially developed for the present study.

For content-analysis purposes, foods were classified into ten food groups: dairy, meat/poultry/fish, bakery and cereals, fruit, vegetables, sweets, convenience foods and snacks, sweetened beverages, other, and non-identifiable food. Examples of the food items included in each category are given in Table 1.

Table 1. Food categories used for the content analysis of food depictions in the series examined.

Dairy	**milk, yoghurt, cheese**
Meat, poultry and fish	all kind of steaks, pork, beef, meatballs, fish, fish fingers
Bakery and cereals	rusks, bread, breakfast cereals
Fruit	all kind of fruit, freshly-squeezed juices
Vegetables	fresh or boiled vegetables, vegetable soups
Sweets	cakes, pancakes, biscuits, lollypops, candies, sweet pies, donuts, ice-cream
Convenience foods and snacks	hamburger, pizza, potato chips, popcorn and other salty snacks
Sweetened beverages	refreshments, cola drinks, prepackaged fruit juices
Other food	coffee, wine, tea, mixed foods (e.g. peanuts with onions in ketchup sauce), condiments, alcoholic drinks, any other foods not classified under any of the other food groups
Non-identifiable	foods that could not be identified

Results of the Content Analysis

Types of food and food consumption

One hundred animated cartoon episodes were analyzed for their food-related content.

Scenes which show food being actually consumed represented a subset of all food-related scenes. Overall, 68 of the 100 episodes showed actual food consumption, at least once. The series main hero was the character who was most frequently seen to eat. The foods consumed were basically processed foods; specifically sweets (in 27 of all episodes), sweetened beverages (in 24 of all episodes), and convenience foods and snacks (in 19 of all episodes). In contrast, the consumption of vegetables, dairy products, and fruit, appeared considerably less frequently, namely in 8, 11, and 12 of the episodes, respectively (Fig. 1). The consumption of "other foods" was recorded in 20 episodes.

Fig. 1: Number of episodes showing actual food consumption by food group occurring at least once during the episode.

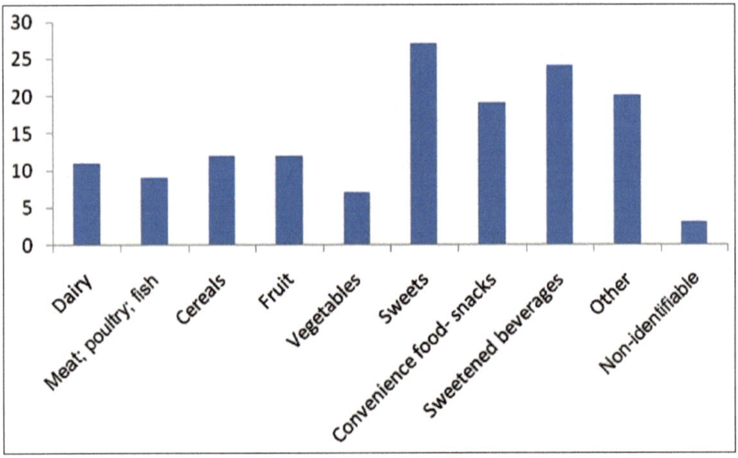

Furthermore, the consumption of sweets, convenience foods, and snacks or sweetened beverages, was found to be in excess of 10 times per episode in 1 or 2 of the episodes in total, while this never occurred in relation to fruit or vegetables in any episode. In fact, the frequency of vegetable consumption never occurred more than 1 to 4 times per episode. On the other hand, the consumption of sweets, or convenience foods and snacks was reported 5 to 9 times per episode in 7 or 8 episodes, while this same frequency of consumption for fruits was found in 3 episodes.

Our analysis shows that food holds a dominant role in the imaginary stories addressed to children. Food depictions and narrations do not always refer to normal foodstuffs, but also to fictional ones, either in natural or processed form. Thus, imaginary foods, such as "sardine ice lollies" and "magic wine" are not relevant to human patterns and are intended for the triggering of children's fantasy.

Messages about food

With regard to the messages accompanying the eating scenes, 60 of them were positive in character, while only 8 of them were negative in tone and referring mostly to vegetables. More than half of the positive messages referred to sweets, such as biscuits, cakes, lollipops and candies; salty snacks, such as popcorn, pizza, and hot dogs; and to fruit, such as carrots, bananas and apples (Fig. 2).

Fig. 2: Number of positive messages displayed by the food group.

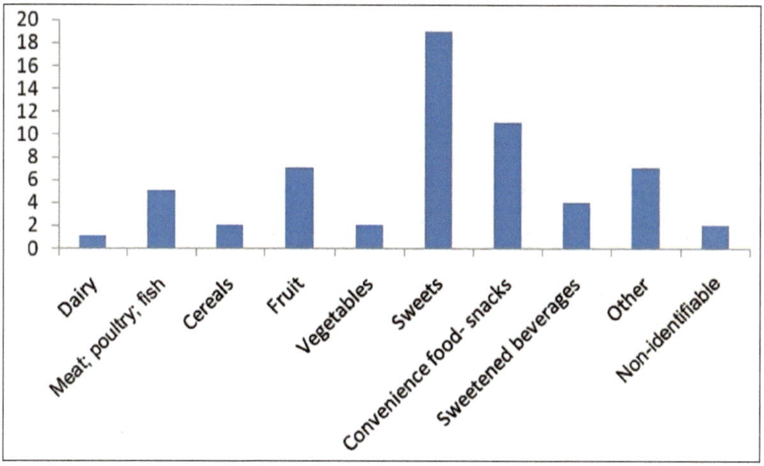

Positive messages for convenience foods and snacks, as well as for sweets, were recorded even on occasions when they were not consumed. Representative examples of positive messages are presented in Table 2.

Table 2. Free text examples of positive messages recorded for foods.

– "Oh no, we've run out of ice cream!"
– "I have few memories from my childhood but I never forgot that marmalade's taste..!"
– "Human's food is so delicious…" (while the hero eats a bowl of biscuits).
– "Look at this perfect burger…..!!"
– "I feel like a sausage in big bread!" (says a hero while dreaming of being a hot dog).
– "Both my need for beauty and my need for a beverage are filled" (says a hero after he had a cold drink).

– "Pizza with tuna, sardines and clam sauce, is paradise" (says a penguin, main hero of a series.
– "It is very good to eat ice cream from time to time."
– "Aaaah there is enough for everybody!" (says the hero while starring at the popcorn while all the others screaming ppppppopcorn!
– "I get crazy with lollipops, now I feel much better" (says a hero after eating the lollipop).
– The special dish of the day is bream with garnish!
– The ice lollies with sardines are so cool!!
– "Who are you? Have you got any sweets?" (asks a hero who likes indulging in sweet eating)
– "Mmm! The chicken is delicious!"
– While a central hero brings in a dish with fruits for a snack the children shout: "woooow!"
The heroes see a coconut and dream of it as freshly-squeezed juice.

On the other hand, the majority of negative or neutral messages were recorded for mainly two food groups: vegetables and fruit. Representative examples of these negative messages are presented in Table 3.

Table 3. Free text examples of negative or neutral messages recorded for foods.

– "Bananas, cherries…just so boring…!" (says a main hero while opening the fridge).
– "What are those things??!!" (while staring in fear at the vegetables).
– "We are out of money…. now we have to buy fruit and vegetables instead of cakes and chocolates!" (All main heroes seem displeased because they are forced to buy vegetables)
– Main hero eats a sandwich which contains a lot of vegetables (no comments available – neutral message).
– Main hero drinks a freshly-squeezed juice (no comments available).
– Depiction of vegetables which are sold unpacked appear in the background of the scene (no comments available – neutral message).
– Main hero eats an apple (no comments available – neutral message).
– Heroes are in a bakery shop, there are breads all around (no comments available).
– Heroes drink tea at home (no comments available).
– Central hero is cooking rice (no comments available).

Our analysis also showed that the scenes projecting food items like sweets or sugary products and sweetened soft beverages, are linked to the elements of joy and entertainment. Young heroes often appear in joyful social events relishing their favourite snacks with their close friends. This is typically expressed either in visual or verbal forms when heroes refer to their favourite foods These meals usually contain beverages, sweets, biscuits, milk shakes, hamburgers, pizzas, ice cream and cakes.

In contrast to this, scenes which present food, such as fruit and vegetables, in its natural form, are neutral or negative in nature, besides being considerably fewer in number when compared to those presenting convenience foods, sweet delicacies, beverages and other processed foods. For example, a neutral presentation includes observing the main hero in many episodes consuming a fruit, but without the inclusion of any verbal overtones or visual connotations. Furthermore, these natural food items often appear in the background of the scenes (figuring in illustrations and images), thus holding but a minimal role in the episodes' plot. At the same time, natural foods are largely absent from pleasant and social gatherings, while they are present in family scenes. Increasing the gap between the appeal of natural and processed food, the consumption of fruit and vegetables is often linked to negative comments. A scene with a group of displeased adolescents who have run out of money and are forced to buy vegetables instead of sweets, as they are cheaper, is indicative of this attitude. Other examples include the depiction of various heroes on opening the fridge door and staring sadly at the tomatoes and lettuce it contains, or a young hero's exclamation, "What are those things", while staring in fear at some vegetables.

Concluding remarks

The aim of the present study is to analyse the food-related content of popular animated series on television and the Internet, addressed to children in Greece. The results reveal that emphasis is placed on the depiction of processed food items, such as sweets, salty snacks, and beverages, and that it is always accompanied by a strong positive affect. On the other hand, forms of "natural" food, such as fruit, vegetables and dairy products, are generally underrepresented and often framed with neutral or even negative comments. Our analysis of animated comic series thus exemplifies the ways in which children's need for imaginative stories may interfere with their food choices and thus perpetuate a sense of dislike towards healthy foods.

List of References

Printed

Bathrellou, E. / Yannakoulia, M. / Voutzourakis, N. / Zisis, P. / Matalas, A. L. / Sidossis, L. S.: "Food Advertisements Targeted at Children: Nutritional Information and Appeals". *Pediatriki* 69, 2006, pp. 127–133 (in Greek).

Birch, L. L. / Fisher, M.: "Development of Eating Behaviours among Children and Adolescents". *Official Journal of the Academy of Pediatrics* 101(2), 1998, pp. 539–549.

Borzekowski, D. L. / Robinson, T. N.: "The 30-second Effect: An Experiment Revealing the Impact of Television Commercials on Food Preferences of Preschoolers". *Journal of the American Dietetic Association* 101, 2001, pp. 42–46.

Byrne, E. / Nitzke, S.: "Preschool Children's Acceptance of a Novel Vegetable Following Exposure to Messages in a Storybook". *Journal of Nutrition Education and Behavior* 34, 2002, pp. 211–214.

Byrne, E. / Nitzke, S.: "Nutrition Messages in a Sample of Children's Picture Books". *Journal of the American Dietetic Association* 100, 2000, pp. 359–362.

De Julio, S.: "The Construction of Fun in Food Advertisements Targeting Children". *Young Consumers* 11(2), 2010, pp. 96–107.

England, K. A. / Linchey, J. / Madsen, K. A. / Patel, A. I.: "Reach Out and Eat: Food and Beverages Depicted in Books for Preschoolers". *Clinical Pediatrics* 54(13), 2015, pp. 1257–1264.

Gentil, D. A. / Walsh, D. A.: "A Normative Study on Family Media Habits". *Applied Developmental Psychology* 23, 2002, pp. 157–178.

Hart, K. H. / Bishop, J. / Truby, H.: "An Investigation into School Children's Knowledge and Awareness of Food and Nutrition". *Journal of Human Nutrition and Dietetics* 15(2), 2002, pp. 129–140.

Halford, G. C. / Gillespie, J. / Brown, V. / Pontin, E. E. / Dovey, T.: "Effect of Television Advertisements for Foods on Food Consumption in Children". *Appetite* 42 2004, pp. 221–225.

Hastings, G. / McDermott, L. / Angus, K. / Stead, M. / Thomson, S.: "The Extent, Nature and Effects of Food Promotion to Children: A Review of the Evidence. Technical Paper Prepared for the World Health Organization". World Health Organization, 2006.

Jones, S., / Fabrianesi, B.: "Gross for Kids but Good for Parents: Differing Messages in Advertisements for the Same Products". *Public Health Nutrition* 11(6), 2008, pp. 588–595.

Korr, J. L.: "Healthy cartoons? A Content Analysis of Foods in Children's Animated Television Programs". *Food, Culture and Society* 11 (2008), 449–462.

Kraak, V. / Pelletier, D. L. : "The Influence of Commercialism on the Food Purchasing Behavior of Children and Teenage Youth". *Family Economics and Nutrition Review* 11, 1998, pp. 15–24.

No, E. / Kelly, B. / Devi, A. / Swinburn, B. / Vandevijvere, S.: "Food References and Marketing in Popular Magazines for Children and Adolescents in New Zealand: A Content Analysis". *Appetite* 83, 2014, pp. 75–81.

Roberto, C. A. / Baik, J. / Harris, J. L. / Brownell, K. D.: "Influence of Licensed Characters on Children's Taste and Snack Preferences", *Pediatrics* 126 (2010), 88–93.

Rozin, P.: "The Meaning of 'Natural': Process More Important than Content". *Psychological Science* 16, 2005, pp. 652–658.

Stead, M. / McDermott, L. / Mackintosh, A. M. / Adamson, A.: "Why Healthy Eating is Bad for Young People's Health: Identity, Belonging and Food". *Social Science and Medicine* 72(7), 2011, pp. 1131–1139.

Verhoogh, H. / Matze, M. / Lammerts Van Bueren, E. / Baars, T.: "The Role of the Concept of the Natural in Organic Farming". *Journal of Agricultural and Environmental Ethics* 16, 2003, pp. 29–49.

Part III:
Alienation and the Handling of Food

Silke Bartsch, Heike Müller, Leif Oppermann and Steffen Schaal

Using Smartphones for Tracing Local Food – Location-based Games on Mobile Devices in Consumer and Nutrition Education

Abstract: *Most young people in Western societies are unaware of the origins of their everyday food. At the same time, adolescents grow up in close contact with smartphones and digital media. MILE*[1] *– Move. Interact. Learn. Eat. – is an interdisciplinary project, which is developing an easy-to-use toolbox for multipliers to create location-based games, in order to encourage adolescents to trace local food products and to become more attentive to the origin of food.*

Introduction

Most adolescents in Western societies have little knowledge about the origin of the food they consume on a daily basis (cf. Spiekermann 1999, pp. 41–56; Bartsch 2008). Furthermore, according to recent research, their knowledge about food in general and their skills in handling food are limited (Dreblow / Schoenheit 2010). The majority of adults in these societies buy their food in supermarkets, and thus have some idea about food supply, product costs, and how eating habits affect their bodies. At the same time, people's actual appreciation of food is often low, and this in turn affects how food is handled. Jörissen / Priefer / Bräutigam 2015, p. 2703 f.) point out that the amount of food wasted is highest among people who shop exclusively in large supermarkets, and that food waste is lowest among people who use a variety of shopping facilities or grow supplementary food themselves. Furthermore, age, lifestyle, and everyday situations influence the quantity of food waste generated in households (WRAP 2008; Jörissen / Priefer / Bräutigam 2015, pp. 2695–2715)), as well as the cooking skills evident among different generations (Brombach / Bartsch / Winkler 2015, pp. 20–25). Thus, the behavioural data concerning waste is a good example of the beneficial effects of acquiring knowledge about the production and handling of food (e.g. Bartsch / Körner 2012, pp. 238–243; Jörissen / Priefer / Bräutigam 2015; Dräger de Teran 2015).

---

1 MILE is the name of the current research project, funded by the Baden-Württemberg State Ministry for Rural Areas and Consumer Protection (MLR). For more information on the project, visit www.mile-bw.de.

At the same time, young people make intensive use of mobile devices such as smartphones or tablet computers, and are often online and virtually connected. Digital data is part of their real world and mobile devices function as personal assistants in everyday life (JIM-Studie 2015; BMFSFJ 2013; Common Sense Census 2015).

Mobile technologies allow for location-aware learning activities and thus they facilitate the transformation of a physical space into a personally relevant place (cf. Harrison / Dourish 1996, pp. 67–76; Lengen 2016, pp. 19–29). Mobile technologies for targeting issues in the field of nutrition on-site offer authentic learning opportunities for young people. As these authentic learning opportunities provide problem-based, collaborative, and reflective activities, they are inherently multi-, trans- or interdisciplinary in nature (cf. Lave / Wenger 1991; CTGV 1993, pp. 52–70).

The aim of the MILE project (2013–2017) is to foster awareness among young people regarding their grocery purchases and eating habits, as well as their knowledge of local food production, by means of a digital game-based learning approach (Bartsch / Schaal 2014, pp. 36–47; Schaal / Bartsch 2015, pp. 47–164). Mobile gaming activities have the potential, to increase adolescents' engagement in the field with regard to obtaining knowledge about food and region, and also to raise awareness about the origins of food. Furthermore, the enjoyment involved in game-based learning is considered to impact positively on adolescents' attitudes and attentiveness concerning the origin and handling of food (Schaal / Bartsch 2015). However, technological barriers for educational staff still exist in this regard. As a solution to this problem, the interdisciplinary MILE team has developed an easy-to-use tool (MILE.designer) to create MILE geogames for adolescents.[2] This paper describes the specific opportunities provided by mobile, location-based learning in order to achieve the aim of the MILE project. In this context, the central research questions are:

1. What opportunities does mobile, location-based learning offer for nutrition and consumer education?
2. How do multipliers use the MILE.designer toolbox to create location-based games?

Method: Theory-based interdisciplinary development of an online toolbox that allows multipliers to create geogames for young people.

---

2 Bartsch / Schaal / Oppermann 2016, retrieved 13.12.2016 from http://www.awer-center.org/abstracts/WCES%202016%20Abstracts%20Book.pdf.

Opportunities Provided by Mobile, Location-based Learning in Nutrition and Consumer Education

The living environment is a topic of study in nutrition and consumer education. Authentic learning (see above) is, therefore, important in this regard. Thus mobile, location-based learning facilities, offer new opportunities for this kind of development. Studies in the context of environmental competence are the basis of the MILE pilot project (Roczen et al. 2013; Lude et al. 2013; Schaal / Bartsch 2015).

Food Production in the Context of Nutrition and Consumer Education

Being educated in the sense of being consumer and nutrition literate includes being critically aware of the environmental impact involved in the groceries we buy (Heseker et al. 2005). The concept underpinning the REVIS model project ("Reform der Ernährungs- und Verbraucherbildung"[3]) considers the role of education in sustainable development. There are overlaps between the two domains mentioned above – education for sustainable development and consumer and nutrition education. For example, goal 9 of the nutrition and consumer education curriculum of the REVIS model is intended to encourage students to develop a sustainable way of life. The overlapping between consumer and nutrition education is also evident in some of the 17 goals of the new (25 September 2016) UN sustainable development agenda 2030, e.g. goal 2: end hunger, achieve food security and improved nutrition and promote sustainable agriculture; goal 12: ensure sustainable consumption and production patterns (http://www.un.org/sustainabledevelopment/sustainable-development-goals/, retrieved 5.12.2016).

Sustainable consumption is also regarded as a part of consumer and nutrition literacy in the REVIS model (Bartsch 2015, pp. 78–92; Marchand 2015). In general, sustainable consumption means that the consumption of goods and services has minimal impact on the environment, is socially fair, and economically practicable (Hauff 1987; UNEP 2008).

When considering sustainability young people often see it as consisting of a merger of local food production and seasonal consumption (Bartsch 2015). Although this is a simplified interpretation of the concept of sustainability, it might be a prerequisite of awareness, which, in the context of nutrition and con-

3 REVIS is an acronym for the project "Reform of the Nutrition and Consumer Education in German Schools", funded by the Federal Ministry of Consumer Protection, Food and Agriculture in the years 2003–2005 (Heseker et al. 2005, www.evb-online.de).

sumer education, involves living and consuming in a more sustainable fashion. Furthermore, region could be part of self-conception in the sense of belonging and creating identity.

From Space to Place

In order to engage with the immediate environment, it is necessary to interact with the particular *space* involved. The distinction between space and place is a traditional construct[4] (cf. Heidegger 1927) and not simply a dualism of space and place. Lengen (2016) summarizes different concepts of spaces as follows: "Spaces are quantifiable and comprehensible, places are perceptible. Direct perception and emotions are connected to places; they are shaped and used accordingly" (authors' translation of Lengen 2016, p. 21[5]). To transform a *space* into a *place*, interaction with the *space* is crucial (Lengen 2016, pp. 19–29; cf. Heidegger 1927; Levi-Strauss 1958; Tuan 1974; Relph 1976; Harrisson / Dourish 1996, pp. 67–76; Dourish 2006, pp. 299–308). In order to make sense of a *space*, people add personal meaning and also often link emotion to what then becomes a *place*.

Kaufmann (2005) distinguishes between "space of flows" and "space of place". The "flows" stimulate the reorganisation of social places, and influence relations and identity. "Flows" and "relations" make it possible to get new "scapes" like "mediascapes" etc. (Appadurai 1990, pp. 295–310; Kaufmann 2005), but this is not helpful for the concept of "local food". In fact, in this regard, it is necessary to get in touch with the non-virtual lives of region and people in order to get a sensuous, meaningful, and an emotionally-linked experience. Harrison and Dourish (1996) have also proposed an analytical distinction between "place" and "space", because it is useful in understanding applications in the context of Computer-Supported Collaborative Work (cf. Dourish 2006). The separation of *space* and *place* into two different domains, the domain of the physical and the domain of the social, is of assistance in understanding interaction processes. For our work dealing with mobile, location-based learning, it is useful to grasp the idea[6] of interaction, as

---

4 The words "Raum" and "Ort" in German make a similar distinction (cf. Heidegger 1927).

5 "Räume sind mess- und verstehbar, Orte sind erlebbar, mit Orten verbinden sich direkte Wahrnehmungen und Emotionen; sie werden entsprechend gestaltet und genutzt" (Lengen 2016, p. 21).

6 Ten years later, Dourish (2006, p. 306) wrote: "However, a closer examination suggests that this distinction cannot hold. Place and space are both products of social practice, albeit different systems of practice." Therefore, he suggests "Re-space-ing Place", instead of "Re-Place-ing Space".

a means of fostering the notion of the personal, social and culturally-meaningful environment as place, in the sense of an existential concept of space ("existenzielles Raumkonzept"; Lengen 2016).

Location-based Games

The MILE project applies a digital game-based learning approach to encourage interaction between the players and the environment in a playful manner. Geogames are digital, location-based games played on mobile devices, which require the players' locomotion in the physical space (Schlieder 2014, pp. 567–574). As the object sought-after (e.g. a task or a cache) can be attained only in the physical environment, the players' geographical position constitutes a game element. Thus, geogames link the physical and virtual worlds. Schlieder proposes a model with three levels of game-design with respect to the specific characteristics of geogames (Fig. 1).

Fig. 1: Levels of game design in geogames (according to Schlieder 2014).

Performative level: Geogames are part of a broader picture, e.g. educational geogames are derived from educational objectives. Game designers need to consider the staging of the game: In which particular setting and moment of time will the game be realized?

Narrative level: The game narrative connects the subordinate tasks within a geogame. The story line influences the game content.

Ludic level: Because of the players' locomotion, prerequisites for geogames are the design and implementation of game mechanics, rules, and assistive technologies, e.g. navigation.

Schaal and Bartsch (2015) provide a theoretical framework for the MILE project based on empirical connections between attitudes and environmental behaviour, their pilot studies in nutrition and consumer education (Bartsch / Schaal 2014, 36–47), and the competence model for environmental education as developed by Roczen et al. (2014). Furthermore, results from concepts for mobile, location-based learning in biology and sustainable-development education, have also been taken into account (Schaal / Schaal / Lude. 2015; Lude et al. 2013).

Using Location-based Games in Nutrition and Consumer Education

The interdisciplinary MILE team consists of educational experts in the fields of outdoor education, nutrition and consumer education, as well as computer science. In order to foster awareness for responsible and sustainable value chains in the everyday lives of adolescents with the help of mobile, digital technologies, the MILE team has developed a toolbox for designing and playing educational geogames based on partner Fraunhofer FIT's tradition of building pervasive games (Oppermann / Slussareff 2016). The tools can be easily authored in a browser and deployed to GPS-enabled smartphones. Nutrition specialists have been trained as multipliers to enable them to use the tools for designing location-based geogames for adolescents.

The MILE Geogames

In a scavenger hunt-like game, the geogames players move to different locations and solve a location-aware-game task at each location (e.g. What does the local bakery do with unsold goods? Ask the bakery salesman).

Fig. 2: The MILE toolbox.

The MILE toolbox (Fig. 2) consists of the authoring system MILE.designer and the native gaming app MILE.explorer. In the web-based MILE.designer, the multipliers are guided step-by-step through the game-design process. Each game consists of a user-defined game narrative and a set of tasks. The MILE.explorer Android app presents the game narrative and the location-aware tasks. In the game, the players earn scores by solving the location-aware tasks, which includes interacting with the content, peers, and / or the local environment. The multipliers are encouraged to top off every mission with a food-enjoyment experience.

Research and Results

The MILE geogames created by the multipliers are assessed using different foci in the accompanying research (e.g. Brosda et al. 2016 on the use of audio). In total, 51 MILE games were designed from March 2015 to May 2016, and 37 MILE games (ready to play versions) from these were involved in this study – the goal of which is to analyse how multipliers use the MILE templates, in order to facilitate interaction between players and location, in location-based learning.

In general, the MILE approach encourages interaction between players and their living environment through location-based, authentic learning opportunities (see above). Analysis of the geogames has identified three ways in which the multipliers use the tools to further strengthen location-based experiences: Game flow, tasks, and cooperation in teams. Bearing in mind Schlieder's (2014) three game-design levels, the MILE geogames can be seen to provide the multipliers with game design templates on the ludic level. On a performative level, the multipliers implement the geogames in leisure-time facilities for nutrition and consumer education. The research question mainly operates on the narrative level, i.e. the game flow and tasks aspects.

Game flow: MILE geogames are embedded in a story. The story lines can be fantasy or historical, etc., but they are generally bound to the region of the specific geogame. Thus transferring a region-bound MILE geogame to another location is not an option. For example, the MILE mission "Pretty Little Genes – Tracing Genetic Engineering in Karlsruhe" is located in the city of Karlsruhe where the Federal Constitutional Court of Germany is located. The narrative deals with the revisiting of the laws concerning genetic engineering in food production at the Constitutional Court. The players are introduced to one of the judges, who they are to support in researching the current impact of genetic engineering on products of everyday consumption.

Tasks: Each MILE geogame consists of several location-based tasks. The toolbox offers ten different types of task formats as templates, such as choosing multiple correct answers, sorting items into groups, going to a designated location to choose the correct answer, or estimating a value. The multipliers need to adapt the task templates to the specific contents of their individual MILE geogame. Thus, the multipliers shape the interaction between the players and the environment when creating a game. In the course of their training, the multipliers are trained to give preference to higher-level location-based tasks than to lower levels of such tasks. We categorize the grade of location-awareness as follows:

Table 1. Grade of location-awareness in the geogame tasks.

Grade 0 (No / Low location-awareness): The task could be solved in any other location. There is no interaction between the players and the location.

Grade 1 (Limited location-awareness): The location offers additional information on-site. The information could help the players to solve the task, but it is not specific for the site. There is limited interaction between the players and the location.

Grade 2 (Essential location-awareness): On-site examination of the location is essential for completing the task, as the location provides critical information. Interaction between the players and the location is essential.

Grade 3 (Exclusive location-awareness): The location is the exclusive information necessary to solve the task.

The analysis of this study includes 290 tasks of 37 geogames concerning nutrition and consumer topics. The results are presented below (Fig. 3).

Fig. 3: Analysis of the grade of location-awareness in the geogame tasks.

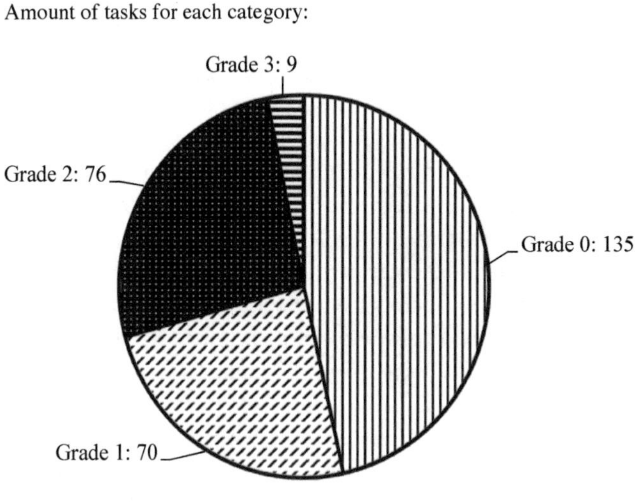

In addition to Schlieder's (2014) three game-design levels, the analysis includes the pre-implementing of team cooperation. Playing in teams contributes to the joyful experience of engaging in a game, in terms of the definition of enjoyment in Tamborini et al. (2010). As the MILE geogames serve educational purposes, cooperative aspects are relevant in the context of learning theories.

Cooperation in teams. The adolescents play the geogames in teams. High teamwork-intensity is useful for cooperative learning (cf. Konrad / Traub 2010) and it fosters interaction between the players and the location. In creating geogames, the multipliers need to adapt the tasks to a specific geogame, and thus they are implicitly forced to provide teamwork among the players. For example, in a task within the geogame "Food from Nature", the players give an award to the most sustainable dish of the day in the menu of the local dining hall. In order to fulfil the task, the players need to discuss the value chains of the ingredients needed for the dishes on the menu.

Discussion

The MILE project aims to foster awareness among young people about their nutrition and consumption habits, and also about their knowledge of local food production, by means of a digital game- and location-based learning approach.

The results of the analysis show that the multipliers adequately use the MILE toolbox to design opportunities for location-based learning.

The MILE toolbox provides templates that need to be adapted to the specific environment involved, as opportunities for location-based learning depend on the location. For example, rural, rather than urban, areas, enable agricultural food-production sites to be explored – for obvious reasons.

The game designer's pre-knowledge and preconceptions further influence the individual MILE geogame, e.g. regarding issues such as "What is local food?"

Some geogames show a tendency to gloss over realities that are contrary to the concept of nutrition and consumer literacy. But it must be borne in mind that everyday life is complex and differs from the ideal. Identifying and analysing issues in food production and consumption form the basis for making informed and reflective consumption choices (e.g. REVIS goal 7).

In the course of their training, the multipliers are trained to give preference to elevated levels of location-awareness in the geogame tasks, as interacting with the location facilitates the transformation of space to place. Since interaction shapes the place, the game designers need to consider possible consequences of the interaction carefully and responsibly. For example, encouraging the players to leave a letter as a form of self-generated information on-site must be done in the context of also considering its future preservation, decay or disposal.

Conclusion

On the basis of a literature review and pilot studies, educational experts from nutrition, consumer, and outdoor education, have developed a framework for using digital game- and location-based learning in nutrition and consumer education. Stemming from a design-based research approach (BBRC 2003), they have co-created the easy-to-use MILE online toolbox with computer scientists. Multipliers use the MILE toolbox for designing educational geogames for adolescents. The geogames encourage interaction between players and the environment, facilitating thereby the transformation from a physical space into a personally relevant place. The research data show that the multipliers use the tools to even fortify the location-awareness of the geogames in three different ways – by means of narrative, tasks, and cooperation in teams. On a task-level, the data indicate that the potential for location-based learning is not yet fully utilized. Challenges for the future development of the MILE project are to multiply the MILE tools through training and mentoring, and to unleash the full potential of location-based learning in the domain of nutrition and consumer education.

List of References

Printed

Appadurai, A.: “Disjuncture and Difference in the Global Cultural Economy”. In *Theory, Culture and Society* 7, 1990, pp. 295–310.

Bartsch, S.: “Subjektive Theorien von Studierenden zur Nachhaltigen Ernährung. Explorationsstudie” (“Students’ Subjective Theories of Sustainable Nutrition. Explorative Study.”). *Haushalt in Bildung und Forschung* 4(4), 2015, pp. 78–92.

Bartsch, S.: *Jugendesskultur: Bedeutungen des Essens für Jugendliche im Kontext Familie und Peergroup* (“Adolescent Food Culture: The Significance of Food to Adolescents in the Context of Family and Peer Group”). BZgA: Köln 2008. (Bundeszentrale für gesundheitliche Aufklärung, Band 30.)

Bartsch, S. / Körner, T.: “Lebensmittel wegwerfen? Wertschätzung von Lebensmitteln als Bildungsaufgabe” (“Wasting Foodstuff? Appreciation of Foodstuff as Educational Task”). *Ernährung im Fokus* 12, 2012, pp. 238–243.

Bartsch, S. / Schaal, S.: “Mit digitalen Medien auf der Spur von regionalen Lebensmitteln – ein Pilotprojekt zum mobilen, ortsgebundene Lernen”. (“Using Digital Media to Trace Regional Foodstuffs – A Pilot Project on Mobile, Location-based Learning”) *Haushalt in Bildung und Forschung* 2, 2014, pp. 36–47.

BBRC. Design-based research: An emerging paradigm for educational inquiry. *Educational Researcher* 32(1), 2003, pp. 5–8, 35–37.

Brombach, C. / Bartsch, S. / Winkler, G.: “Ernährungsverhalten im Verlauf von drei Generationen” (“Nutritional Behaviour in the Course of Three Generations”). *Schweizer Zeitschrift für Ernährungsmedizin*, 5(5), 2015, pp. 20–25.

BMFSFJ. Bundesministerium für Familie, Senioren, Frauen und Jugend (Hrsg.): *14. Kinder- und Jugendbericht. Bericht über die Lebenssituation junger Menschen und die Leistungen der Kinder- und Jugendhilfe in Deutschland* (“14th Youth Reprort. Report on the Living Situations of Young People and the Performance of Youth Welfare Services in Germany”). Berlin 2013.

Brosda, C. / Bartsch, S. / Oppermann, L. / Schaal, S.: “On the Use of Audio in the Educational Location Based Game Platform MILE”. In MobileHCI ‘16: 18th International Conference on Human-Computer Interaction with Mobile Devices and Services Adjunct Proceedings, (2016).

CTGV. “Anchored Instruction and Situated Cognition Revisited”. *Educational Technology* 33(3), 1993, pp. 52–70.

Dourish, P.: “Re-Spaceing Place: “Place” and “Space” Ten Years On”. In: *CSCW ’06 Proceedings of the 2006 20th anniversary Conference on Computer-supported Cooperative Work. Banff, Alberta*, 2006. ACM: New York 2006, pp. 299–308.

Dourish, P.: "Re-Space-ing Place: Place and Space Ten Years On". Paper presented at the Computer Supported Cooperative Work Conference, November 4–8, 2006, Banff, Albert, Canada.

Dräger de Teran, T.: *Das große Fressen* ("The Great Feeding"). WWF Deutschland (Hrsg.): Berlin 2015.

Harrison, S. / Dourish, P.: "Re-Place-ing Space: The Roles of Place and Space in Collaborative Systems". In: *CSCW '96 Proceedings of the 1996 ACM Conference on Computer-supported Cooperative Work*. ACM: New York 1996, pp. 67–76.

Hauff, V.: *Unsere gemeinsame Zukunft. Der Brundtland-Bericht der Weltkommission für Umwelt und Entwicklung* ("Our Common Future. The Brundtland Report of the World Commission for Environment and Development"). Greven: Eggenkamp Verlag 1987.

Heidegger, M.: *Sein und Zeit* ("Being and Time"). (Unveränderter Nachdruck 1953, 2006 der 15. Gesamtausgabe). Tübingen: Max Niemeyer Verlag 1927.

Jörissen, J. / Priefer, C. / Bräutigam, K.-R. "Food Waste Generation at Household Level: Results of a Survey among Employees of Two European Research Centers in Italy and Germany". *Sustainability* 7, 2015, pp. 2695–2715.

Kaufmann, S.: *Soziologie der Landschaft* ("Sociology of Landscape"). VS Verlag: Wiesbaden 2005.

Konrad, K. / Traub, S.: *Kooperatives Lernen. Theorie und Praxis in Schule, Hochschule und Erwachsenenbildung* ("Cooperative Learning. Theory and Practice in Schools, Universities, and Adult Education"). Schneider: Hohengehren 2010.

Lave, J. / Wenger, E.: *Situated Learning: Legitimate Peripheral Participation*. Cambridge University Press: Cambridge 1991.

Lengen, C.: "Places: Orte mit Bedeutung" ("Places: Locations with Meaning"). In Gebhard, U. / Kistemann, T. (Hrsg.). *Landschaft, Identität und Gesundheit*. Springer Fachmedien: Wiesbaden 2016, pp. 19–29.

Lévi-Strauss, C.: *Anthropologie structural*. Plon: Paris, 1958. German translation by Naumann, H.: Strukturale Anthropologie I. Suhrkamp: Frankfurt am Main 1967.

Lude A. / Schaal, S. / Bullinger, M. / Bleck, S.: *Mobiles, ortsbezogenes Lernen in der Umweltbildung und Bildung für nachhaltige Entwicklung*") ("Mobile, Location-based Learning in Environmental Education and Education for Sustainable Development"). Schneider Verlag: Hohengehren 2013.

Marchand, S. *Nachhaltig entscheiden lernen. Urteilskompetenzen für nachhaltigen Konsum bei Jugendlichen* ("Learning to decide sustainably. Adolesecents' Competencies to Assess Sustainable Consumption"). Bad Heilbrunn: Klinkhardt 2015.

Oppermann, L. / Slussareff, M.: "Pervasive Games". In Dörner, R. / Göbel, S. / Kickmeir-Rust, M. / Masuch, M. / Zweig, K. A. (Hrsg.). *Entertainment Computing and Serious Games*. Springer Lecture Notes in Computer Science 9970, 2016. DOI: 10.1007 / 978-3-319-46152-6, pp. 475–520.

Relph, E.: *Place and Placelessness*. Pion: London 1976.

Roczen, N. / Kaiser, F. G. / Bogner, F. X. / Wilson, M.: "A Competence Model for Environmental Education". *Environment and Behavior*. Published online 30 June 2013; DOI: 10.1177/0013916513492416.

Schaal, S. / Bartsch, S.: "Jugend im Web 2.0 – Spielorientiertes Lern- und Informationsangebot zur Herkunft unserer Nahrung im Projekt MILE " ("Youth on Web 2.0 – Offering Game-oriented Opportunities for Learning and Informing on the Origin of Our Food in the MILE Project"). In Dr. Rainer Wild-Stiftung (Hrsg.).: *Jugend und Ernährung. Zwischen Fremd- und Selbstbestimmung*. Dr. Rainer Wild-Stiftung: Heidelberg 2015, pp. 47–164.

Schaal, S. / Schaal, S. / Lude, A.: "Digital Geogames to Foster Local Biodiversity". *International Journal for Transformative Research* 3(1), 2015, pp. 16–29.

Schlieder, C.: "Geogames – Gestaltungsaufgaben und geoinformatische Lösungsansätze" ("Geogames – Design Task and Geoinformatic Solution Approaches"). *Informatik-Spektrum* 37(6), 2014, pp. 567–574.

Spiekermann, U.: "Esskultur heute. Was, wie und wo essen wir?" ("Food Culture Today. What, How, and Where We Eat?"). In Dr. Rainer Wild-Stiftung (Hrsg.): *Gesunde Ernährung zwischen Natur- und Kulturwissenschaft*. (Healthy Eating between Natural Sciences and Cultural Studies). Rhema: Münster, 1999, pp. 41–56.

Tamborini, R. / Bowman, N. D. / Eden, A. / Grizzard, M. / Organ, A.: "Defining Media Enjoyment as the Satisfaction of Intrinsic Needs". *Jounal of Communication* 60, 2010, pp. 758–777.

Tuan, Y.F.: *Topophilia: A Study of Environmental Perception, Attitudes and Values.*: Prentice-Hall: Englewood Cliffs, NJ, 1974.

Internet

Bartsch, S. / Schaal, S. / Oppermann, L.: "Location Based Games with Smartphones – Developing a Toolbox For Educators Presentation". 8th World Conference on Educational Sciences 4–6 February 2016, University of Alcala, Madrid, Spain. Retrieved 13.12.2016 from http://www.awer-center.org/abstracts/WCES%202016%20Abstracts%20Book.pdf.

"Common Sense" (2015). "The Common Sense Census: Media Use by Tweens and Teens", retrieved 5.12.2016 from https://www.commonsensemedia.org/sites/default/files/uploads/research/census_ researchreport.pdf.

Dreblow, M. / Schönheit, I.: "Konsumkompetenz von Jugendlichen. Ein Überblick über Kernaussagen aus aktuellen Jugendstudien" ("Adolescents' Competencies in Consumption. An Overview on Core Messages from Contemporary Youth Studies"). Berlin 2010. Verbraucherzentrale Bundesverband e. V. (Hrsg.), retrieved 5.12.2016 from http://www.vzbv.de/sites/default/files/mediapics/konsumkompetenz_jugendliche_studie_imug_vzbv_2010.pdf.

Heseker, H. / Schlegel-Matthies, K. / Heindl, I. / Methfessel, B.: *REVIS Modellprojekt. Reform der Ernährungs- und Verbraucherbildung in Schulen (REVIS) 2003–2005* ("REVIS Model Project. Reform of the Nutrition and Consumer Education in Schools 2003–2005"). Paderborn 2005, retrieved 30.3.2015 from www.evbonline.de/evb_revis_schlussbericht.php.

MPFG. Medienpädagogischer Forschungsverbund Südwest (Hrsg.). "JIM-Studie 2015. Jugend, Information, (Multi-)Media. Basisstudie zum Medienumgang 12- bis 19-Jähriger in Deutschland" ("JIM Study 2015. Youth, Information, Multimedia. Basic Data on the Media Use of 12–19 Year Olds in Germany"), retrieved 30.3.2015 from www.mpfs.

"Mile – Move – Interact –Learn – Eat.", retrieved 5.12.2016 from www.mile.bw.de.

UNEP. United Nations Environment Programme (2009). *Annual Report* 2008, retrieved 1.12.2016 from www.unep.org.

WRAP (2008). Executive summary. "The Food We Waste. A Study of the Amount, Types and Nature of the Food We Throw Away in UK households". Version 2. Branbury, retrieved 5.12.2016 from www.bhfood.org.uk/pdfs/WRAP_-_The_Food_We_Waste_08_-_EXEC.pdf.

Rogéria Campos A. Dutra

Bottled Water Consumption in Brazil: A Matter of Taste?[1]

Abstract: *This paper presents a study of the consumption of bottled water in Brazil. It explores some features of this new and increasing drinking habit in the country. It raises questions about private and public interests and the commodification of nature, by employing exploratory qualitative research based on a transdisciplinary bibliography focusing on a variety of water issues.*

Since it is essential to human life water can be considered an intersecting theme, not only because of its omnipresence but also because of the transdisciplinary literature that deals with the phenomenon. Water has been studied from different perspectives, ranging from analyses of its chemical composition and related soil types, to global governance. Amongst these, specific mention can be made of studies on social and cultural aspects of water in human cultures undertaken by anthropologists (Orlove / Caton 2010, pp. 401–415). The investigation of different forms of valuing water provide us with an opportunity to broaden our perspective on this natural resource, thus contributing to a better understanding of contemporary challenges involved in its management, challenges which have given rise to debates about urbanization, technology, commodification and governance.

Concerning the management of drinking water in ancient and indigenous cultures James Salzman (1995, pp. 1–33) has pointed out that, in general, it was not common for societies to view water as a commercial good, due to its importance for survival. Water was a resource associated with divine beneficence; in times of need, access to drinking water seems to have been a basic right as we can see, for instance, in the rules governing drinking water expressed through the Jewish and Islamic Water Laws.

Although its water fountains were important for the townspeople's water supply, Rome can be considered the first major city that managed drinking water as a priced resource. Due to their engineering and management skills, the Romans enabled efficient water distribution networks to be constructed, the planning of which had been largely neglected by feudal societies with predominantly agrar-

1 The author thanks Fundação de Amparo a Pesquisa do Estado de Minas Gerais (FAPEMIG) for financial support to attend the SIEF 21st International Ethnological Food Research Conference, Heidelberg, 30 August – 2 September 2016.

ian and subsistence economies. In medieval European towns and cities water was considered potentially dangerous to drink, lacking the prestige afforded to wine, beer and ale as hydration choices.

Little progress was made in water supply and sanitation systems until the advent of the Industrial Revolution. The growth of cities, the emergence of pollution and contamination problems as part of city life, and the increasing incidence of disease as a consequence, led to the expansion of waterworks and pumping systems in urban areas. John Snow's mid-19th century London investigation of the spread of cholera through contaminated water had a great impact on future water treatment systems. His findings gave rise to water chlorination as an effective disinfection process, which was adopted, allied to sand filtering, by several cities before distributing water to the public. Continuing advances in science and technology were important factors in consolidating the dominant view of water quality in Western industrialized societies: that it was no longer enough for water to be pleasant-tasting, odorless and clean-looking; it also had to be safe to drink.

In fact, it can be stated, that massive urbanization gave rise, not only to growth in the planning of public water management, but also, as a consequence, once proper sewage and fresh water was available, to major increases in life expectancy and improvement in public health. This can be viewed as part of the scientific project of imposing the human will on nature – defining and measuring water, using rational infrastructural methods of water provision such as channeling and damming of water courses, cleansing water by such means as chemical treatment and purification, and delivering water through organized distribution processes – which has brought, along with many benefits, some challenges as well (Wilk 2006, pp. 303–325). Although urban populations in Third World countries are still struggling over access to water, there is, on the other hand, a growing suspicion concerning water quality around the world, particularly in industrialized countries.

Access to clean and affordable water has been defined as one of the greatest challenges facing developing countries, a situation that is apparently beset with serious problems, such as social inequalities, and mismanagement and inefficiency on many levels and in different contexts. According to The United Nations World Water Developing Report (2015), about 748 million people worldwide lack access to an improved drinking-water system and 2.5 billions do not have access to an improved sanitation facility, an estimate that reveals close connections between poverty and water access. The Cochabamba water war, a series of protests that occurred in the Bolivian city of that name, in response to the privatization of the city's municipal water-supply company – and the consequent increases in the price of the water provided to the consumer – is a good illustration of potable water consumer demands. This is not only because it highlights persistent public inefficacy in relation to potable water management in developing countries, but also because it deals with the consequences for consumers of water-supply privatization as a solution to water scarcity and its unequal distribution. The commodification of water, presented as a solution to potable-water access problems, has been inspired by neo-liberal ideas referencing the virtues of the marketplace rather than the realities of the situation – inefficient government bureaucracy to provide basic public services for citizens.

On the other hand, the recent surge in the contamination of water sources, and the risks arising from chemical byproducts used for water treatment purposes, indicate, that concerns about drinking water are no longer focused only on the elimination of pathogens from the water supply. The water crisis in the city of Flint, Michigan, in the United States, in which contaminated tap water gave rise to lead poisoning, illness and even death among children (https://www.rt.com/usa/329881-flint-water-lead-poisoning-usa/, retrieved 17.10.2016), can be pointed to as one of many incidents that are contributing to an increasing level of distrust of public water supplies, in both rich and poor countries. Conversely, such problems provide new opportunities for the expansion of the market for bottled water, the production of which is part of a larger process of commodification of nature within a capitalist commodity-culture.

The packaged water narrative has a long history, arising, as it does, from deep-rooted ideas about magical and healing powers associated with water. Sacred springs and wells were viewed as sources of vitality, connecting people to the power of nature, as can observed with reference to the contagious magic of baptism, libation, bathing, and drinking, present both in pagan and Christian traditions. Water from the Apollinaire springs, for example, had been transported in vessels throughout Europe since classical antiquity. Recognizing the benefits of drinking and bathing in natural waters, the Romans built thermal and public baths in many parts of the Empire (Salzman 1995, pp. 1–33; Wilk 2006, pp. 303–325). There are controversies concerning the name "Spa", but some authors affirm that it is derived from the Latin expression *Salus per Aqua* (Health through Water), referring to the Roman tradition of water treatments, which, later on, inspired the term Spa for the Belgium city of that name, because of the curative properties of its thermal spring (Crook / Whitfield /Jackson 2009).

Although mineral springs and pools retained some cultural significance in medieval times, it was in the 18th and 19th centuries that spa culture came to popularity. Apart from the revival of medical uses for spring water promoted by the Enlightened physicians of the second half of the eighteenth century (https://www.researchgate.net/publication/49719636_Enlightened_Physicians_Setting_Out_on_an_Elite_Academic_Career_in_the_Second_Half_of_the_Eighteenth_Century, retrieved 18.10.2016), bathing and water-drinking practices were also encouraged by an emerging bourgeoisie class searching for refinement and distinctive healthy habits. In contrast to lavish aristocratic meetings – marked by excesses and carnal components, which were manifestly incompatible with the bourgeoisie's notions of productivity and well-being – spa visiting became a respectable way of spending free time (Mackaman 1998). Taking the healthful waters home became a common practice among such visitors.

By the end of 19th century, bottling plants emerged throughout Europe and the United States, and, gradually, over the last century, bottled water became more widely distributed in stores, cafés and restaurants. Global bottled-water sales increased as a result, and the rate of consumption more than quadrupled between 1990 and 2005 (Li 2007, retrieved 18.10.2016 from http://www.worldwatch.org/). Currently, it is the fastest growing segment of the non-alcoholic beverage market, to the extent that it is projected to exceed carbonated soft-drinks' consumption in the coming years (Esterl 2015, retrieved 14.6.2016 from http://www.wsj.com/articles/water-water-everywherein-bottles-1440581400).

Drinking bottled water, however, may be more than a practical way of quenching thirst out of home – a common reality for the greater part of contemporary societies involved in office work. It touches on a full cultural complex involving the pursuit of the purest water, which is driven by the desire for health and in order to come close to nature, or even to social distinction. The semiotics of bottled-water labels and advertisements deal efficiently with our water imaginary, by appealing to the deep-rooted values of our modern industrialized society. The budgets earmarked for the publicity campaigns of the bottled-water industry leapt from 43 million dollars per year in the 1990s to 20 million dollars for the outdoor campaigns of a single bottled-water brand, ten years later (Doria 2006, pp. 271–276). Some of the campaigns emphasize water purity and health, presenting their products as tokens of nature and talismans of health, as the pictures of pristine mountains, glaciers, and islands on their labels would seem to demonstrate. Others emphasize the idea of distinction in branded-water consumption, since the bottled water of famous brands, such as Dasani and Perrier, has been promoted as a life-style drink or as a status symbol. This distinctive consumption can be demonstrated by the rise of water sommeliers, who are to be found in some of the finest and most fashionable hotels in cities such as Tokyo, Paris and Los Angeles, advising premium customers on their choice of branded water, thus elevating bottled water to a status that rivals the culture of wine.

The reasons for increasing consumption of bottled water worldwide, are not straightforward, however, once diverse possibilities, according to region and country, as can be seen in the case of Brazil, for example, are involved.

A Matter of Taste?

It is estimated that about 12 % of the world reserves of freshwater are located in Brazil, thus placing this country in a privileged position worldwide in this respect. Nevertheless, the notion of abundance obscures serious problems regarding water access due to geographical features in different regions in the country, as well as widespread social inequalities. Besides the large number of poor Brazilians still living in urban slums and in rural areas without access to treated water and sanitation, there are other factors that contribute to Brazilian water-management challenges, such as the postponement of investments in water-management facilities that would allow for more efficient use of water and the implementation of water-resource protection policies.

Since the second half of 20th century, Brazilian water resources have been adversely affected by population growth and by the transformation of the country's economic profile. Industrialization, and the consequent migration of workers from rural to urban areas, as well as the growth of agricultural irrigation in order to produce food, greatly increased demand for water.

Water quality in Brazil has been seriously affected by untreated sewage effluent – one of the major causes of water pollution in the country. That this has led to the undermining of the quality of life and health of people living in large cities, can be demonstrated by the fact that in the year 2000, according to the National Survey of Basic Sanitation (PNSB),[2] only 35 % of collected wastewater received any treatment, leading inevitably to the contamination of water sources, feeder rivers, and lakes.

In 2015, São Paulo, Brazil's largest city, suffered its severest water crisis in almost a century. But climate change, leading to rain shortfall, was only partly to blame for the daily water shutoffs that affected the city's population at that time. This city of approximately 20 million inhabitants has been plagued by the effects of a failing water-supply infrastructure, particularly in the poorer overpopulated districts, for some considerable time. The shortage of water hit, then, the entire southeastern region of the country – the most populated and industrialized part, which also includes Brazil's second largest city, Rio de Janeiro – giving rise to a

2 Brazilian Institute for Geography and Statistics (IBGE): National Survey of Basic Sanitation (PNSB) 2000.

public debate about inefficient water-management policies by public authorities. All of these factors have been contributing to a growing suspicion of the quality of tap water, thus enabling the market for bottled water to expand in Brazil.

Perceptions of water quality have been the object of a considerable amount of research in the last 50 years in order to improve the implementation of technical solutions regarding water supply. However, as Doria (2010, pp. 1–19) points out, if until the 1990s, water quality standards based on scientific parameters were broadly accepted, since then, the judgment of drinking water safety has been changing. Water quality standards have also become a matter of debate, due to the emergence of the general public as an important social actor in water management, whose opinions should be considered. Political decisions should then be made, taking into account social and cultural perceptions of what an acceptable level of risk in relation to drinking water, is.

Bottled water consumption varies according to gender and social position, something which has been demonstrated by Brazilian researchers in recent times (Queiroz et al. 2013, pp. 520–531). Having conducted an investigation into drinking water preferences in Brazil, they have pointed out that while essentially the same factors drive bottled-water sales in South America as in North America and Europe, there are also differences to be observed. In Brazil, for example, health and risk concerns were the most obvious factors that justified bottled water consumption, according to research carried out in three municipalities, while it was mainly organoleptic aspects, such as water taste and odor, which were of concern in First World countries. Concerns about tap-water quality and supply have also influenced household bottled-water consumption in Brazil, especially among the poor population, according to the research (Coelho / Cardoso 2010), with more than 80 % of poor, low-income households living in Vitoria, the State of Espírito Santo's capital, spending more money on bottled water than on tap water.

The same investigation conducted in the three Brazilian municipalities also revealed the role which women played as the main actors in choosing drinking water sources for their families, as they appeared to have a higher perception of water-related health risks than men. However, those "… in charge of water supply infrastructure and management, including water related campaigns and bottled water distribution, are often men" (Queiroz / Doria / Heller / Zhouri 2013, pp. 520–531). Thus, the integration of gender equality into water-management processes would seem to be necessary in order to achieve a more risk-aware approach to public water provision.

Because many Brazilian consumers have only a basic knowledge about water composition, confusion has arisen with regard to the features that make mineral water different from tap water. Although fluoride is not a criterion for mineral-water classification according to Brazilian law, nevertheless, from the 1980s, the National Department of Mineral Production (BNPM) regarded any kind of bottled water containing the mineral fluoride as qualified to be accorded the status of mineral water. Thus, even a minute concentration of the mineral fluoride in bottled drinking-water was enough to allow it to be classified as "mineral water". This gave rise to the banal use of the term with the result that all bottled water was referred to simply as "mineral water" (ibid.).

Bottled water consumption in Brazil has been continuously growing over the last twenty years, thus following the global trend towards expansion in the bottled water market. Presently the country is the fifth major market of this commodity worldwide. Though the existing market, involving many regional companies, is largely fragmented, the trend towards global expansion, by mega-corporations, through investment in the drinking water business in developing countries, can also be identified in Brazil (Junior / Reydon / Portugal 2015, pp. 413–430). The four leading companies in this segment – Nestlé Waters, Danone, Coca-Cola and PepsiCo – are targeting the drinking-water market in Brazil for focused investment, which in turn is giving rise to public debates about the need for control regarding this strategic and finite resource.

The presence of the multinational company, Nestlé Waters, in developing countries has been controversial. Launched in Pakistan towards the end of 1990s, *Pure Life* – a Nestlé bottled-water brand – was then the object of a massive marketing campaign. This consisted, not only of contributions to "awareness seminars" with government officials, with the aim of having the population officially warned about the risks of contamination of urban water supplies, but also of the distribution of leaflets and samples of the product, backed by the campaign slogan "Welcome to purity" (Rosemann 2005, retrieved 27.8.2016 from (http://www.alliancesud.ch/en/policy/climate/downloads/nestle-pakistan.pdf). In Brazil, *Pure Life* production was based on the process of demineralizing water obtained from a spring in the water park of the historic spa town of São Lourenço. This had an adverse impact on others springs in the water park and also on the local tourism business. Furthermore, water demineralization is not allowed under Brazilian law, and this massive operation in this hydromineral station, has also had negative environmental impacts (Ninis / Drummond, retrieved 13.9.2016 from (http://www.alliancesud.ch/en/policy/climate/downloads/nestle-pakistan.pdf). An analysis of the social and environmental conflicts associated with *Pure Life* production has revealed that the bottling industry is incompatible with the continuation of the hitherto relatively stable and prosperous economy, derived from tourism, of this small town.

Nevertheless, sales of bottled water seem to keep growing in Brazil, not only with regard to market share, but also in terms of added value. This is particularly so after local companies invested in portfolio differentiation following the example of imported brands. If, previously, Brazilians paid little attention to brands and were only concerned about whether the water served in restaurants was of the still or sparkling variety, nowadays consumers have started to buy premium bottled water. The sub-segmentation of the bottled-water market is noticeable because of the growing number of products being offered for consumption, such as, the "purest" types, those with calibrated pH levels and minerality, and those with additional elements. Spa culture, and the diffusion of the body-health industry, are closely connected with the rise of bottled-water consumption, and also with the increased intake of nutritional supplements.

As we can see, bottled water as a form of cultural consumption, has been guided either by values that emphasize its close connection to nature – thus conferring power and health to the consumer – or by those associated with technological convenience. The drinking of water, with ideally-balanced levels of elements, therapeutic compositions and flavours, and available in different bottle designs – options which accord with individual preferences – is becoming a meaningful part of daily life (Wilk 2006, p. 306). Furthermore, the plastic packaging of water – associated with cultural meanings of purity, cleanliness and controlled contamination – references the very same ideas that earlier gave rise to public-water treatment strategies.

Wilk (2006, p. 310) points out that our ambivalence towards nature refers to "... unresolved and longstanding conflicts in western cultures about technology and the body", indicating two healing traditions in the West: a Gnostic one that deals with the utopian possibilities of technology to transform and heal nature and the body, and a Romantic one that treats technology with suspicion because of its capacity to move humans from nature. As a commodity, water touches on conflicts between market and moral values, a theme present in debates since the beginnings of capitalism.

The trade in commoditized water reveals dissident perspectives that defend water as a public good, either regarding it as a part of Nature, or as a collective resource that claims to be well managed. However, it seems that water marketing forms a symbiotic and entangled relationship with commodification resistance once anti-commercial attitudes give rise to new branding and commodification opportunities. Based on criticism of industrialization, nature destruction, and scientific water-manipulation, the pursuit of the *purest* water has given rise to creative branding, such as the bottling of deep-sea water. Likewise, concerns about unequal water distribution in capitalist culture have led to the appearance of the bottling labels of some corporations guaranteeing philanthropical financial support for initiatives to provide water for the poor.

Therefore, as noted by Salzman (1995, pp. 1–33), the viewing of drinking-water management as a binary conflict between rights and markets, and between public and private management forces, leads to a false dichotomy. It is also an ahistorical perspective on water management, since it ignores societies that, throughout history, have left examples of public and private arrangements with regard to drinking water provision and access. Perhaps it is by considering drinking water to be, ultimately, a *unique* resource, that strategies for dealing with contemporary challenges in drinking-water management can be best and fairly resolved.

List of References

Printed

Brazilian Institute for Geography and Statistics (IBGE): National Survey of Basic Sanitation (PNSB) 2000.

Crook, M. / Whitfield, T. W. A. / Jackson, S.: *The Commodification of H_2O: How Water became a Designed Product.* Swimburne Research Bank, Swinburne University of Technology and RMIT University: Melbourne 2009.

Doria, Miguel: "Factors Influencing Public Perception of Drinking Water Quality". *Water Policy* 12, 2010, pp. 1–19.

Doria, Miguel: "Bottled Water Versus Tap Water: Understanding Consumers' Preferences". *Journal of Water Health* 4(2), 2006, pp. 271–276.

Ferrier, C.: "Bottled Water: Understanding a Social Phenomenon". Report commissioned by the World Wide Fund for Nature (WWF), 2001.

Junior, Pedro dos Santos Portugal / Reydon, Bastiaan Philip / Portugal, Nilton dos Santos: "As águas minerais no Brasil: uma análise do mercado e da institucionalidade para uma gestão integrada e sustentável ("Mineral Waters in Brazil: An Analysis of the Market and Institutional Framework for Integrated and Sustainable Management"). *Rev. Ambiente & Água* 10(2), June 2015, pp. 413–430.

Mackmann D. P.: *Leisure Settings: Bourgeois, Culture, Medicine and the Spa in Modern* France. The University of Chicago Press: Chicago / London 1998.

Orlove, B. / Caton, S.: "Water Sustainability: Anthropological Approaches and Prospects". *Annual Review of Anthropology* 39, 2010, pp. 401–415.

Queiroz, Emanuel T. de / Silva, João Da Goméa Fidelis da / Baretto, Alencar Moreira: *Águas minerais do Brasil: distribuição, classificação e importância econômica* ("Mineral Waters in Brazil: Distribution, Classification and Economic Importance") Brasília: Departamento Nacional de Produção Mineral, Diretoria de Desenvolvimento e Economia Mineral 2004.

Queiroz, J.T. / Doria, Mde F. / Heller, L. / Zhouri, A.: "Perceptions of Bottled Water Consumption in Three Brazilian Municipalities". *Journal of Water and Health* 11(3), 2013, pp. 520–531.

Salzman, James: "Thirst: A Short History of Drinking Water". *Duke Law School Legal Studies*. Research Paper 92, December 1995, pp. 1–33.

The United Nations World Water Development Report 2015: Water for a Sustainable World. United Nations Education, Scientific and Cultural Organisation: Paris 2015.

Wilk, R.: "Bottled Water: The Pure Commodity in the Age of Branding". *Journal of the Consumer Culture* 6(3), 2006, pp. 303–325.

Internet

"Enlightened Physicians: Setting Out on an Elite Academic Career in the Second Half of the Eighteenth Century", retrieved 18.10.2016 from https://www.researchgate.net/publication/49719636_Enlightened_Physicians_Setting_Out_on_an_Elite_Academic_Career_in_the_Second_Half_of_the_Eighteenth_Century.

Esterl, M.: "Water, Water, Everywhere – In Bottles". *The Wall Street Journal* 27 August 2015, retrieved 14.6.2016 from http://www.wsj.com/articles/water-water-everywherein-bottles-1440581400.

"Flint water crisis triggers debate over lead poisoning of children across US", retrieved 17.10.2016 from https://www.rt.com/usa/329881-flint-water-lead-poisoning-usa/.

Li, Ling: "Bottled Water Consumption Jumps". *Worldwatch Institute*. November 8, 2007, retrieved 18.10.2016 from http://www.worldwatch.org/.

Ninis, Alessandra B. / Drummond, José A.: "Mineral Water Production in São Lourenço (Minas Gerais, Brazil) – Private or Public Matter?" retrieved 13.9.2016 from https://www.academia.edu/3894693/Mineral_Water_Production_in_S%C3%A3o_Louren%C3%A7o_Minas_Gerais_Brazil_private_or_public_matter.

Rosemann, Neal: "Drinking Water Crisis in Pakistan and the Issue of Bottled Water: The Case of Nestlé's 'PureLife'". Action Aid Pakistan. Swiss Coalition of Development Organizations. April, 2005, retrieved 27.8.2016 from http://www.alliancesud.ch/en/policy/climate/downloads/nestle-pakistan.pdf.

Håkan Jönsson

One Hundred Years of Solitude and Commensality – A Study of Cooking and Meals in Swedish Households

Abstract: *This article aims to unwrap changing practices and attitudes to meals and cooking in Sweden through a comparative study of open-ended questionnaires. The most prominent changes are the re-gendering of cooking, and the new forms of commensality created by meals and cooking. It is argued that kitchens should be seen as living laboratories where societal changes such as globalisation are handled and incorporated into everyday life.*

Introduction

From sourcing food to the meal itself, the preparation and intake of meals in Swedish households have undergone significant changes in recent decades. The transitions which are taking place in meals and cooking in these households are affecting not only the food intake of individuals, but can also can be seen as being an important part of emerging cultural processes involving views on gender, family and social positions. This paper aims to shed some light on these processes by combining material concerning them collected from the 1970s until the present day. A comparison made between the different periods in this time frame is used in order to unwrap changing practices and attitudes to meals and cooking during the periods in question. The food ingredients, as well as the beverages, the cooking, and the meal situations, are described and analysed. Special emphasis is placed on issues of eating and community. The title, playing with that of Gabriel Garcia Marquez's famous novel, refers to the dialectics between solitude and commensality that cooking and meals imply. Generally, meals have been commensal, while cooking is carried out in solitude. This article tries to explain, and, at the same time, to give a more nuanced picture of this phenomenon than what has hitherto been provided. The reverse situation – the fact of communal cooking and the taking of meals in solitude is also evident in the empirical material used in this paper.

The article starts by considering the actual food and drinks consumed according to the source material. Three things are highlighted by most of the informants: an increasing consumption of (fresh) vegetables, an increasing amount, and a larger variety of, spices being used, and changing habits with regard to the kind of beverages consumed. After describing and discussing the new consumption habits evident in the empirical material, the article moves on to deal with the cooking practices involved. It asks, for example, about who does the cooking, and when the cooking tasks are performed in the kitchens. In this context, gender divisions and their relation to power are regarded as central issues to be discussed. Finally, the article concludes with a comparison being made between cooking and eating, and between how solitude and commensality were, and are, lived out in the Swedish households.

Notes on Material and Methodology

The empirical basis of this article consists of responses to three questionnaires issued to respondents by Folklife Archives in Sweden. In 1972, 1988 and 2016, similar open-ended questionnaires about cooking practices, household appliances, and meal structure and content, were sent out by these archives. Those from 1972 and 1988 were issued from the Uppsala Folklife Archive, while the later questionnaire, dating from 2016, which I composed, was sent out from Lund. The issuing of open-ended questionnaires has a long tradition in Swedish ethnological research. Such questionnaires have been used for collection, documentation, and research purposes by Folklife archives there since 1932. They have been, and are, distributed to the archives' network of so-called solid respondents – those who tend to reply on a fairly regular basis to requests for information on various ethnological topics – and this means of gathering reliable data has been shown to be an effective qualitative method of research (Hagström 2015). The lists of questions on different topics are sent out three to four times a year. At present, there are 130 respondents connected to the Folklife Archive in Lund, and each questionnaire usually generates between 60 to 80 responses, each being in essay form and each averaging between four to six pages in length. For the 2016 questionnaire on cooking and meals (LUF 244), 59 answers have been registered to date (July 2016). In addition to the full-length questionnaire, a shorter-web based questionnaire has been issued and has received 72 responses so far (2016). The questionnaire from 1972 (S 27) on dietary changes and that from 1988 (M 239) about the kitchen and its artifacts, have been used both as primary source material for this study and also for developing LUF 244. Many of the questions from the early questionnaires have been reused in order to allow comparisons in time to be made.[1] Since many of the older informants who responded to the early questionnaires were referring

1 The questionnaire deals with a large number of questions related to food, cooking and the household. Several questions deal with the kitchen, and the artifacts within it, and

back to their youth in the first decades of the 1900s, the responses in total from the three questionnaires cover a period of, and deal with, one hundred years of cooking and eating in Sweden.[2]

The use of the term "Swedish" in this article is not intended to mean that there is but a single Swedish meal-order or food-culture. There are certainly differences observable in the questionnaire replies between the various informants' practices, ideals, and experiences, related to social position, gender, ethnicity, generation, health status, regional variations, and so on. Having said that, I would also like to stress the fact that the period under investigation here is one in which cooking practices and meals had specific national characteristics evident throughout the country. It was a time in which the food-producing companies in Sweden, and, to an even larger extent, the period also when the distribution and retail companies, developed into national enterprises and created national standards for the range and variety of goods available in retail stores. The rapid development of meals in the public sector (especially school lunches) established national standards for meals, and national television and radio were important communication channels for the provision of information about cooking and meal provision. The very fact of cooking and eating in Sweden means that one has shared, and still shares, experiences and practices with other cooks and eaters in Sweden. Therefore I argue that it is fruitful to speak about cooking and meals in national terms, and also to use the results of the aforementioned questionnaires sent out from both the Lund (Southern Sweden) and Uppsala (Central Sweden) archives in this context.

Vegetables and the Death of the Proper Meal

The statement that "I / we eat much more vegetables these days", is the most common first answer to the question: "If you look at the food / ingredients you use in your cooking, what are the key differences that these have undergone during your time as cook, and what do you believe has contributed to these changes?" A

---

with the meal order. These questions are being left out in this article, which focuses on other aspects of the material.

2 In addition to the questionnaires, interviews and participant observations complement the contemporary material. 27 interviews and 5 observations have been conducted as part of the project. Since there is a bias towards older people with families living in Sweden for generations among the solid respondents, interviews have been collected in order to get material that covers a broader diversity of life experiences. Younger people with a family background from other countries are better represented in the interview category.

large number of informants stated that they had started to eat vegetarian meals on a regular basis. Some are indeed fully committed vegetarians, but most of the respondents who mention these meals are in fact referring to something that adds variety to their eating habits and that also provides them with a way in which to live up to values involved for living a healthy and sustainable life, rather than to a vegetarian diet.

If the respondents' view of how their eating habits have changed is compared to the statistical data available in this regard, it is noticeable that the consumption of fresh fruit and vegetables has indeed increased in Sweden; in fact it has almost tripled since 1970. Another striking feature evident in the statistics is the overall increase in the consumption of meat (especially of poultry, pork and beef), which has more than doubled since 1970 (*Statistics from the Swedish Board of Agriculture, Report 2013:04*). But none of the informants say that they themselves consume more meat than formerly. On the contrary, they highlight how they believe that they eat less meat-based meals nowadays. But the stories from the statistics, and those from the informants, are not as incompatible as they may seem at first sight. The situation is related to what I would like to call "the death of the proper meal", with reference to Mary Douglas's investigation of meal components (Douglas 1972, p. 1). The proper meal, as defined in British studies (Murcott 1995, pp. 89–99; Charles / Kerr 1998), was substantially similar to its counterpart in the Nordic countries for much of the twentieth century. A proper meal should consist of potatoes (normally boiled), meat or fish, gravy, and supplements (boiled or pickled vegetables, jam, jelly, etc.). But not even the older generation sticks to this meal concept any longer. A woman, aged 79 years, described the situation in this regard as follows:

> The former classical alimentation with meat or fish, gravy and potatoes changed significantly some years ago. I would say that now I always have some vegetables on the plate, and very often neither gravy nor potatoes, but definitely vegetables in some format (LUF 244 / M27474).[3]

The reasons that many informants think that meat has more or less disappeared from meals, when in fact more meat is actually being consumed, are most likely due to a combination of factors. Firstly, there does not appear to be a realization that when meat is actually served that the portions have become larger; or that products such as sausages have a higher meat content than formerly; or that meat-

3 The references to the responses to the open-ended questionnaires are written as follows: Name of the questionnaire (e. g. LUF 244) / number of the specific answer (e. g. M27474).

loaves and meat balls served at home also contain more meat nowadays as there are less fillers such as bread crumbs, mashed potatoes, or rice, included. Another reason for this view is probably the decrease in the consumption of what are actually vegetarian meals though not considered as such. Porridge, for example, which was until quite recently (the 1980s) a common dish for both morning and evening meals, is now quite unusual in these contexts. When replaced by sandwiches with ham or salami, or by a full meal in the evening, meat consumption was actually increasing without being noticed.

Another disruption of norms related to the idea of proper meals concerns the serving of specific dishes on specific days. In the early questionnaires, the meals followed a weekly rhythm. Among the frequently-mentioned dishes that marked a distinction between the weekdays were salted herring being served on Mondays, pea soup on Thursdays, and steak on Sundays. Although the tradition to serve pea soup on Thursdays is not totally abolished, it is clear that the previous rather strict norms in this regard are now easily ignored. A woman, aged 70 years, related a striking example of this:

> The other day I asked my partner: Can one have pork pancake (a typical simple mid-week dish) on a Sunday? I was hungry for it, and the partner caught on (LUF 244 / M27473).

The disruption of norms concerning what a proper meal is, and when it should be served, could potentially evoke sentiments of nostalgia is this regard. But none of the informants expressed such views. On the contrary, if they touched upon the subject at all, they did so in positive terms, invoking a sense of freedom from customary meal systems rather than having a sense of a loss of traditions.

Spices – The Domestic Kitchen as a Melting Pot

Until quite recently, one of the main characteristics of food in Sweden was, apart from its high salt content, the absence or low degree of spices used. "We use salt. And (white) pepper", is the brief comment from an informant to the 1988 questionnaire, in response to the question about what spices they used in his household. Although other informants mention spices such as thyme, marjoram, savory, lovage, bay leaf, and allspice, in actual fact the regular use of spices in the preparation of everyday meals in Swedish households was limited. When it came to baking, the story was a bit different, however. Bread with caraway, fennel (kernels) and anise, and buns and cookies with cinnamon, saffron, ginger, cardamom and cloves, were commonly baked in these households during the 20th century.

The diversity of spices mentioned in the answers from the informants to the 2016 questionnaire is considerably greater than that found in the earlier questionnaire responses. Many of the respondents mention how they really enjoy spicy food, and how the introduction of spices such as chili, garlic, and fresh ginger, as well as dried spices and mixtures, has changed their cooking habits. Garlic is one of the spices that has made a long journey from being exotic and strange to being an everyday staple item in Swedish culinary culture. As a restaurant chef during the 1980s, I was instructed not to include garlic in food prepared for staff, since the guests should not be exposed to the unpleasant breath of a garlic-eating waiter. Nowadays garlic is considered to be both commonly used and to be unproblematic by the informants. The use of spices was often brought up when the introduction of dishes originating from other countries was mentioned. An 80-year-old woman, stated:

> Lots of new dishes have come over the years; in my youth there was no pasta apart from macaroni, which was stewed and served with sausage. Now, there are lots of pasta varieties, both dried and fresh. I buy mostly tagliatelle or papardelle; I like the wide bands (LU 244: 5).

Osso, bucco, Thai food, and tacos, are some examples of other dishes mentioned by the informants as having been included in their standard repertoire.

The international influences involved when it comes to food and eating is a worldwide phenomenon, since few areas have been so affected by globalisation as eating habits have. The interesting thing here is the degree to which dishes originating in other countries have become part of a standard repertoire in domestic cooking in Sweden. The most common dish cooked in a Swedish household today is Spaghetti Bolognese. Although a visitor from Bologna is unlikely to recognize the dish bearing the name of his or her home city, it says something about the transformation of Swedish domestic cooking during recent decades. The most popular dish for Friday night dinner among families with children is tacos, to mention another example in this context. Since the 1960s, cookery-book authors, as well as radio and television programmes, have successfully introduced dishes and cooking techniques (woking, steaming, stir frying) from other countries and adapting them to ingredients available in Sweden.

It may look as if this situation has come about as a result of a weak sense of national identity. But one has to take into account, that one of the main characteristics of Swedish (middle class) identity, which developed during the second part of the 20th century, was the embracing of modernity. Being Swedish was not necessarily about guarding traditions. On the contrary, the ideal Swedish citizen should be open to new influences, whether introduced by means of new technologies or through international inspiration (Löfgren 1992, pp. 91–115). The domestic kitchen became a melting pot, where international aspects were introduced, negotiated, and domesticated, and where they became what they are today: an unproblematic part of everyday kitchen practice in Sweden.

Becoming "European" – New Drinking Habits

The kinds of beverages consumed in Sweden have also undergone quite dramatic changes. Most notable in this regard is the introduction of wine as a regular beverage during meals. Until the 1950s, wine drinking was uncommon in Sweden, with an average consumption of not more than 1 to 5 litres per person per year (Sundström / Ekström 1962). In 2015, the consumption had increased dramatically to more than 20 litres per year, which means that Sweden is somewhere around 15th place in the world when it comes to wine consumption per individual. One informant, a former military officer in his late 70s, wrote in 2016: "Wine has become a beverage used several times a week. Bottled water has replaced other drinks" (LUF 244 / M27446).

This quote also points to the other most prominent change in relation to beverages: the drinking of water. In the earlier questionnaires, water was said to be rare as a drink taken with meals. The common beverages included in meals at that time were milk, (light) beer and sometimes drinks based on berries, principally lingonberries. The absence of references to water being included as a beverage in the early questionnaires does not necessarily mean that it was not consumed during meals, as it could have been regarded as not being a "real beverage" and could, therefore, have been excluded from the answers. Another reason that it might not have been mentioned was the existing common association between being poor and the drinking of water; in other words, milk or beer could not be afforded. People who preferred water for different reasons may have been unwilling to mention it, so as not to be considered poor or stingy. From the 1970s onwards, however, the taking of water as a beverage became more and more associated with having a healthy lifestyle. The massive introduction of bottled carbonated water in the 1990s, and the availability of carbonators for domestic use, established water consumption as something positive and healthy.

Until the 1980s, milk was essentially the standard beverage taken with an everyday meal, but its use decreased almost at the same pace as water and wine consumption with meals increased. The consumption of milk, which was 160 litres per person per year in 1960, had dropped to just over 80 litres in 2013 (*Statistics from the Swedish Board of Agriculture, Report 2013:04*). Taking into account that a large portion of the milk bought nowadays is consumed as a part of coffee drinking, or taken with cereals, or used in cooking, it is clear that the drinking of milk as a beverage is no longer common.

The scale of international influences evident in household beverage consumption has been just as dramatic as in food change. From the 1980s onwards, a deliberate attempt to break away from norms and habits considered to be "typically Swedish" – that is boring, modest and non-hedonistic – can be seen. In some cases, the decision to drink water instead of milk for lunch or dinner may be due to something as simple as having an idea that milk was not a fit accompaniment for Thai or Mexican food, for example. But the abandonment of milk as a typical beverage during meals had more to it than this. Milk had special status as a "Swedish" beverage. In earlier works I have interpreted the changing status of milk in Swedish eating habits as being part of Sweden's transition from being an industrial society to an experience economy (Jönsson 2005, pp. 105–116; 2013, pp. 127–142). The drinking of water and wine has become a means by which to perform an identity linked to being an outward-looking and tolerant person with a lifestyle that leaves room for both healthy practices and indulgence. The term "continental", referring to the European continent south of Scandinavia, achieved very positive overtones in the Swedish context, and the copying of some of the eating and drinking habits of Southern Europe has become part of the cultural capital of the Swedish middle class.

Who's Cooking? – Towards a Re-gendering of Cooking

Cooking has always been an important part of gender relations and the division of labour among men and women (Adams 1990; Counihan 1999). Critical feminist research has argued that the traditional female role of feeding the family has been an important part of the reason why women have tended to be excluded from public power (DeVault 1991). However, it can be argued, that there is also a dimension of power in the act of cooking as it determines what kind of food other members of the family should eat (Avakian 2006). The person who controls food intake can affect not only bodily functions, but can also thereby imprint values and virtues onto other members of the household. In most societies, changing gender norms, when it comes to cooking, can be noted. The transformation of the labour market, new ideals with regard to family relationships and the rearing of children, as well as the upgrading of professional cooking and male chefs becoming stars of the television era, are all factors that have led to more and more men taking an active part in domestic cooking.

This development is certainly notable in the source material used in this article. Some of the male respondents to the early questionnaires found it hard to answer questions about cooking. A few even let their wives answer the specific questionnaire although it was the man who was the regular respondent, with the excuse that he did not have much to say about the topic. No such dilemma is evident in the contemporary material, however. There are still examples of relationships where the woman performs most of the cooking tasks, but there are also plenty of examples of the opposite situation. Some women state that they have learned to cook with the assistance of their more skilled male partner. The ideal of seeing cooking as a joint task that should be (fairly) equally distributed between partners is a common aspect of the questionnaire replies.

Of special interest here is the long process of emancipation in Sweden. The traditional gender roles had already started to crack in the early 1960s. Among the 2016 questionnaire informants was an 80-year old man who was doing all the cooking in the household, although his wife is in good health. Plenty of others describe, not only their own households as one in which cooking is a shared activity or even a male-dominant task, but they also indicate that their parents' households were ones in which the father took responsibility for cooking. The development is further supported by recent quantitative research which shows that men cook more than one third of all meals prepared in Sweden, and that the proportion is even larger among the younger generation (Holm et al. 2015, pp. 589–610).[4] Domestic cooking in Sweden is about to lose its role as a female practice.

The term "mothering" used to describe the female role of cooking in families has proven to be a fruitful concept for gaining an understanding of the negotiations and practices that women perform in relation to cooking (Molander 2011). Cooking is certainly still an important part of the caring for and the raising of families. But the contemporary material poses some important questions for future research. When fathers have the main responsibility for domestic cooking, is the food served any different from mothers' home-cooked food? There has been a lot of pressure on women to foreground health and household aspects when it comes to cooking, while men have been allowed to have a more sensory and hedonistic perspective on cooking. If this is still true, the re-gendering of cooking may potentially have a large impact on views on domestic cooking, and eventually on the health status of the population. This is related to another question – what happens to cooking as a form of caring? Or to put it differently: how is *fathering* performed in cooking?

4 Among the interesting conclusions of this study is that there are no longer any significant differences between social classes. While middle-class men, in 1977, were more likely to cook than men from other social groups, no such differences could be found in 2012.

Our Meals but My Cooking – Some Notes on Commensality, Knowledge Transformation, and the Power of Cooking

The idea of a decline in commensal eating, especially as regards the family meal, leading to individualized eating and constant nibbling, with harmful effects on public health, is something that has been highly debated in recent years. However, the empirical research that has been done on the subject, has established a more nuanced picture in this regard (Short 2006; Kjærnes 2001). Most people still want to eat together, and most families devote a lot of time and energy to the establishment of commensal eating patterns. However, there are other factors, such as demographic changes, that certainly make it more difficult to eat together with others. Even though there are still cultural values creating normative pressures towards commensal eating, there is also a form of structural individualization related to changing living conditions, which lead to a kind of dietary individualization (Sobal / Nelson 2003, pp. 181–189). The high level of single households, and of divorce among married couples with children, are factors that make it difficult for many people to eat together with the family, no matter how strong the ideal of a proper family meal might still be for them. This picture is confirmed by the material in this study. While the actual number of meals eaten with others has decreased, the ideal of the family meal is still attractive for many people. Although most informants mention conflicts related to meals in the household, they still (with few exceptions) highlight the joys of communal eating.

When it comes to cooking, the picture is different. As Frances Short has noticed in her study about what cooking means "in everyday life", cooking is normally an individual task (Short 2001). Most cooks want to cook alone, and if others are involved, their task should preferably be to take over the cooking on specific days or occasions (thereby allowing for leisure activities), or to help out with simple tasks, such as peeling potatoes or setting the table.

The individualistic character of cooking may explain why many of the informants claim that cooking skills have not been transferred from one generation to the next. The informants from the 1970s, 1980s, and also from the present day, have, with some exceptions, the same story to tell in this regard. They learned to cook after they had left the family household, either by "practice and my own mistakes", by using cookery books, or by picking up skills from a partner with more cooking ability than themselves. Stories about how the respondents' mothers did not want them in the kitchen while cooking are quite common in the source material. Some mention how they discuss housework with friends, but that is not without its problems, either. There is a certain fear about admitting ignorance about cooking: “I rarely discuss housework with anyone. I feel inferior with wives talking about making cakes and puddings and such” (M239/35015).

Having inferiority feelings in relation to cooking is certainly a good enough reason for not discussing it, and for avoiding cooking, with others. But most parents would probably not feel inferior to their children in terms of their cooking abilities. Still, many informants claim that they were never involved in the cooking process at home. This could be related to the power aspect of cooking, as described by David Bell and Gill Valentine (1997, pp. 63 ff.), which suggests that having control over cooking is to have control over one’s position in the family, thereby ensuring that one is vital for its existence. Thus, to give up space in the kitchen is to give up domestic power, no matter how many other benefits are to be gained thereby, such as having more leisure-time for oneself or preparing children for the management of their own households.

In the earlier questionnaires, there are common references to a pre-history of communal cooking. These refer to certain kinds of cooking connected with special events, such as hunting, harvest, or festive occasions which, traditionally, have involved a group of people cooking together. Informants answering the questionnaire in 1972 tell of practices connected with their early years in the first decades of the 1900s, when such cooking took place at events like slaughtering, but also when baking, and the taking care of fruit and apples, involved several people. The reasons suggested by the respondents for the decline of communal cooking, vary. Some relate it to the urbanization, others to the small kitchens in modern apartments, and one informant says it has to do with the cost of household appliances. She did not dare borrow equipment or go to her friends when she had apples to press, since she was afraid that she would break the machine, which would be impossible for her, cost-wise, to replace. It was different when she was young when they gathered together at the farm that had a large manually-driven apple press which she could use.

Thus, individualization is evident not just in the eating practices of Swedish households. Shared meals are still highly appreciated and are a strong norm, but this ideal is often difficult to live up to. The individualization of cooking, on the contrary, is not normally seen as a problem. The sharing of this specific household task has more to do with dividing the days for cooking purposes between the partners, than to actually do the cooking together.[5]

5 Which makes cooking different from other kinds of domestic labour. Jean Claude Kaufmann and Tim Putnam, in a study of laundry practices, pointed to the importance that young couples, who wanted to have an equal relationship, afforded the idea that laundry should be a joint task. See Kaufmann / Putnam 1998.

However, it should also be said that there are exceptions to this. Some of the informants refer to cooking as a joint enterprise, something they enjoy doing with their partner. Especially in situations where there are no children, or, at least, no small children, present, cooking can be a kind of floating practice that is both necessary domestic work and a hobby. The changing gender dimension of cooking, therefore, has not necessarily led to friction in terms of the balance of power, with men taking over the kitchens, because, at least in some households, cooking has become a kind of bonding practice between partners. In terms of social relations, this is one of the more promising developments in contemporary cooking, and it is far from the stories of decline, social positioning, conflicts and frustration, that are regularly brought up when it comes to discussion of domestic cooking.

Concluding Remarks

Kitchens are more than rooms for the preparation of food. They are also living laboratories where societal changes are handled and incorporated into everyday life. This comparative study of meals and cooking in Swedish households during the last century has tried to highlight three such processes. One relates to the globalisation of everyday life. Domestic kitchens are melting pots where international influences have changed daily cooking practices. Most informants embrace these developments, although some critical remarks about effects on the environment can be noted. Another relates to the re-gendering of cooking. Cooking is no longer a distinct female practice in Swedish households. Finally, the commensality element of meals and cooking is undergoing fundamental change. There is ongoing individualization in this regard, but also a constant struggle to uphold commensal meals when possible. The period investigated will, in retrospect, probably be seen as the peak of individualized cooking practices. From the 1940s onwards, cooking has been mostly an individual task. It will be interesting for future research to see if the current tendencies towards a remaking of communal cooking will evolve into a new form of cooking commensality.

List of References

Printed

Adams, Carol: *The Sexual Politics of Meat: A Feminist-Vegetarian Critical Theory*. Continuum Publishing: New York 1990.

Avakian, Arlene Voski (ed.): *Through the Kitchen Window. Women Writers Explore the Intimate Meanings Food and Cooking*. Oxford: Berg, 2006.

Bell David / Gill, Valentine: *Consuming Geographies. We Are What We Eat*. Routledge: London 1997.

Charles, Nickie / Kerr, Marion: *Women, Food and Families: Power, Status, Love, Anger*. Manchester University Press: Manchester 1988.

Counihan, Carole: *The Anthropology of Food and Body. Gender, Meaning and Power*. Routledge: New York 1999.

DeVault, Marjorie: *Feeding the Family: The Social Organisation of Caring as Gendered Work*. University of Chicago Press: Chicago 1991.

Douglas, Mary: "Deciphering a Meal". *Daedalus* 101(1), 1972, pp. 61–81.

Hagström, Charlotte: "Questions and Answers in the Archives: Knowledge Production through Open-ended Questionnaires". Abstract from SIEF Congress, Zagreb, Croatia, 2015.

Holm, Lotte / Ekström, Marianne Pipping / Hach, Sara / Lund, Thomas Bøker: "Who is Cooking Dinner?". *Food, Culture & Society* 18(4) 2015, pp. 589–610.

Jönsson, Håkan: "Wholesome Milk". In Rykönen, P. / Hernandez, G. / Jonsson, U. (eds.): *From Local Champions to Global Players: Essays on the History of the Dairy Sector*. Stockholm University: Stockholm 2013, pp. 127–142.

Jönsson, Håkan: "A Land of Milk and Money. The Dairy Counter in an Economy of Added Values". In Löfgren, Orvar / Willim, Robert (eds.): *Magic, Culture and the New Economy*. Oxford: Berg, 2005, pp. 105–116.

Kaufmann, Jean-Claude / Putnam, Tim: *Dirty Linen. Couples as Seen Through Their Laundry*. Middlesex University Press: London 1998.

Kjærnes, U. (ed.): *Eating Patterns. A Day in the Lives of Nordic Peoples*. Report no. 7–2001. SIFO: Oslo: 2001.

Löfgren, Orvar: "Modernizing the nation – nationalizing modernity". *Etnol. Trib.* 15 (1992), pp. 91–115.

Molander, S.: *Mat, kärlek och metapraktik. En studie I vardagsmiddagskonsumtion bland ensamstående mödrar* ("Food, Love and Meta-Practices. A Study of Everyday Dinner Consumption among Single Mothers"). Stockholm University: Stockholm 2011). Dissertation.

Murcott, Anne: "'It's a Pleasure to Cook for Him': Food, Mealtimes and Gender in Some South Wales Households". In Jackson, S. / Moore, S. (eds.): *The Politics of Domestic Consumption*. Harvester Wheatsheaf: Hemel Hempstead 1995, pp. 89–99.

Sobal, Jeffrey / Nelson, Mary K.: "Commensal Eating Patterns: A Community Study". *Appetite* 41(2), 2003, pp. 181–189.

Short, Frances: *Kitchen Secrets: The Meaning of Cooking in Everyday Life*. Berg: Oxford 2006.

Sundström, Å. / Ekström, J.: *Dryckeskonsumtionen i Sverige* ("Beverage Consumption in Sweden"). Stockholm: Industriens utredningsinstitut, 1962.

Statistics from the Swedish Board of Agriculture, Report 2013:04. Swedish Board of Agriculture: Stockholm 2013.

Questionnaire responses

LUF 244 / M27474.

LUF 244 / M27473.

LUF 244 / M27446.

M239 / 35015.

Una A. Robertson

Alien Shadows: Elements of Alienation in the Diet of Scotland

Abstract: *The dominance of the supermarkets causes concern on many counts. Change is coming from different directions, including the supermarkets themselves. Does the situation today differ from that in the past? Has Scotland's food always been healthy, seasonal and locally-produced? And finally, a look at how Scotland's traditional food is interpreted today.*

Many shades of meaning lie within the words "alien" and "alienation" including attributes of belonging to something else, extraneous, repugnant, inconsistent, incompatible, estranged; a foreigner, an outsider. A significant nuance comes with "plant introduced by man but maintaining itself" (Macdonald 1972, p. 30). This presentation incorporates two distinct but entwined strands: feelings of alienation aroused by the supermarkets and elements alien to our diet.

Looking into the history of our food, little is truly indigenous. Much has been introduced from elsewhere that has then acclimatized to Scotland's environment. Truly native sheep, cattle and poultry still exist;[1] other breeds were incomers but have been here long enough as to be regarded as "traditionally Scottish".[2] The majority of our vegetables and fruits are "aliens" – even those now regarded as the basics – cabbage, potatoes, turnips and rhubarb, for example.

The last 50 years or so have seen the increasing dominance of our supermarkets on our food habits. An abundance of choice greets us in the aisles with produce available from every corner of the world. Seasonality is forgotten. Geographical origins are obliterated. After taking such abundance, such choice, for granted and at ever-decreasing prices, concerns are being raised. People find themselves alienated, estranged or even hostile to the supermarkets' dominance.

What are these issues? The lengthy "food chains" with the potential for dubious practices, surfacing, for example, in the horsemeat scandals of 2013;[3] intensive factory farming and the reliance on chemicals; the wastage inherent in the

1 Soay, North Ronaldsay, Shetland sheep: Shetland, Highland and Galloway cattle; the Aberdeen Angus developed from two East Coast breeds; the Scot's Dumpie is an ancient type of hen.

2 Cheviot and Blackface sheep; Ayrshire and Shorthorn cattle; Scots Grey hens.

3 In 2013 horsemeat was discovered in a consignment of beef products sold in a UK supermarket.

system; the means used to keep suppliers in thrall and prices low for the shopper; the "air miles" that cause such environmental problems and obliterate both season and geography; queries over the "freshness" of "fresh" produce (Renton 2011, retrieved 15.6.2016 from www.dailymail.co.uk/news/article.../Just-fresh-fresh-food-supermarkethtml); long-distance transport of animals for slaughter; additives incorporated into processed foodstuffs; profits going to distant conglomerates and the difficulties of local suppliers and independent shops in the high street; and, not least, the general ignorance as to where food comes from or how it is produced – dubbed "food without thinking". With issues such as these it is no wonder that a reaction has set in and supermarkets have seen a drop in sales.

Change has come from several directions: From the supermarkets themselves who are now addressing the problem of waste. Several chains are selling "wonky" or misshapen vegetables and fruit and send their "out-of-date produce" to good causes or school feeding programmes. Some have pledged to increase the proportion of British fruit and vegetables on sale, in order to protect growers and improve the relations between producers and retailers.

On the consumers' side the Slow Food Movement, founded in Italy, now has a worldwide membership with branches in Scotland. It has evolved "to develop a comprehensive approach to food that recognizes the strong connection between plate, planet, people, politics and culture" (www.slowfood.com/international/7/history, retrieved 15. 6. 2016). Farmers' Markets encourage small-scale producers to sell direct to the public. They also serve to lessen the distance between town and country. Farm Shops offer further opportunities – although some would query the meaning of "local" when many sell olive oil, lemons, dried fruit, rice and other imported products. Growers deliver "Vegetable Boxes" to the door each week offering a selection of locally-grown fresh items.

To further these ambitions of persuading people to "eat local", a project called "The Fife Diet" was set up in which only food sourced within the county was eaten.[4] As a reasonable and nutritious diet it was perfectly possible but somewhat limited; one journalist who followed it for a year described his joy, at the beginning of May, when offered fresh strawberries (Jardine 2016, p. 27).

Demand for allotments has soared after years of decline. So-called "guerilla gardening" has seen city folk taking over neglected corners to grow flowers and vegetables. Urban beekeepers have multiplied – to the benefit of honey production and pollination generally. The keeping of pigs in a public park proved surprisingly popular – until the time came for slaughter which provoked a storm of protests

4 Fife: an area on the east coast, north of Edinburgh and the Firth of Forth.

and a barrage of online abuse. It has to be said, though, there was a high demand for the meat ("Pigs in city park …", retrieved 15.6.2016 from www.dailyrecord.co.uk/news/scottish-news/pigs-city-park-slaughtered-meat).

Since lack of education is considered the root of the problem, initiatives are centred on "the young". Schools have started gardens or orchards; children are taken to city farms, agricultural shows or farm trails where they learn about food production: one supermarket runs "Farm to Fork" trails within its stores and suppliers, to help children build a healthier relationship with food (www.ourtesco.com//our-commnity/the-tesco-eat-happy-project/, retrieved 17. 6. 2016). Food Festivals are held across the country, centered on the local specialities. The year 2015 was promoted as "The Year of Food and Drink" although rather than encouraging people to "eat local" it aimed to enhance an already thriving export sector in the economy which is on target to reach £16.5 billion by 2017 ("The Taste for Success, Vision Scotland, Food and Drink 2015").

Over and above, there exists a multiplicity of projects, action plans, schemes, programmes, challenges, awards and the like, set up by charities, focus groups and other well-meaning parties.

The need is serious. A survey reported in 2014 that 63 % of adults did not know British farmers grew blueberries, 62 % did not know they grew sweet corn (maize), and 29 % that cauliflowers were a local crop. In addition, 19 % were ignorant of apples being grown here while 41 % denied all knowledge of British-grown strawberries. Of those born in the 1990s, 16 % optimistically thought oranges were grown here commercially (Buckland 2014, p. 14).

That is the situation today: widespread ignorance, supplies originating anywhere in the world, the dominance of the supermarkets alienating sections of the public (i.e. those who have the luxury of choice in these matters) together with the concept of a return to former days – fresh, locally-grown, healthy food sold by independent shops in the High Street. Looking at the evidence, how does today's situation compare with our food in the past?

Was Our Food Always Healthy?

A long-held belief considers the modern diet as detrimental to health, especially where refined carbohydrates in white bread and sugar are involved. Organizations such as the Soil Association and the Henry Doubleday Research Foundation worked to change attitudes to modern production methods. They were joined by individuals such as Doris Grant who also campaigned against the multiplicity of chemicals in processed foods (Grant 1973, 14–34). Elizabeth David, the cookery writer, was scathing with regard to commercially-produced white bread (David

1977, pp. 33–39). More recently, concern has focused on salt and fat in processed foods. The spotlight is now on sugar again, amid the current disturbing situation regarding obesity and diabetes.

Edinburgh's (and Scotland's) first Medical Officer of Health was appointed in 1862. He set up an investigation into the city's meat supply, which uncovered a disturbing list of unhygienic and unsavoury practices. A later investigation revealed the dubious situation regarding milk and ice cream (Littlejohn 1865).[5] Today's Trading Standards Officers continue to uncover instances of malpractice and fraud – such as the "horsemeat scandal" above.

Was Our Food Always Seasonal in Character?

To a certain degree, methods of preserving extended the seasons. Cheaper sugar saw an upsurge in the making of jams and jellies, previously confined to the gentry's kitchens. A novel describes how the year 1787 was notable for the parishioners making use of the berries from their own gardens: "not without the plausible pretext that jelly was an excellent medicine for a sore throat, and jam a remedy as good as London candy for a cough, or a cold, or a shortness of breath" (Galt 1911, pp. 173–174).

Meanwhile, root vegetables could be stored in "clamps" covered with straw and earth; cabbage might be salted while peas and beans were dried, prior to being ground into meal. As to fish, it is said that the methods of curing – with salt, smoke or in the wind – are Scandinavian in origin and arrived with the Vikings, although it was a Dutchman in the 14th century who perfected the salting technique (Hope 1987, p. 51). Meat was generally salted for winter use and the story was told of an Edinburgh lady who conscientiously ate her way from nose to tail along the carcass (Cockburn 1977, p. 66). Surplus milk was turned into hard cheese and two forms of butter were made: one for domestic use and one to pay the rent. Whether in its fresh or preserved forms the underlying seasonal character of the food remained.

The development of tinned and bottled goods during the 19th century expanded the range of foods available and introduced many to such novelties as peaches, pineapple and Canadian salmon. Board of Trade records for the early 1890s reveal the UK consumed each year a total of about 70,000 tons of imported tinned foods, and that excluded tinned fruits and vegetables and the tinned meats made up in this country. The total was made up of about 30 million pounds of tinned

5 For a wider view of the subject see Tait 1974.

salmon, 7 of lobsters, 18 of sardines, 66 of meats [including tongues] and 35 of milk (Law c. 1896, p. 711).

The domestic refrigerator did away with shopping every day but the deep freeze had the greater impact on choices available to the housewife and contributed to year-round availability.

Was Our Food Always Local?

It was the coming of the railways in the 19th century that really altered the supply system and began to lessen both seasonal and geographical dependency. Fresh produce from the warmer south of England could be sent north to start the season earlier while produce from the colder north when sent south extended it there. Cities such as Edinburgh and Glasgow could be supplied with milk from 100 miles away, whereas previously the limit had been 10 miles and a fast-trotting pony. Scottish meat and fish were sent 500 miles overnight, to be sold in London the next morning. Prior to this canals had eased the transport of non-perishable goods.

Later in the century refrigerated steamships brought in produce from all over the world: meat and butter from Australia and New Zealand, eggs and wheat from Canada, "green fruit" from South Africa and elsewhere. These products were mostly duplicating what was familiar but some newcomers appeared. It was noted in the 1890s that "tomatoes or love-apples", regarded here with the greatest suspicion, "… have advanced in general favour, both raw and cooked, more than any other fruit" and immense quantities were imported, both fresh and in tins and bottles. The same authority says of avocado that "a taste for it is soon acquired" and that the aubergine or egg-plant is "more popular in France or America than in England" (ibid., pp. 711, 59, 271).

Mrs. Somerville's cookery book agreed: "The same remarks are applicable to fruits as to vegetables, … Besides our own country supply, other countries contribute largely to supplying the market" (Somerville c. 1875, p. 37) and she provided recipes for an impressive list of such items. However, the author M. V. Hughes writing in the 1930s of her London childhood 60 years before, contradicts this: "Oranges in summer were unknown then, as well as all the foreign apples and other fruit to be had in London today" (Hughes 1977, p. 89). Whether her experience was based on the family's personal circumstances or not, vast quantities of plums, peaches, apples, pears, tomatoes, onions and similar produce were being imported.

By the 1930s even the most basic items that could grow here continued to be brought in – 91 % of onions, for example, and 80 % of fresh fruit. Near-starvation during the First World War meant the Government was better prepared in 1939. Imports virtually ceased: the focus was again on self-sufficiency. An extra 0.5 million allotments were needed, enough to feed 1 million adults and 1.5 million children for 8 months of the year. Under the slogan "Dig for Victory" the Government promoted not only home-grown fruit and vegetables, especially leafy green ones, but also advised on keeping poultry, bees, pigs and rabbits (Buchan 1977, pp. 34, 36, 50). Culinary advice was forthcoming on making the most of what there was – such as the [in]famous "Woolton Pie" consisting of diced root vegetables, spring onions, a little oatmeal, vegetable extract, all covered with potato and baked in the oven.[6] Recipes made use of the sweetness of carrots in cakes and biscuits – which suddenly became fashionable about 25 years ago!

The evidence shows little has changed over the last 200 or even 250 years: the desire to return to "how things were" has no basis. Our food for many a long year has been neither healthy, nor local nor eaten in its season. UK food security (self-sufficiency) has steadily declined over the past 20 years and currently stands at 68 %, down from 87 % (Beament 2014, p. 11).

Although many imports were replicating what could be produced here, cookery books published in Scotland, setting out to inspire or educate their readers, often called for items that were truly "alien".

In the 1820s, before any impact from the railways, Mrs. Dalgairns assumed the ready accessibility of sugar, wine, brandy, dried fruits, citrus fruits and several spices (Dalgairns 1829). Her contemporary Meg Dods included a section on "Scottish National Dishes" where even the most basic are flavoured with pepper (both black and white), lemon juice or spices. Many of her soups or stews use the humbler parts of the animal and are enhanced with cayenne, allspice, mace, lemon peel, Seville orange juice and claret. The celebrated haggis, based on lamb offal, requires a dash of cayenne and lemon juice while her recipe for Lambs' Haggis specifies nutmeg (Dods 1827, pp. 354, 355). Orange Marmalade is generally considered a Scottish invention but the sugar and bitter oranges never grew locally. The countless varieties of cakes and biscuits – scones, diet loaf, shortbreads, gingerbreads, Dundee Cake, Hogmanay's Black Bun, all long term favourites – call for sugar, dried fruits and spices.

If cookery books are considered aspirational or over-optimistic, then domestic account books reveal the nation's purchases. Slightly earlier, an Edinburgh household was buying many of these non-local items, together with vermicelli or maca-

6 Named after Lord Woolton, wartime Minister of Food.

roni, curry powder, ketchup and several types of sugar (Private ms. 1810–1814). In fact household accounts over the previous 150 years bear a remarkable similarity, whether belonging to families in Edinburgh in the 1750s, the 1700s or even the 1670s. Raisins, currants, ginger, coffee beans, various sugars, tea and spices such as cinnamon, nutmeg, mace and pepper often feature.

Entries regarding oranges are noticeable, sometimes specified as being "sweet" or "bitter", sometimes in large numbers and in close proximity to accounts for sugar. In 1710 Lady Grizell Baillie used a consignment to make orange wine and had "two dusone (i.e. 24) oranges to preserve" (Scott-Montcrieff 1911, p. 90) while the Innes of Stowe accounts in 1754 specify the purchase of "8lbs of bitter oranges for marmalade" (Innes of Stow 1754). At this level of society it would seem that the "traditional Scottish" cuisine had always been innovative and prepared to accept the unfamiliar.

However, many had no need for a cookery book, subsisting, as they did, on a few staple foods. In the 1790s the diet of Dalmeny, then a small village outside Edinburgh, can be taken as typical: "Their food consists of oat-meal porridge, oatcakes and pease bannocks, barley broth, with greens, potatoes, buttermilk and water. Some begin now to use wheaten bread and small beer, but seldom eat any butcher meat (i.e. fresh meat). The luxuries in which they indulge are tea, and what is worse, whisky" (Sinclair 1979, p. 729).

Although the range of food widened during the 19th century it is these items, surely, that should be considered as the traditional foods of Scotland.

Today one can eat one's way around the world, courtesy of the supermarket and the professional chef: A recent series of adverts for a supermarket here started with the words "As Scottish as …" and showed five processed items: prominent among the ingredients were coconut, pecan nuts and fiery chillies.[7]

Restaurants, bistros, gastro-pubs and the like often offer our visitors a "Scottish menu" which might mean "modern Scottish" or "traditional Scottish". Either way its "Scottishness" should surely come from the use of local ingredients and flavourings. While many are unexceptional, although rarely offering a truly authentic traditional experience, (i.e. based on oatmeal, barley broth, the cheaper cuts of meat, buttermilk and kail), with others one can but admire the ingenuity and imagination involved. It must be puzzling to meet a menu offering chermoula crumbed fillet of lamb, served with an aubergine and tahini puree and shoestring

7 It is uncertain whether coconuts originated in the East Indies or tropical America. Pecan nuts are generally from the southern states of North America; and wild chillies originated in Mexico. They need a warm night-time temperature to fruit satisfactorily.

sweet potatoes.[8] Doubtless such ingredients can be grown here with sufficient heat, light and protection but they are hardly "Scottish" in essence.

A menu for a Burns' Night Dinner, that most Scottish of Scottish occasions held on 25th January, offers: Cullen Skink, a smoked-fish soup, while unusual for the occasion is definitely a traditional dish. The roast lamb with onions and potatoes is, again, unexceptional although the centre-piece has always been haggis; however, the "spiced winter fruit" on a vanilla cream rice pudding base is questionable: the 25th January is mid-winter for us. The fruits used – apple, pear – store well, but fresh plums are long-since past and ripe brambles (blackberries) are unlikely. The rice for pudding is a "traditional" import as is the cinnamon, but the star anise used as flavouring is definitely a newcomer on the scene.

And don't even ask about the option of a vegetarian haggis! (www.scotland.org/recipes/, retrieved 15.6.2016).

List of References

Printed

Buchan, Ursula: *A Green and Pleasant Land*. Hutchinson: London 2013.

Buckland, L.. "'Britons don't know their onions'", say experts. Survey conducted by L.E.A.F. (Linking Environment and Farming), *The Scotsman*, 2.6.2014, p. 14.

Cockburn, Henry: *Memorials of Our Time*. The Mercat Press: Edinburgh 1977.

David, E.: *English Bread & Yeast Cookery*. Allen Lane: London 1977.

Galt, John: *Annals of the Parish*. T. H. Foulis: London & Edinburgh 1911.

Grant, Doris: *Your Daily Food: Recipe for Survival*. Faber & Faber: London 1973.

Hope, Annette: *A Caledonian Feast*. Mainstream Publishing Co.: Edinburgh 1987.

Hughes, M. V.: *A London Child of the 1870s*. Oxford University Press: Oxford 1977.

Innes of Stow, National Archives of Scotland, GD 113, v.397, 22 February 1754.

Jardine, Steven: "Food for Thought: Arrival of Strawberries the Sweetest of Times". *The Scotsman*, 18.6.2016.

Law, James T.: *Law's Grocer's Manual*. J. T. Law: Liverpool c. 1895.

8 Chermoula: a Morrocan/North African marinade or sauce, with many variations, generally used for fish and seafood. It usually incorporates preserved lemons/lemon juice, several fresh herbs, assorted spices and olive oil. Tahini is a paste made from sesame seeds, a plant widely grown in ancient times in Egypt, the Middle East and India. Sweet potatoes originated in tropical South America, possibly Peru.

Littlejohn, Dr. H. D.: *Report on the Sanitary Condition of the City of Edinburgh.* Colston & Son: Edinburgh 1865.

Macdonald, A. M. (ed.): *Chambers Twentieth Century Dictionary.* Edinburgh: W & R. Chambers Ltd., 1972.

Somerville, Mrs.: *Mrs. Somerville's Cookery & Domestic Economy.* Glasgow, c. 1875, 4th ed. p. 37.

Tait, H. P.: *A Doctor and Two Policemen: A History of the Edinburgh Health Department, 1862–1974* Mackenzie & Storrie: Edinburgh 1974.

"The Taste for Success, Vision Scotland, Food & Drink". *The Scotsman*, Winter 2015.

Internet

"Pigs in city park are slaughtered for meat despite fierce campaign to save the popular porkers", *Daily Record*, 4.12.2014, retrieved 15.6.2016 from www.dailyrecord.co.uk/news/scottish-news/pigs-city-park-slaughtered-meat.

Renton, Alex: "Just how fresh is fresh food at the supermarket?" *Mail Online*, 26th March 2011, retrieved 15.6.2016 from www.dailymail.co.uk/news/article.../Just-fresh-fresh-food-supermarkethtml,

www.ourtesco.com//our-commnity/the-tesco-eat-happy-project/, retrieved 17.6. 2016.

www.scotland.org/recipes/, retrieved 15.6.2016.

www.slowfood.com/international/7/history.

International Commission for Ethnological Food Research: Conferences, Themes and Publications (1970–2017)

Year	Place	Theme / Publication
1970	Lund, Sweden	*Theme*: 'Ethnological Food Research: Development, Methods and Future Tasks'. *Publication: Ethnological Food Research in Europe and USA.* *Editors:* Nils-Arvid Bringéus & Günter Wiegelmann. *Publisher:* Otto Schwartz & Co. Göttingen, 1971, 213. Also in: *Ethnologia Scandinavica* 1971, 1–187 and *Ethnologia Europaea* 5 (1971), 1–213.
1973	Helsinki, Finland	*Theme*: 'Dominant Traits in Regional. Food Systems in the Twentieth Century'. *Publication*: *Ethnologische Nahrungsforschung. Ethnological Food Research.* *Editors:* Niilo Valonen & Juhani U. E. Lehtonen. *Publisher:* Sonderdruch aus/Offprint from: *Kansatieteellinen Arkisto* 26. Suomen Muinaismuistoyhdistys, Helsinki 1975, 340pp.
1977	Cardiff, Wales	*Theme*: 'National Food'. *Publication*: *Food in Perspective.* *Editors*: Alexander Fenton & Trefor M. Owen. *Publishers:* John Donald Publishers Ltd., Edinburgh 1981, 425pp.
1980	Stainz, Austria	*Theme*: 'Nahrung als Kommunikation'. *Publication*: Proceedings Unpublished. Review in: *Österreiche Zeitschrift für Volkskunde* 1980, 252–263.
1983	Matrafüred, Hungary	*Theme*: 'Sequences and Periods of Change in the History of Popular Dict'. *Publication*: *Food in Change. Eating Habits from the Middle Ages to the Present Day.* *Editors:* Alexander Fenton & Eszter Kisbán. *Publisher*: John Donald Publishers Ltd., Edinburgh 1986, 166pp.

Year	Place	Theme / Publication
1985	Karniowice, Poland	Theme: 'Innovations in Food Habits'. *Publication:* Proceedings unpublished. Review in: *Ethnologica Scandinavica* 1986, 161–163.
1987	Søgndal, Norway	*Theme*: 'Food Preservation and Conservation'. *Publication*: *Food Conservation. Ethnological Studies.* *Editors:* Astri Riddervold & Andreas Ropeid. *Publisher*: Prospect Books, London 1988, 224pp.
1989	Philadelphia, USA	*Theme*: 'Food as Symbol'. *Publication*: Proceedings Unpublished.
1992	Dublin & Kilfinane, Co. Limerick & The Burren, Co. Clare, Ireland	*Theme*: 'Milk and Milk Products'. *Publication*: *Milk and Milk Products, from Medieval to Modern Times.* *Editor*: Patricia Lysaght. *Publisher*: Canongate Academic, Edinburgh 1994, 229pp.
1994	Freising, Germany	*Theme*: 'The Potato'/'Die Kartoffel'. *Publication*: *Kulturprägung durch Nahrung: Die Kartoffel.* *Editors:* Sigrid Weggeman & Gertrud Benker. *Publisher*: Edition infotainment Verlags GmbH., München 1997. (Part publication of the Conference Proceedings), 94pp.
1996	Nicosia, Cyprus	*Theme*: 'Food and the Traveller. The Impact of Migration, Immigration and Tourism on Ethnic Traditional Food'. *Publication*: *Food and the Traveller. Migration, Immigration, Tourism and Ethnic Food.* *Editor:* Patricia Lysaght. *Publisher:* Intercollege Press, in association with the Department of Irish Folklore, University College Dublin. Nicosia 1996, 342pp.
1998	Umeå & Frostviken, Sweden	*Theme*: 'Making the Most of Nature'. *Publication*: *Food from Nature. Attitudes, Strategies and Culinary Practices.* *Editor*: Patricia Lysaght. *Publisher*: The Royal Gustavus Adolphus Academy for Swedish Folk Culture, Uppsala, Sweden. (*Acta Academiae Regiae* Gustavi Adolphi 71), 1998, 398pp.
2000	Ljubljana, Preddvor & Piran, Slovenia	*Theme*: 'Food and Celebration: From Fasting to Feasting'. *Publication: Food and Celebration: From Fasting to Feasting* *Editor*: Patricia Lysaght. *Publisher*: Založba. ZRC/ZRC Publishing, ZRC SAZU, in association with the Department of Irish Folklore, University College Dublin. Ljubljana 2002, 428pp.

Year	Place	Theme / Publication
2002	Basel and Vevey, Switzerland	*Theme*: 'Changing Tastes. Food Culture and the Process of Industrialization'. *Publication*: *Changing Tastes. Food Culture and the Processes of Industrialization.* *Editor*: Patricia Lysaght with Christine Burckhardt-Seebass. *Publisher*: Verlag der Schweizerische Gesselschaft für Volkskunde, Basel, in association with the Department of Irish Folklore, University College Dublin. Basel 2004, 332pp.
2004	Dubrovnik, Croatia	*Theme*: 'Mediterranean Food and Its Influences Abroad'. *Publication*: *Mediterranean Food: Concepts and Trends.* *Editor*: Patricia Lysaght with Nives Rittig-Beljak *Publisher*: Biblioteka Nova Ethnografia, Zagreb, 350pp.
2006	Innsbruck, Austria & Merano, Italy	*Theme*: 'Sanitas per Aquas. Foodways and Lifestyles in the Search for Health and Beauty'. *Publication: Sanitas per Aquas*. Spas, Lifestyles and Foodways. *Editor*: Patricia Lysaght. *Publisher*: Studien Verlag, Innsbruck, Austria 2008, 379pp.
2008	Oslo, Norway	*Theme*: 'Cultural Crossroads. Food and Meals at Cultural Crossroads'. *Publication*: *Cultural Crossroads. Food and Meals at Cultural Crossroads.* *Editor*: Patricia Lysaght (with Ann Helene Bolstad Skjelbred). *Publisher*: Novus, Press, Oslo 2010, 341pp.
2010	Åbo/Turku, Finland	*Theme*: 'Time for Food'. *Publication*: *Time for Food. Everyday Food and Changing Meal Habits.* *Editor*: Patricia Lysaght. *Publisher*: Åbo Akademi University Press 2012, 366pp.
2012	Lund, Sweden	Theme: 'The Return of Traditional Food'. *Publication*: *The Return of Traditional Food.* *Editor*: Patricia Lysaght. *Publisher*: Lund Studies in Arts and Cultural Sciences 1, Lund 2013, 311pp.
2014	Łódź, Poland	*Theme*: 'Food and the Internet'. *Publication*: *Food and the Internet.* *Editors*: Violetta Krawczyk-Wasilewska and Patricia Lysaght. *Publisher*: Peter Lang, Frankfurt am Main, 2015, 275pp.

Year	Place	Theme / Publication
2016	Heidelberg, Germany	*Theme:* 'Places of Food Production. Origin, Identity, Imagination'. *Publication*: *Places of Food Production. Origin, Identity, Imagination.* *Editors*: Silke Bartsch and Patricia Lysaght. *Publisher*: Peter Lang, Frankfurt am Main, 2017, 291pp.

Compiled by Patricia Lysaght, 2017

List of Contributors

Albala, Ken, Professor of History and Chair of Food Studies at the University of the Pacific in Stockton and San Francisco, California. He is the author or editor of 25 books including academic monographs, reference works, textbooks and cookbooks. His latest is about noodle soup around the world (kalbala@PACIFIC.EDU).

Bathrellou, Eirini, Ph.D., dietician- nutritionist, is a teaching assistant in the Laboratory of Nutrition and Clinical Dietetics of the Department of Nutrition and Dietetics, Harokopio University, Athens, Greece (ebathrellou@hua.gr).

Bartsch, Silke, is Professor for nutrition and home economics and specialized didactic at the University of Education Karlsruhe since 2010. She studied home economics and biology at the Technische Universität Berlin and earned her Ph.D. degree with her work on the eating culture of young people at the University of Education Heidelberg. Her research interests focus on eating behaviour and nutrition and consumer education (bartsch@ph-karlsruhe.de).

Báti, Anikó, Ph.D., is a senior research fellow at the Institute of Ethnology of the Hungarian Academy of Sciences, since 2009. Her current fields of interest include questions concerning foodways, lifestyle, and the eating habits of children in Budapest (bati. aniko@gmail.com).

Beyers, Leen, is curator of the MAS exhibition *Antwerp à la carte. On cities and food.* She is head of the curatorial department of the MAS museum, which displays, researches, and updates the MAS collection of about 500,000 objects associated with the city and port of Antwerp and with cultural diversity in the world. She has a Ph.D. in history and an M.A. in anthropology. Her expertise as a researcher and curator mainly relates to urban history, migration, food culture, oral history and memory (leen.beyers@gmail.com).

Bongard, Stefan, Professor Dr. His main field of research is electric mobility. All research activities are bundled in the Ludwigshafen Research Center for Electric Mobility (LUcem). A central platform for publication and communication can be accessed on www.elecarda.com, a project directed at users providing relevant information about available electric cars in an electric car database. Stefan Bongard has held a professorship for Business Administration and Logistics at the University of Applied Sciences Ludwigshafen am Rhein, Germany, since 2008 (Stefan.Bongard@hs-lu.de).

Cherkasky, Shirley, is an independent scholar and culinary historian who, since her retirement from the Smithsonian Institution, has pursued research interests in American confectionery, food and beverage museums worldwide, and Upper Midwest foodways (shircher@gmail.com).

D'Auria, Déirdre, completed her Ph.D. on the influence of Italian food on Irish foodways in the twentieth century, at University College Dublin, in 2013. She is Assistant Editor on the Historical Dictionary of Modern Irish, *Foclóir na Nua-Ghaeilge*, in the Royal Irish Academy, Dublin (deirdre.dauria@gmail.com).

Dutra, Rogéria Campos A., is Professor of Anthropology at the Federal University of Juiz de Fora, Brazil, and carries out research on food and culture. She graduated in the Social Sciences at the Federal University of Juiz de Fora, and she also has a Master's degree and a Ph.D. in Anthropology from the Federal University of Rio de Janeiro, Brazil (rcadutra@uol.com.br).

Godina Golija, Maja, Ph.D. in ethnological science, is a scientific adviser with the Institute of Slovene Ethnology, ZRC SAZU and Associate Professor of Ethnology at the Faculty of Arts, University of Maribor, Slovenia. Her research is focused mainly on food, economy, and urban life. She has written over 90 scientific papers, and five ethnological monographs about everyday life and food culture in Slovenia, for example: *Hunger and Misery: The Influence of the First World War on the Diet of Slovenian Civilians* (Farnham: Ashgate, 2011): *La pomme de terre dans les habitudes alimentaires slovènes : de l'hostilité à la consecration*, Tours: Press Universitaire François-Rabelais, 2011; *The Revitalisation of Rural Products in Slovenia: From Simple Food to Culinary Attraction* (Lund: Lund University Press, 2013); and *The Impact of Weather on Rhythms and Structure of Meals in Slovenia* (Paris: Hermann 2015) (Maja.godina@zrc-sazu.si).

Hanson, Adelia, was an independent scholar who worked as a researcher for the centennial of Oklahoma State University College of Arts & Sciences and wrote the history, called "The Centennial History of Arts and Sciences". She also worked as registrar at the Sheerar Museum of Stillwater. Besides history she was interested in herbs and cooking. Adelia passed away on 24 November 2016. May she rest in peace.

Jönsson, Håkan, is Associate Professor in European Ethnology at Lund University. His research has focused on food and consumption in the new experience economy. He has conducted several applied cultural analysis projects encompassing food-concept development, regional foresight, and culinary tourism. He teaches classes in Food Studies and European Ethnology and is the coordinator of the interdisciplinary platform, Lund University Food Studies (hakan.jonsson@kultur.lu.se).

Kılıç Zeynep, Ph.D., Associate Professor, is a qualitative sociologist who studied immigration, belonging and identity. Her current research explores cultural identity through food, how food is racialized in the Global North, and how social class and ethnicity interact with food. A Fulbright scholar, her documentary *Tables of Istanbul* has been screened and received awards at film festivals around the world. Currently on a sabbatical, she is working on her book about contemporary food discourses in Istanbul (zkilic@alaska.edu).

Kisbán, Eszter, D.Lit., emeritus Univ.prof., Dept. of European Ethnology and Cultural Anthropology, University of Pécs, Hungary; specialist in food history in Hungary and neighbouring regions, particularly in a European context. Author of numerous articles on food and related subjects. Major contributor on "food culture" in the handbook "Hungarian Ethnology", vols. I.1. and IV. (in Hungarian), Budapest, 2009, 1997, and in the "Hungarian Ethnological Atlas", vols. VI–VII., Budapest 1989, 1992. Author of *Népi kultúra, közkultúra, jelkép: a gulyás, pörkölt, paprikás* (English summary: "Goulash: a popular food item that became a national symbol") Budapest, 1989 (ekisban2@yahoo.co.uk).

Köstlin, Konrad, born 1940, was educated (among others) in Volkskunde (the later European Ethnology), Sociology and Philosophy. He taught at the universities in Kiel (1968–2000), Regensburg (1980–1988), Tübingen (1988–1994), and in Wien (Vienna) since 1994, and was a Guest Professor at the University of Prishtina, Kosovo (2002–2008). He acted on boards of scientific organisations such as SIEF and the German Society for European Ethnology. His main interests accentuate the relations between the *ideas* of Folk Culture and Modernity, on which he tries to shed light, more or less as an old-fashioned generalist (konrad.koestlin@univie.ac.at).

Ličen, Daša, is a research assistant at the Institute of Slovenian Ethnology at the Research Centre of the Slovenian Academy of Sciences and Arts (ZRC SAZU) and a doctoral student at the University of Ljubljana. Her research interests are in historical anthropology, identities, social organizations, food, and nationalism (dasa.licen@zrc-sazu.si).

Lysaght, Patricia, Professor em. of European Ethnology, University College Dublin, is currently Chair of the SIEF Food Working Group. She has edited most of the proceedings of previous Food Conferences, including the recent volume (with Violetta Krawczyk-Wasilewska), entitled *Food and the Internet*, Proceedings of the

20th International Ethnological Food Research Conference, Department of Folklore and Ethnology, Institute of Ethnology and Cultural Anthropology, University of Łódź, Poland, 3–6 September 2014 (patricia.lysaght@ucd.ie).

Matalas, Antonia-Leda, Ph.D. Professor, teaches nutrition at the Department of Nutrition and Dietetics, Harokopio University, Athens. She holds a B.Sc. in Chemistry and a Ph.D. in Nutrition from the University of California, Davis (amatala@hua.gr).

Minami, Naoto, Professor of History at Kyoto Tachibana University; Doctor of Literature at Osaka University. Publication: *Shoku Kara Yomitoku Doitsu Kindai Shi* ("A History of Modern Germany from the Viewpoint of Food") (Kyoto: Minerva Shobo, 2015) (mnm-f@zeus.eonet.ne.jp).

Müller, Heike, is a junior scientist for nutrition and consumer education at the University of Education Karlsruhe. She has a state examination degree in bilingual education, home economics, English as a Foreign Language, and theology. She received a top score with her final project on considering meat in the content and language-integrated classroom and her award-winning thesis on language support in nutrition and consumer education (heike.mueller@ph-karlsruhe.de).

Nakazawa, Hiroko, is a Professor of the Faculty of Human Life Sciences at Nagano Prefectural College, Japan. She graduated in Domestic Science at Ochanomizu University and has a Master's degree in Food Science from Ochanomizu University. She also graduated in Medical Science at the University of Tokyo and has a Ph.D. in Health Science from the University of Tokyo (hirokon@nagano-kentan.ac.jp).

Oppermann, Leif, is Head of the Mixed and Augmented Reality Solutions (MARS) group at the Fraunhofer Institute for Applied Information Technology FIT in Sankt Augustin. He has a background in real-time computer graphics, a Diplom in Mediainformatics, and earned a Ph.D. degree with his work on "Facilitating the Development of Location-Based Experiences" at the Mixed Reality Lab, University of Nottingham, UK (leif.oppermann@fit.fraunhofer.de).

Richter, Marcus, is a research assistant at the Institute for European Ethnology of the Philipps University of Marburg. Recent publication: "Between Arrival and Departure: Some Ethnographic Notes on Time and Space in Motels" (with Peter F. N. Hörz), in W. Kuligowski and A. Standisz, eds., *Cultures of Motorway: Localities through Mobility as an Anthropological Issue, Poznańskie Studia Ethnologiczne* 19, 2015, 31–46 (marcus.richter@staff.uni-marburg.de).

Rydz-Żbikowska, Ph.D. (Economics), University of Łódź, The Faculty of Economics and Sociology, The Department of The World Economy and International Relationships, Poland (annarydz85@wp.pl).

Robertson, Una A., is a freelance historian who focuses on Scottish social and domestic history. For many years she lectured at Edinburgh University's Office of Lifelong Learning but also spoke to other organizations, cooked dinners to 18th century recipes and helped set up a Butler's Pantry as a Visitor attraction at nearby Hopetoun House. She is the author of *The Illustrated History of the Housewife 1650–1950* (Stroud: Sutton Publishing Ltd., 1997] and "Coming out of the Kitchen: Women beyond the Home" (Stroud: Sutton Publishing Ltd., 2000).

Schaal, Steffen, is professor for biology and biology education at the University of Education Ludwigsburg. He is dean for Study Affairs of the faculty for Cultural and Natural Sciences and leads several projects in the field of location-based and mobile learning in science education. He has a background in outdoor and experiential learning, in human biology and health promotion, a Masters-degree in biology, educational sciences and sports, and earned a Ph.D. degree with his work on interdisciplinary learning with digital technology in science education (schaal@ph-ludwigsburg.de).

Spalvēna, Astra, Ph.D. degree in Arts (Latvian Academy of Culture). Her Ph.D. thesis topic was: "Cultural-Contextual Analysis of Food Adaptation in Sign Systems". Her research interests include: food semiotics, food and language, representation of food in arts and media, Soviet cuisine in Latvia. Papers, presented and published, deal with Latvian food traditions focusing on contemporary habits. Course provision in the Riga International School of Economics and Business Administration includes "Media Semiotics" and "Language of Advertising" (astra.spalvena@gmail.com).

Tzoutzou, Milia, M.Sc., is a Doctoral candidate at the Department of Nutrition and Dietetics, Harokopio University, Athens, Greece (miltzou@hua.gr).

van Winter, Johanna Maria, born in 1927, is Professor emerita of Medieval History at Utrecht University. She has published mainly about Knighthood and Nobility in Western Europe, including works about The Order of St John in the Netherlands, as well as about Local History of the Low Countries, and Food and Health in Medieval Europe (J.M.vanWinter@uu.nl).